Golden Cables
of Sympathy

Golden Cables
of
Sympathy

The Transatlantic Sources
of
Nineteenth-Century Feminism

Margaret H. McFadden

THE UNIVERSITY PRESS OF KENTUCKY

Publication of this volume was made possible in part by a grant
from the National Endowment for the Humanities.

Scholarly publisher for the Commonwealth,
serving Bellarmine College, Berea College, Centre
College of Kentucky, Eastern Kentucky University,
The Filson Club Historical Society, Georgetown College,
Kentucky Historical Society, Kentucky State University,
Morehead State University, Murray State University,
Northern Kentucky University, Transylvania University,
University of Kentucky, University of Louisville,
and Western Kentucky University.
All rights reserved.

Editorial and Sales Offices: The University Press of Kentucky
663 South Limestone Street, Lexington, Kentucky 40508–4008

99 00 01 02 03   5 4 3 2 1

Library of Congress Cataloging-in-Publication Data

McFadden, Margaret.
    Golden cables of sympathy : the transatlantic sources of
nineteenth century feminism / Margaret H. McFadden.
        p.   cm.
    Includes bibliographical references and index.
    ISBN 0-8131-2117-5 (cloth : alk. paper)
    1. Feminism—History—19th century. 2. Women's rights—
History—19th century. 3. United States—Civilization—
European influences. 4. Europe—Civilization—American
influences. 5. Feminism—International cooperation—
History—19th century. 6. Women's rights—International
cooperation—History—19th century. I. Title. II. Title:
Transatlantic sources of nineteenth century feminism.
III. Title: Transatlantic sources of 19th century feminism.
HQ1154.M3965   1999
305.42'09'034—dc21   98-49993

Manufactured in the United States of America

To
Gerda Lerner
and
Karen Offen

Twentieth-Century Mothers of the Matrix

Contents

Preface

I began this project, first envisioned as a collection of early nineteenth-century feminist theory documents, in 1984, with a month-long stay in Cambridge, Massachusetts, when I had a chance to examine the resources of the Schlesinger Library on the History of Women. As I found more and more evidence of transatlantic networking among these women, however, the project was gradually transformed into its present monograph status. Over a twelve-year period I did research in nine countries—the United States, England, Ireland, the Netherlands, France, Germany, Finland, Sweden, Australia—and many libraries. I came to feel like one of Maikki Friberg's *kvinnosakskvinna*, women's movement women, for the search was rewarded with wonderful helpers and friendships on three continents.

During many summers and my Fulbright year in Finland in 1991–92, I was able to build up, bit by bit, a body of data showing the dense network of connections women made during the nineteenth century. Although archival research was very much a part of what I did, printed nineteenth-century sources, especially autobiographies and memoirs, were similarly valuable. And then there were the spectacular finds: Anne Knight's heavily annotated copy of Marion Kirkland Reid's *Woman, Her Education and Influence* (also titled *A Plea for Women*), in her collection at the Friends House Library, London; Anna Doyle Wheeler's house in Ballywire, County Tipperary, Ireland, and the search for and discovery of her death certificate at the Public Records Office in London (to lay to rest the question mark after 1848 in her dates in many reference books); the correspondence between Sophia Sturge and Aleksandra Gripenberg; the Selma Borg photographs and music manuscripts at the Sibelius Museum in Åbo, Finland; the diary and letterbook of Julia Gertrude Stewart, an international governess, at the Mitchell Library in Sydney, Australia; Frances Power Cobbe's letter revealing her life-long "romantic friendship" with Mary Lloyd at the Fawcett Library; Fredrika Bremer's American correspondence; Maggie Walz's letters from the United States to Aleksandra Gripenberg in Finland; Caroline Healey Dall's and Ednah

Dow Cheney's 1837 teenage correspondence showing their familiarity with the woman question. These and more cheered and energized, convincing me that there was much more evidence out there than I had time to find.

Here is a list of the institutions that were my most important sources of information:

International Archives of the Women's Movement, Amsterdam
Fawcett Library, City of London Polytechnic, London
Schlesinger Library on the History of Women, Cambridge, Mass.
Harvard Divinity School Library, Cambridge, Mass.
New York Public Library
Library of Congress
Perkins Library and Special Collections, Duke University,
 Durham, N.C.
Divinity School Library, Duke University, Durham, N.C.
Davis Library, University of North Carolina, Chapel Hill
Finnish Literature Society, Helsinki
Åbo Akademi University Archives, Turku, Finland
Sibelius Museum, Åbo Akademi University
University of Turku Library
Friends House Library, London
British Library, London
Royal Library, Stockholm
University of Helsinki Library
State Archives, Helsinki
Interlibrary Loan at Appalachian State University, Boone, N.C.
Western Carolina Regional Library Network
Virginia Polytechnic Institute and State University Library,
 Blacksburg
Bobst Library, New York University
Stowe-Day Foundation and Library, Hartford, Conn.
Mortlock Library, State Library of South Australia, Adelaide
Mitchell Library, State Library of New South Wales,
 Sydney, Australia
Library of Sovereign Hill, Ballarat, Victoria, Australia
Regional Library of Ballarat, Victoria, Australia
Trinity College, Library, Dublin
Representative Church Body Library, Dublin

Diocesan Library, Cashel, Ireland
Friends Historical Collection, Guilford College, Greensboro, N.C.
Stanford University Libraries, Stanford, Calif.

A project like this one, spanning more than a decade, depends not only on friends and colleagues, scholars, and professional archivists and librarians but on what I read and taught over the years, the conferences I attended and the people I met, my students and the people with whom I team-taught, the changes in my scholarly directions, my mentors and my heroes, both living and dead. No matter how many I mention here, I will inadvertently omit some, but they have all been important in the process of writing this book and in my ongoing work.

In 1982 I spent a sabbatical year, first in Europe, and then at the University of Wisconsin-Madison, trying to sort out the theoretical basis for different kinds of feminisms, past and present, in the United States and in Europe. That work led me to make a kind of sea-change in my scholarly direction, toward the nineteenth century and women's history.

Renate Klein and Jan Pahl in England (and David Doughan at the Fawcett Library, who introduced me to Anna Wheeler and William Thompson's 1825 *Appeal*), Mineke Bosch and Anneke van Doorne-Huiskes in the Netherlands (and all the staff at the International Archives of the Women's Movement), Sheila Briggs in Tübingen and Johanna Kootz, Barbara Duden, and Barbara Schaeffer-Hegel in Berlin; Hélène Cixous's student Marguerite Sandré, Françoise Basch, and Christine Delphy in Paris—all these folk and more were invaluable in that European year.

At the University of Wisconsin-Madison in 1982, the people at the Women's Studies Research Center, especially Elaine Marks and Sophie Colleau; Gerda Lerner ("the Mother of Us All") and her women's history students in the feminist theory and historiography course; Betsy Draine and the feminist research and writing group; and my sister Edith Collins, who took care of my four-year-old daughter in Oshkosh during the week—all these gave me more than they know.

In 1986 a Stanford National Endowment for the Humanities Summer Seminar, "The Woman Question in Western Thought," helped to clarify my thinking and begin the work on Anna Doyle Wheeler. I was given supportive readers in my fellow seminarians and a splendid mentor in Karen Offen.

In New York in 1987 and again in 1991 and 1994 as director of

Appalachian's residential facility in Tribeca, I was able to take advantage of colleagues and libraries in Manhattan: Columbia University's Women and Society Seminar, NYU's Bobst Library, the Lydia Maria Child Collection at the New York Public Library, and wonderful colleagues Claire Sprague, Dorothy Helly, Bonnie Anderson, Sandi Cooper, and Miranda Pollard.

At Duke University when I was on a leave of absence in 1987, Director of Women's Studies Jean O'Barr and her Feminist Thought Seminar; Christina Greene and the Women's Studies Research Center; Toril Moi and her Feminist Theory Seminar; historians Nancy Hewitt and Anne Firor Scott; and Elizabeth Clark and Kathy Rudy of the Divinity School were all helpful.

During a Fulbright year in Finland in 1991–92, I became indebted to all my colleagues at the Institute of Women's Studies at Åbo Akademi University, especially Solveig Bergman, Elizabeth Ettorre, Maria Grönroos, Elianne Riska, Harriet Silius, and, in the Department of History, Sune Jungar and Marianne Liljeström. Special gratitude is owed to my graduate assistant Ann-Catrin Östman, women's history scholar, translator, and colleague; and to Elisabet Kurtén and Monica Nyland, assistants in Women's Studies. Feminist biochemist colleague Carita Peltonen (and Salla and Per), offered advice, child care, food, and love during and after my year in Turku. In Helsinki, Paivi Settälä welcomed me at the Christina Institute at the University of Helsinki; Liisa Husu consulted with me at the State Equality Office; and librarians at the Finnish Literature Society, State Archives, and the Unioni (League of Finnish Feminist Societies founded in 1892) made up for my lack of language skills. Colleagues Aino Saarinen at the University of Oulu and Pirjo Markkola at the University of Tampere invited me to their campuses and gave me new contacts and ideas.

In Sweden, Ulla Wikander provided hospitality and great conversation on two visits to Stockholm and Uppsala; Mona Eliasson, Barbro Werkmäster, and Birgitta Holm welcomed me to Women's Studies at Uppsala; and Ingrid Claréus of the Fredrika Bremer Society gave me hospitality, a visit to Årsta Slott (Bremer's home), information, and continued international communication with other Bremer scholars.

Anka Ryall of the English Department at the University of Tromsø, Norway, has given friendship and advice in three countries, beginning with our meeting at the Fawcett Library in London and continuing with visits, consultations, and mutual connections with colleagues and students.

In Australia, I thank especially Barbara Caine of the Department of History, Monash University; Renate Klein, Women's Studies, Deakin University, friend and colleague for nearly twenty years; and Kay Lovell Rankin and Sandra Lovell Lynch, Australian pen pals for more than forty years—international women's connections indeed continue.

Helena Lewis, chair of the Biography Seminar at Harvard's Center for Literary and Cultural Studies, Dave McFadden at Fairfield University, Leila Rupp of the Ohio State University, Loralee MacPike of Cal State-San Bernardino, Antoinette Burton of Johns Hopkins, Christine Lattek of St. Louis and London, and Karen Offen of Stanford University have all read parts of the manuscript and made helpful suggestions. Two anonymous reviewers, the editorial staff at the University Press of Kentucky, and Pat Sterling all have my thanks for close readings and suggestions in the revision and copyediting stage.

At Appalachian State University, my debts are many and varied. First, my thanks go to the Department of Interdisciplinary Studies, to my colleagues, and three department chairs—Marv Williamsen, Kay Smith, and Cynthia Wood—for supporting my scholarly work and travel over the years, including two Off-Campus Scholarly Assignment years, reassigned time, and excuses for numerous missed faculty meetings. I thank also the College of Arts and Sciences and Dean Don Sink for supporting my work and especially the Fulbright to Finland; Graduate Studies and Research and Dean Joyce Lawrence for a University Research Committee Grant, travel moneys, copying and scanning costs; and the Office of International Studies for a Travel Grant for Finland and Estonia in 1993, as well as additional smaller grants. Special thanks go to Diana Moody and the efficient and enthusiastic Interlibrary Loan Staff at Belk Library; to Liz Bordeaux, secretary extraordinaire of Interdisciplinary Studies; to Jim Young, cartographer in the Department of Geography; and to Pat Pilchard and Beth Jacquot, Media Services, for their graphics talents. Thanks also to more than a decade of students in women's history and feminist theory classes for asking perceptive questions and helping refine my thinking. Finally, my Feminist Research and Writing Group at Appalachian, 1992–97—Pat Beaver, Tina Groover, Janet Hutchison, Kathryn Kirkpatrick, Marilyn Smith, Susan Staub—read my writing, helped me set priorities, suggested sources, and provided warm support on many difficult occasions.

Three other individuals remain to thank: Dana Greene, professor of history at St. Mary's College of Maryland, graduate school compatriot at Emory University's Institute of the Liberal Arts, friend and role-model for thirty years, who started me in feminist activism with our protest about female fellowship quotas at Emory University; Brian Anderson, coauthor of the original version of Chapter 2, "Paving the Way" (presented at the Nineteenth Century Interdisciplinary Studies Association, University of California, Santa Cruz, in 1995), and long-time editorial assistant; and Leslie E. "Bud" Gerber, after thirty years of marriage still my severest and best critic.

Introduction

On Beginning to Tell a "Best-Kept Secret"

Hereafter there will be a golden cable of sympathy between you and us. Every victory you will win shall be ours; you work not only for the women of your country, but for the women of the whole world.
    —Alli Trygg-Helenius, 1888, at the International Council of Women.

Social criticism originating in the urban centers of France or England crisscrossed the Channel, traveled north via the North and Baltic Seas to the capital and port cities of Scandinavia, Poland, and Russia, and to the seaports of the old Hanseatic League, and quickly sailed west to the Americas. Thus, ideas elaborated in London or Edinburgh rapidly reached a reading public not only in the Low Countries and in New England but in Stockholm, Hamburg, Königsberg, and St. Petersburg as well. Within months of publication the works of the Marquis de Condorcet, Mary Wollstonecraft, George Sand, and John Stuart Mill found translators (many of whom were women), reviewers, advocates, and detractors in other countries. In the nineteenth century intellectual networks soon assumed organizational forms through loose international alliances—a development that held true as much for partisans of the women's movements as for the better-known antislavery, socialist, and pacifist movements. Indeed, it would not be amiss to state that the international intellectual ferment surrounding the cause of women has, until recently, been one of Western civilization's best-kept secrets.
    —Susan Groag Bell and Karen Offen,
Women, the Family, and Freedom: The Debate in Documents, 1983.

The first dependable transatlantic telegraph cable link was completed in 1866. Stretching from Heart's Content, Newfoundland, to Valentia Island and Queenstown in Ireland, it culminated an engineering and financial effort of almost mythic dimensions; the participating steamships bore such names as *Agammemnon, Gorgon, Valorous, Terrible,* and *Niagara.* Directing the Anglo-American Telegraph Company were economic titans such as Sir Daniel Gooch (chairman of the Great Western Railway Company), Henry Ford Barclay, and the legendary Cyrus W. Field of New York City.[1] Their submarine link destroyed Western Union's audacious project to build a land telegraph line from British Columbia across the Bering Straits and through Siberia to St. Petersburg, Russia. Defeated, the Western Union company sold glass insulators to Siberian peasants as American teacups.[2]

With its massed teams of physicists, electrical engineers, cable manufacturers, surveyors, financiers, and ship captains, the transatlantic cable operation was a thoroughly masculine undertaking. Promethean in scale, it nevertheless served first the down-to-earth ends of profit and efficient trade. In the words of Henry Field (his father Cyrus's biographer), the cable was a "reporter of markets, giving quotations of prices to counting rooms and banking houses."[3] The rhetoric of celebration surrounding the link's establishment bristled with separate-spheres assumptions. Cyrus Field proudly noted that "the ladies . . . have had their appropriate place" in the venture, "for when the cable was laid, the first public message that passed over it came from one of their own sex"—Queen Victoria.[4] And Henry Field appealed to women by observing that "the slender cord beneath the sea had finer uses" than the merely economic: to link "hearts and homes on opposite sides of the ocean, bearing messages of life and death, of joy and sorrow, of hopes and fears."[5]

By the century's end the 1866 cable had been supplemented by scores of others, webbing the Atlantic world into a grand structure of electrical communications (see Figure 1). This structure generated its own world of metaphors, one of which Alli Trygg-Helenius drew upon in her Finnish-accented address to the International Council of Women in 1888. Underlying (in the most literal sense) the "golden cable of sympathy" was a material system of copper and iron in the cold Atlantic. But also beneath—or, better, "behind"—the system of sympathy lay something else: a very long pre-cable history of linkages between women in the Atlantic community, a history that attested to something Trygg-Helenius's very presence in Washington embodied: the movement of "ladies" out of their "appropriate places" to virtual and actual sites where intense woman-to-woman communication could take place.

One can, I believe, speak legitimately of a tradition of transatlantic female communication far older than either the cable or the steamer. Indeed, it is a tradition older even than many historians of women's international organizations and international feminism are aware; this is at least the central thesis of this book. Formal organizations grew up in the late nineteenth century, and the extensive scholarly attention directed to them has been more than justified.[6] But what has not come clearly enough into view is the fact that such organizations sprang out of ground that had been well prepared. The "best-kept secret" noticed by Susan Bell and Karen Offen needs to begin to be told. Such is my aim here, although I believe something a good deal "thicker" than "intellectual ferment" is involved.

Evidence of a Pre-Organizational Matrix

The gradual building up of international relationships and contacts between women in Europe and North America, across borders of nations, languages, ethnic groups, and sometimes class, intensified throughout the nineteenth century. Although this process had been going on even earlier, the transformation of travel, magazine and book dissemination, and the international post combined with nineteenth-century advances in literacy and education to create a virtual explosion in the number of physical and verbal connections between women. It is my contention that the building up of these connections—an accretion, like the slow dripping of minerals that forms stalactites in caves or the deposits leading to the emergence of coral reefs—enabled the establishment of more formal international women's organizations by the turn of the century.

My research on the origins of international feminism in the nineteenth century has thus led me to postulate the existence of a pre-organizational matrix or network of international experiences and relationships, which then served as the basis upon which an autonomous movement and explicit feminist consciousness could later develop in the Atlantic community. Elements of this development can be spotted in the very early decades. At first only implicit and incipient, the network gradually emerged as a recognizable (to the historian, at least) infrastructure created by increasingly intense, multileveled, transnational "traditions of communication" among women. In the process, rudiments of a feminist consciousness began to form, albeit not always directed toward the creation of an autonomous movement. Indeed, some of the most important fashioners of the matrix were in many senses antifeminist, but ironically, their work helped produce structures whose existence was an indispensable precondition to feminism's future.[7]

To research what Bell and Offen usefully termed "loose international alliances" among women in the nineteenth century has required a multidimensional procedure. The "best-kept secret" yielded only gradually (and incompletely), as I investigated a variety of sources and testimonies. Evidence hails from several kinds of nineteenth-century material, both printed and archival.

At least six domains or avenues of woman-to-woman international connectedness can be identified, each exhibiting such vitality that one cannot ignore it without distorting the overall picture: (1) the rise of new communications systems—including the travel industry—and women's vigorous use of them, especially the female adventurers' exploits whose deeds served to make travel appealing to newly literate publics; (2) the work of Protestant evangelists and Catholic women religious, who, despite their mostly conservative ideas about women's place, displayed in their actions bold and imaginative modes of international communication and organization; (3) the complex international bonds developed among women working in reform movements— abolitionism, temperance, peace, antiprostitution; (4) the personal and institutional interconnectedness which developed in the utopian community movement, both secular and religious; (5) the transatlantic and intra-European networks of support, affiliation, and common purpose that linked political revolutionaries, refugees, and expatriates; (6) the emergence of female literary celebrities—Harriet Beecher Stowe and George Sand, for example—whose works and personal example served to call into existence "virtual communities," international in scope and significance.

Other avenues of female "outreach" that have attracted my attention include international diplomacy, socialism and labor movements, translation, entrepreneurship, immigration, correspondence, artistic and scientific communities. Material from these areas plays a smaller role in the book, however.

The plethora of Nordic and Scandinavian materials is partly explained by my work with these sources during a Fulbright year and in subsequent visits. But the intriguing fact remains that the number of international connections made by Nordic women was disproportionate to their population; more important, these women and their internationalism are relatively unknown to American readers.

Degrees of Consciousness as an Organizing Principle

As shown by the sorts of internationalists and proto-internationalists already mentioned, the hypothesized pre-organizational matrix out of which a mature Atlantic community sisterhood would grow was itself the result of both feminist and nonfeminist elements and interactions. Some nonfeminist women limned patterns of action that had unintentionally but objectively positive implications for the women's movement. Others had little idea that their activities would have profound consequences both for female emancipation and for the eventual global linking of women. Still others sought internationality and did so in full awareness of their attempts to change women's position.

After a chapter that analyzes as paradigmatic the scheme of influence begun by Lucretia Mott's 1840 visit to the British Isles, I discuss the implications for women of the communication and travel revolution of the nineteenth century (Chapter 2). Turning then to the contributions of international female religious orders and female evangelists such as Cornelia Connelly, Phoebe Palmer, Catherine Booth, Amanda Berry Smith, and Hannah Whitall Smith, I explore the positive implications of their antifeminism (Chapter 3). Theirs was an ironic path, for their conception of women's place often belied the actual roles they themselves undertook—a theological matter that I explore in some detail. Harriet Beecher Stowe and George Sand are the focus of Chapter 4. I call them "unwitting allies" of female internationality because such a goal was hardly part of their literary intentions. Yet these two authors—in both what they wrote and how they handled their fame—advanced networking activity in quite wonderful and unexpected ways.

The next two chapters examine a developing consciousness of the significance of Atlantic community connections among women. Revolutionaries, political emigrés, reformers, and utopians were sources of very important communicative endeavors over astonishing distances. Because they all (even many early nationalists) drew their key ideas and motives from the universalist progressivism of the Enlightenment, such ventures seem logical, but the extent and intensity of their efforts sometimes reached epic proportions—those, for example, of Flora Tristan, Suzanne Voilquin, Margaret Fuller, Mathilde Anneke, Cristina Belgiojoso, and Frances Wright. Political women—revolutionaries, refugees, and expatriates (Chapter 5)—are placed before the reformers in this study because they were relatively less conscious of their position and work as women. Even though many of them established connections with other women across national borders only during or after the 1848 European upheavals, I tell their stories here before those of the earlier socialists and reformers. Reformers and utopians (Chapter 6) were often quite conscious of themselves as women and reached out to like-minded counterparts across geographical boundaries—thus earning a position in this book closer to the four foremothers given pride of place.

Internationalist women who saw clearly the value of creating strong ties of friendship and advocacy among women in the Atlantic community are the subject of Chapters 7 and 8. Although I view all the figures who make an appearance in the book as what I call "mothers of the matrix," some deserve to wear this appellation as a distinct title of honor. I thus single out Anna Doyle Wheeler, Elizabeth Cady Stanton, Fredrika Bremer, and Frances Power Cobbe for special treatment. Despite their considerable philosophic differences, they demonstrated a capacity for adding great substantiality to the emerging web of communication binding together women from very different cultural settings and situations.

The book closes with a consideration of the figure of Aleksandra Gripenberg in relation to the 1888 International Council of Women (Chapter 9). My purpose is to present this threshold moment—the movement from the pre-organizational matrix to accomplished international organization—in such a way as to remind readers of the rich lines of connection that preceded and make explicable this signal event in women's history in the Atlantic community. As Stanton's and Mott's "spiritual granddaughter," Gripenberg wrought ties with Sophia Sturge (daughter of Mott's arch-enemy Joseph Sturge) and with American-Finnish immigrant Maggie Walz, thus revealing how vitally strong an infrastructure was already in place. Other "granddaughters" such as Ida B. Wells-Barnett used the transatlantic network built by Lucretia Mott and the abolitionists in developing (much later) the international antilynching movement.

Several appendixes offer additional supportive data and invite further research in this neglected area, pointing the way, I hope, to future inquiry.

Concerning Boundaries: Time, Territory, Class

For most purposes, the period from the Congress of Vienna (1815) to the International Council of Women (1888) adequately delimits my material. The two boundary decades are thus the 1820s and 1880s. The 1820s witnessed the beginning of the era when Europeans started to visit the American experiment in some numbers, and international travel in Europe became more feasible as the tourist industry emerged. The end of the 1880s saw the founding of the first international women's organization, the International Council of Women—a formalized structure. Although earlier international organizations (antislavery, temperance, and various religious groups) had many female members, no other authentic women's international organizations appeared until after the 1880s, most of them in the period just before World War I. The study thus focuses on the seven decades in the middle of the nineteenth century, with some references to both earlier and later years.

Geographic boundaries are somewhat more problematic. Like chronological eras, national borders too often delimit the study of history, and thus a resolutely international focus creates difficulties. My project trains its attention on "the Atlantic community": that is, Europe and North America, loosely defined. In the western portion I have occasionally included the Caribbean or Canada, but the emphasis is on the United States. Europe encompasses Great Britain and Ireland as well as the Continent, including Scandinavia, Finland, and non-Asiatic Russia. I make some reference also to international travel in the Mediterranean world: the Holy Land, Egypt, and the Ottoman Empire. Students of European history will understand this, recalling the scope of the Roman Empire, the routes of the Crusades, and the old relation of Byzantium with Latin Christianity.

The core of the book is generally the transatlantic United States–British Isles axis, although I regularly point to France and Sweden or Finland. The language-and-idea nexus of the North Atlantic was clearly the basis of many of the connections made by women, and therefore of the network that would gradually grow into the formal women's international organizations of the turn of the century. Obviously, language was a factor here, both as connector and separator. But educated nineteenth-century women simply knew more languages than their modern counterparts, and of course English was not yet the *lingua franca* it has become. Although the nineteenth century saw the apogée of the imperialism of Western Europe, the geographical boundaries of empire do not form the outlines of my study. Rather, I explore a difficult-to-map but very concrete historical reality: the transatlantic world. Figure 1 maps the undersea cables linking the continents by 1890. The busy traffic and

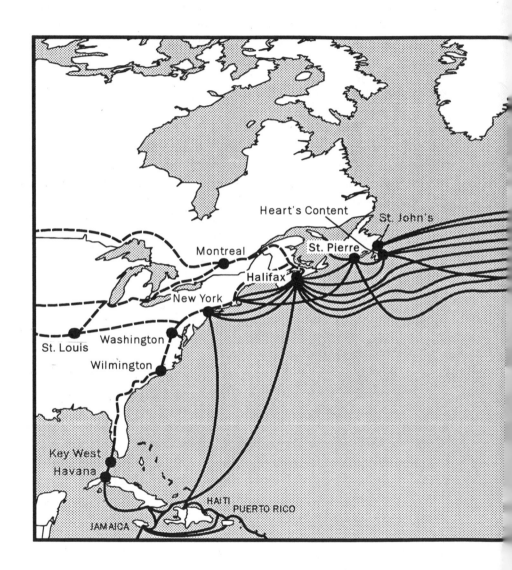

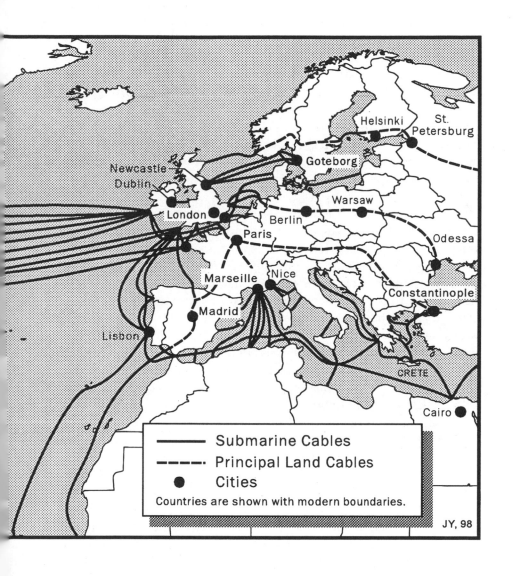

Newcastle
Dublin
London
Paris
Marseille
Nice
Madrid
Lisbon
Goteborg
Helsinki
St. Petersburg
Berlin
Warsaw
Odessa
Constantinople
CRETE
Cairo

—— Submarine Cables
- - - Principal Land Cables
● Cities
Countries are shown with modern boundaries.

JY, 98

bustling life it represents make the national boundaries historians too often use seem not only chauvinistic but unreal.

I am encouraged by the fact that others have usefully viewed the Atlantic as a bridge rather than considering it a barrier, as comparative studies of slavery and modernizing processes during this period do.[8] For example, Paul Gilroy's influential *The Black Atlantic* identifies and explores a thoroughly internationalist black culture taking shape in the late nineteenth and early twentieth centuries. He argues for the use of metaphors highlighting transition and boundary effacement; therefore, hybridity, blending, crossing, and passing become central phenomena. He advises, "[C]ultural historians could take the Atlantic as one single, complex unit of analysis in their discussions of the modern world and use it to produce an explicitly transnational and intercultural perspective."[9] These words precisely describe the cultural and geographic presumptions of my work.

The class bias of this study must be acknowledged at the outset. Since most of the linkages women established were predicated on literacy (books and articles, letters, written introductions, organizations), and since such connections assume some level of financial security (for travel, hosting, or books), it is obvious that most of the women whose stories I have found were members of the educated middle or upper class. Occasionally, I have come across a literate servant or working-class woman—Robert Louis Stevenson's nanny and maid "Cummy," Jamaican entrepreneur Mary Seacole, Finnish immigrant-entrepreneur Maggie Walz, the Saint-Simonian embroiderer Suzanne Voilquin—but these examples serve to point up their exceptionality and highlight the undeniable fact that only a tiny minority of women could become internationally engaged. Grassroots labor organizations did not become international until late in the century, and even then it was the intelligentsia (figures such as Clara Zetkin and Emma Goldman) who played the leading roles.

Three Usefully Related Metaphors

The inherently international character of the nineteenth-century women's movement suggests one reason why it has not been much studied: it was both too obvious and too elusive. Cracking Bell and Offen's "best-kept secret" necessitated envisioning by means of several organizing metaphors a process spreading out over time and space.

The central metaphors used here are "matrix," "network," and "web."[10] An extremely rich word, "matrix" is often encountered today in its mathematical sense of a rectangular grid or chart composed of vertical and horizontal lines that define cells or small fields. Geologists employ the term when speaking about the surrounding material from which one extricates fossils or crystals and to which one may look for an impression or mold of them. Printers have used the word to denote the mold in which the face of a piece of type is cast. But its original sense is *that from which a structure grows*. More precisely and interestingly for my purposes here, it means that in which something develops or takes shape or, in anatomy, the formative cells of a structure such as a fingernail. According to the *Oxford English Dictionary*, "matrix" was used as late as 1896 with its figurative meaning of "a place or point of origin and growth." In Latin the word literally means "womb" or "breeding animal" and derives from *mater, matris,* mother. Thus, "matrimony" and "matron" come from the same root, as does "matriculate," which originates in the medieval Latin *matricula,* diminutive of *matrix,* womb, origin, or public roll.

A mathematical matrix is, almost literally, a network. Indeed, in computer science, "networks" and "matrices" are closely allied concepts. While I often use the terms as near synonyms in this work, I am aware that they carry different metaphoric burdens. "Net" and "network" derive ultimately from the Indo-European root *ned,* to twist together. The fundamental activities pointed to are, thus, threadmaking and the production of open-weave fabrics to be used to hold, contain, or trap. Related are the Latin *nodus,* knot, and *nectere,* to bind—as well as the German word *netz.* The oldest sense of "network" is that of a fabric of parallel threads or wires crossed at regular intervals by others, so as to form a mesh or lace pattern. Later, of course, a network became any interconnected physical system, such as of canals, tracks, or transmitting stations.

"Network" as a noun was defined in Samuel Johnson's 1755 *Dictionary of the English Language* as something with the form or construction of a net; according to the *OED,* its figurative meaning as an interconnected chain or system was used in 1816 by Samuel Coleridge in his *Lay Sermons.* Its contemporary meaning as a group of "interconnected or cooperating individuals" did not emerge until much later. According to *A Feminist Dictionary* (1985), "network" as a verb is a word "coined and used by women," meaning "to establish good connections with other women and provide for each other information, concrete help, and personal or professional support."[11] A networker would then be "one who networks." Note that this definition picks up the weblike connotations of a net.

Recent developments in linked-computer communication have served to fuse the meanings of "net" and "web." Thus, "Internet" is often synonymous with "Worldwide Web." Further complicating matters, a 1995 dictionary defines "Internet" as "a matrix of networks" connecting computers globally.[12] I occasionally contribute to this confusion by referring to web construction and networking in the same context. Yet here again, a somewhat different etymological source furnishes similar meanings and connotations: since "web" derives from the Indo-European word for "weave," it is closely associated with "net."

One is also reminded of the structures made by spiders. Female spiders build webs by spinning out silk, beginning with a bridge thread, to which the first radius is fastened. This becomes the hub; all other radii are secured from there, and only after they are complete does the spider spin out the sticky spiral threads connecting them. Each web has only one hub, but radii are connected not only to the hub but to each other by means of the spiral threads. The example of spiders brings us back to the powerful interplay between "matrix" and "web." In a classic text on spider webs, one reads: "The spider catches its food in a silken web, swathes its prey in a silken bag, and wraps its eggs in a silken cocoon."[13] Thus, the notion of a web or network being a site of new birth is far from an illogical mixing of metaphors.[14]

The appeal of these etymological reverberations in a work such as this hardly needs pointing out. What I am exploring here are the modes of communicative action that came to exist for nineteenth-century women. Such actions and modes were generative, creating a point of origin and growth. They came to constitute a kind of womb, gestating and thus enabling the subsequent development of a more formal organizational structure.[15]

A concluding note: it will have occurred to many by this time that these three metaphors are central to late modernity, with its dazzling revolutions in electronic communication, transport, and information storage and delivery. I hope that I have drawn upon them not because they are so profoundly up-to-date but because they are profoundly apt. In so doing, however, I have had to reckon with the significant fact that "network analysis" is the province of not one but two different disciplines outside of history: computer science and "structural" sociology. The former, as might be expected, offers few invitations to the interdisciplinary historian. The latter I have found interesting and occasionally suggestive.[16]

Network theory has since its beginning become a complicated quantitative part of sociometry, using Boolean algebra; it has its own journal, called *Social Networks,* and its own section in the *Annual Review of Sociology.*[17] But it is the basic concept with which I am concerned: that is, understanding and mapping the connections between women—the meetings, the letters, the introductions—and finding the "brokers," the nodes in the net, the mothers of the matrix, the beginnings of an "old girls' network" in the nineteenth century. I am interested in how these connections became friendships, cliques, organizations, and also ultimately hierarchies and conflicts—resulting in either a glossing over of disagreements or actual splits on the basis of difference in politics, nationality, or language.[18]

The basics of network analysis are very simple; in the words of Jeremy Boissevain, "It asks questions about who is linked to whom, the nature of that linkage, and how the nature of the linkage affects behaviour."[19] It is the transatlantic linkage among women in the nineteenth century that I am seeking to document.[20]

1

Weaving the Delicate Web

Lucretia Mott and Succeeding Generations

A "kvinnosakskvinna" [women's movement woman] could travel
through continents and would everywhere find some centre for
"kvinnosaken," where she would be met with sympathy and friendship,
in the same way as medieval monks were sure to find shelter in the
numerous monasteries.
    —Maikki Friberg c. 1897, quoted in Annie Furuhjelm, *Gryningen*

The disfranchisement of a whole sex, a condition which has
existed throughout the civilized world until a comparatively recent date,
has bred in half the population an unconscious internationalism.
    —Katharine Anthony, *Feminism in Germany and Scandinavia*, 1915

The great Lucretia Mott offers a superb demonstration of the validity of
metaphors of cables, webs, networks, and matrices. Indeed, her legacy of
connections shows the impact a single well-placed individual could make.
The 1840 World's Anti-Slavery Convention in London, which began with
a futile two-day battle over the seating of the American female delegates
(the opposition was led by Manchester Quaker Joseph Sturge), was a
vivid watershed of women's internationality. Lucretia Mott was at the
center of the transatlantic controversy, since her status as a female Quaker
preacher had already divided American Quakers in the Hicksite split.
The fact that the women lost the battle to be seated as delegates brought
the question of a woman's right to be a public person to the fore. The
convention's venue and surrounding gatherings provided Mott a forum,
allowed her to meet many important women, and established her as an
indispensable linking element in a multiplex system of relationships which
formed and informed her actions. Her "centrality" (in network analysis
terms, both the number of her contacts and her accessibility) make her

an essential figure.[1] The web of those relationships later received further strengthening through the activities of Barbara Bodichon and then Aleksandra Gripenberg. The result was the matrix itself, a structure of friendships, acquaintances, ties, and cross-linkages which was the precondition for mature feminist internationality. Thus, I seize on the example of Mott as a figure whose activities during a single year both point to a wider field of similar efforts and invite the use of some specialized concepts and analytic strategies.

I begin with a diagram. It is easy enough for the historian to locate and describe an important individual in relation to a key event, a single famous time and place. But the mothers of the matrix resist such static fixing, for in an unusually intense way the effects of their lives and work reverberate, criss-crossing geography and chronology. Figure 2 therefore attempts to represent the connections of one person, Lucretia Mott, over time and space. Mott is at the left because as an American she lived on the western side of the Atlantic. Englishwoman Barbara Bodichon is at the center, and the Finn Aleksandra Gripenberg is on the "eastern" side of the page, with Continental connections. The smaller names are also placed, roughly, in their relative geographic positions, and the lines represent their connections (meetings, letters, books, etc.). Bold caps denote more important figures.

Temporal development is also important, and thus the diagram represents three generations of activity beginning with Mott, whose birth predates that of Bodichon by some thirty-four years and that of Gripenberg by sixty-six. Mott is represented in the upper left, Bodichon is in the middle as the next generation, and Gripenberg is in the lower right as the third and youngest generation. So ideas are not only effacing space; they are also crossing time; in an intellectual sense Mott, Bodichon, and Gripenberg represent three generations of connectors—a mother, daughter, and granddaughter of the matrix. The diagram springs from my effort to pay close attention to Mott and her successors as kinds of "communicative experts." This results in a narrative whose meaning can be elucidated by networking terminology. Each of the other mothers of the matrix (Chapters 7 and 8) could be the focus of a similar diagram.

The Formative Stage: Lucretia Mott's 1840 Tour

During her remarkable 1840 journey Lucretia Mott kept a diary; this document provides a wealth of information about her activities as a liai-

Lucretia Mott, A "Mother of the Matrix"

During and After Attendance at 1840 World's Anti-slavery Convention, London

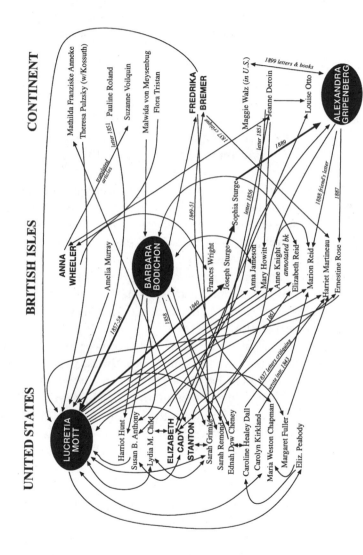

UNITED STATES   BRITISH ISLES   CONTINENT

Dates and lines = face to face visit, unless otherwise noted • Caps = Most Important Networkers • Arrows indicate initiation of contact

son figure for women on an international scale.[2] It vividly displays the interrelation of abolitionism and women's rights—but not just these, for Mott also moved through such topics as temperance, moral reform, the Irish question, evangelicalism, religious differences (especially among Quakers), and class questions (she met the aristocracy and the working class as well as the usual middle class). The diary bristles with names. The extensiveness of her contacts is surprising—in England, Ireland, Wales, Scotland. She traveled in all four areas of the British Isles after the London meetings and often lectured, or at least met and talked with dozens of people. Her true passion was for these various causes and the people involved, rather than the touristic sights that she dutifully visited. Thus, she fell asleep in the British Museum, refused to weep over Shakespeare's grave, and remained unimpressed by the Walter Scott sites in Scotland.

Not only did Mott pay visits, organize meetings, and discuss the position of women—both in and out of the formal abolitionist movement—but she also debated the controversy over women preachers, the "free produce" movement, Frances Wright's plans for abolition and universal education, the India question, the colonization scheme for slaves, female education, and moral reform (antiprostitution). She met prison reformer Elizabeth Fry, Quaker activist Anne Knight, translator Mary Howitt, liberal writer Harriet Martineau, art critic Anna Jameson, traveler-critic Frances Trollope, liberal aristocrats Lady Byron and Lady Sutherland, and many men, including Robert Owen. She encountered most of these people not just once but several times, and so discussions matured. Individuals asked her to speak, to carry letters to friends in America, to send them copies of Sarah and Angelina Grimké's books. Many sent boxes or bags of goods for the famous fundraising Anti-Slavery Fair, held annually by the Female Anti-Slavery Societies in the United States, and Mott asked Harriet Martineau to write something for the book that the Anti-Slavery Fair published each year. William Rathbone's wife requested that Mott discuss the comparative situation of women and, "after we had travelled over England and had seen their women, that we would let her know, how far we considered their minds fettered and crushed by public opinion and external restraints" (76). It is important to note that Mott was in a position to represent to her London interlocutors an interestingly complex set of ideas and impressions of persons derived from her experiences in America. Martineau and Frances Trollope were authors and persons with whom she was well ac-

Lucretia Mott, from *History of Woman Suffrage,* ed. Elizabeth Cady Stanton, Susan B. Anthony, Matilda Joslyn Gage, vol. 1 (New York: Fowlers and Wells, 1881).

quainted, and she was entirely conversant with the radical schemes of Frances Wright.

Mott probably met Marion Kirkland (Mrs. Hugo) Reid, who attended the 1840 Anti-Slavery Convention with her husband and in 1843 wrote an impassioned tract for women's rights, *A Plea for Women,* in answer to Sarah Lewis's *Woman's Mission* (1839). An adaptation and translation of Rousseau's disciple Louis Aimé Martin, *Woman's Mission* was a popular and influential treatise defining woman's moral superiority and her special duties; Lewis thus embraced the ideology of "separate spheres." As Elizabeth Helsinger, Robin Sheets, and William Veeder say, "The terms Lewis helped define—'mission,' 'sphere,' and 'influence'— were invoked throughout the period to awaken women's aspirations and to curtail their activities."[3] Marion Reid answered Lewis in terms of equal rights; she called for women's right to gain financial independence and to have political equality by means of the vote. Interestingly, Reid's work was more popular in the United States than in Britain, going through five editions between 1847 and 1852.[4]

The connection between Mott and Reid is an intriguing one because the book that Reid wrote was not on abolition but on women's rights. Very significant is the direct influence that the argument over the seating of the American abolitionist women had on Reid. Like Mott and Stanton, she saw that women had no more political rights than slaves. It thus appears likely that influences and relationships experienced in the context of abolitionism were laying down a matrixlike structure that joined women with women in the cause of female emancipation. Put another way, Reid was probably a friend of Mott's friends; in network analysis, such proximate relationships are indisputably important, if also "causally" indeterminable. They should be construed as part of "a field of activity" rather than a definable sequence.[5]

A few years after 1840 these ideas and personal contacts were continued and developed when Anne Knight (1786–1862), a British Quaker who had also attended the convention and met Mott, heavily annotated a copy of Reid's work and inserted clippings about women in both French and English plus some stickers she had had printed with feminist quotations and slogans (these she also affixed to her correspondence). On the title page, under the printed "Can man be free, if woman be a slave," she wrote, "No! Emancipate her then!" Calling the book "excellent," she nevertheless quarreled with some of the more reformist proposals. Reid had said that women should not be allowed to sit in Parliament; Knight wrote in the margin, "The point at issue must be equalization of human privilege if my brother have a right to sit there his sister has the same right give it up to her pay your debts ye dis'honourable men'" (no punctuation in original).[6] In the volume on this page is enclosed a pressed flower, a tiny daisy.

Anticipating a future development, I would note that much later, in 1889, Aleksandra Gripenberg came in contact with Reid via her new British friend, Caroline Ashurst Biggs, who remembered Reid as a foremother: "I met today for the first time an old lady who wrote the first 'women's movement' book that I ever read. This was Mrs. Hugo Reed [sic] & she wrote 'A Plea for Woman' [in 1843]. It was very pleasant to see how interested & fresh she was in all our questions having watched their progress for many years. She is really a pioneer for she began working before the first women's convocation in America was summoned."[7] Reid thus functioned as a liaison between Mott and Gripenberg, transmitting congeries of influence and feminist affiliation. Ernestine Rose played a very similar role (see below). Both were in the early generation, and late in life were grandmother-teachers to their third-generation granddaughters.

The scholar who attends carefully to the dynamics of international travel and association will notice points of crossing, overlapping, and lines of connection. French delegates attended the London convention in 1840, including Adolphe Crémieux (1796–1880). Englishwomen Anne Knight and Elizabeth Fry had both worked on the Continent. Present as well were Dutch persons opposed to slavery in the colonies, although slavery was not abolished in Surinam until 1876. Charles Remond, a "free person of color" from the United States, was another delegate; he lectured in England after the convention's end. Eighteen years later his sister, Sarah Remond, traveled to England for an antislavery speaking tour (see Chapter 6). She lectured around the country and remained in England for several years. In 1861 she attended Bedford College for women, founded in London by Elizabeth Reid (not related to Marion Kirkland Reid), another of Mott's English friends who had attended the 1840 convention.[8]

Thus, the linkages that Lucretia Mott forged in 1840 continued their repercussions as the transatlantic stream of visitors and writings against slavery went in both directions. A visit to Lucretia Mott became de rigueur for anyone interested in abolition or women's rights who toured the United States at midcentury, and so we find Fredrika Bremer (Swedish;

Marion Kirkland Reid on the cover of *Woman, Her Education and Influence* (New York: Fowlers and Wells, 1847).

The Homes of the New World, 1853), Theresa Pulszky (Hungarian; *White, Red, Black: Sketches of American Society in the United States*, 1853), and Barbara Bodichon (English; *An American Diary*, 1857) all describing their visits. Even those favoring slavery usually had something to say about Mrs. Mott (Amelia M. Murray, *Letters from the United States, Cuba, and Canada*, 1856).

A number of terms from network analysis may be applied to Mott. Her primary or "first order" network was of course the Society of Friends. Many members of that historic religious body were also "universal reformers," engaged simultaneously in several movements.[9] These may be thought of as constituting different "zones" within a broad network structure. Mott, however, had an originating role, pulling together schemes of relationships to form a potentially separable protofeminist network. She is thus a centralizing figure, a dynamic facilitator of communication. For Jeremy Boissevain, "centrality is an index of the degree to which a person is accessible to the persons in a particular (non-egocentric) network."[10] Her accessibility, even over great distances, certainly is historically striking. An alternative network analysis metaphor for Mott is "broker," a commercial term that usefully emphasizes her work as a go-between or feminist entrepreneur.[11] Boissevain's analysis of the broker figure stresses the for-profit nature of broker transactions and the omnipresence of manipulation; that Mott was not motivated by pecuniary aims shows the limits of this metaphor. Readers more comfortable with feminist terminology might prefer Mary Daly's word "webster," which emphasizes Mott's capacity as a spinner of bridges between continents and diverse groups of women.[12]

The Second Generation:
The Circles Widen to Bodichon and Rose

Barbara Leigh Smith Bodichon (1827–91), only thirteen years old in 1840, is representative of the next generation, whose connections built upon earlier contacts as the diameter of the web moved outward and its density developed. On her wedding trip to the United States in 1857 she explored and exploited the various acquaintanceships and contacts she had earlier made, including that with Mott. Bodichon, more than many, continued to relate abolition and women's rights and everywhere pursued the linkages along that axis. Aboard a Mississippi steamer, on December 11, 1857, after a long conversation with many southern whites, she reflected: "Slavery is a greater injustice, but it is allied to the injustice to women so closely that I cannot see one without thinking of the other and feeling how soon slavery would be destroyed if right opinions were entertained upon the other question."[13]

Bodichon was well positioned by her background to be an extraordinarily productive point in the matrix. By the time of her visit to Mott she was a seasoned internationalist and women's advocate. In 1850 (at twenty-three, and already with an independent income fixed on her by her liberal father, Benjamin Smith) she and her friend Bessie Rayner Parkes had traveled and sketched all over the Continent, chaperoning each other. These two "unprotected women" in corsetless, loose-fitting clothing and blue-tinted spectacles caused quite a stir in small towns of Germany, Austria, and Switzerland. On their return Bodichon founded the Portman School in London, a progressive, coeducational, secular elementary school that enrolled Catholics, Jews, freethinkers, and Unitarians. The absence of religious education marked it as a radical experiment.[14] According to Kathryn Gleadle, Bodichon and Parkes were much influenced by Mary Howitt and other English and American Unitarians in their early years.[15]

In 1854 she had published *A Brief Summary in Plain Language of the Most Important Laws of England concerning Women,* which was revised and expanded several times in the next few years. The spectacularly successful pamphlet cost only a few pence and explained the law as it related to single and to married women. It did more to further the cause of women and especially of married women's property laws than decades of debate on the issue. Partly as a result of the renown of this work, late in 1855 Bodichon (then still Barbara Leigh Smith) and others formed the Married Women's Property Committee, the first organized feminist group in England. It came to be known as the Langham Place Group and included Mary Howitt, Anna Mary Howitt (her daughter), Anna Jameson, Bessie Parkes, Maria Rye, and Mrs. Bridell Fox. The group began with petitions to Parliament and a signature campaign.[16] This unsuccessful effort lasted for more than two years; significant change in the laws for married women would not be made for two more decades.

In 1857 Barbara Leigh Smith married Eugène Bodichon, a French Algerian doctor she had met on family holidays in Algeria, and their year-long honeymoon trip to the United States provided the occasion for visiting Lucretia Mott. The two women talked of people they knew in common and the women's rights struggle in both countries. Bodichon's

Barbara Leigh Smith Bodichon, courtesy of Girton College, Cambridge.

description of Mott shows her admiration and respect for this foremother: "I never saw such a beautiful old lady, really beautiful and so exquisite in her dress, like a pearl. I fell in love with her immediately. She looks 'full of grace' in every sense of the word. I do not wonder her preaching has stirred so many souls, her aspect is eloquent, her smile full of good things." Bodichon was conscious of the importance of fostering the ties between women, for she wrote in her letter diary, "Please let Mrs. Reid [Elizabeth Reid, founder of Bedford College where Bodichon had attended art classes] know that I have seen her friends and how pleasant it was to me to feel a link between such good people."[17]

Bodichon met other notables from the American women's rights movement, especially in the Boston area: medical doctor Harriot Hunt, abolitionists Sara Clarke and Maria Weston Chapman, educator Elizabeth Peabody, and art critic Ednah Dow Cheney, among others.[18] All these women were decisively transatlantic, if only because of the books and magazines they read and wrote for; for example, as a teenager in 1837, Cheney had written on women's rights, criticizing Harriet Martineau.[19] Bodichon also explored her interest in other reform efforts—prisons, women's education, and orphanages. She spent more than a week with Theodore and Angelina Grimké Weld at Eagleswood School, Raritan Bay Union, New Jersey, saying, "I never saw such a satisfactory group of young people in my life. Mr. Weld is working out every day his principles of equal advantages for black or white or male or female."[20] She had nothing to say about either Sarah or Angelina Grimké's earlier works on women, however.

After their prolonged wedding trip to the United States (during which Bodichon also saw slaves and slave markets in the South), the couple spent winters in Algeria at the doctor's clinic and summers in England, where Bodichon could carry out her feminist campaigns. She continued her painting and sketching wherever she was—Algeria, the United States, England—often seeing a "moral landscape" mirrored in the aesthetic one. For example, she interpreted "swampy, slimy Louisiana" as suggestive of the immorality of the institution of slavery in 1858 New Orleans.[21]

Bodichon's concern with abolition widened to include various women's rights campaigns and focused particularly on the legal situation of English women. The *English Woman's Journal*, published by Emily Faithful and others in the Langham Place Group, became the first British feminist periodical, and in true international fashion Bodichon wrote for it a series of articles on her trip to the United States and another about women in Algeria, among other pieces.[22] The first suffrage proposal presented to Parliament also came from the Langham Place Group, as did concern for the unemployment rate of middle-class women (Maria Rye began the Female Middle-Class Emigration Society in 1861 as an outgrowth of the Society for Promoting Employment of Women; see Appendix D: International Governesses).[23] The group also advocated higher education for women and fought for women's medical training. Appropriately, in 1869 Bodichon helped Emily Davies found Girton College at Cambridge, the first university-level college for women in England.

Networks grow because of a multiplicity of links; that Mott is a "centering" figure does not mean that the structure emanated only from her. In the context of Bodichon's relation to Mott, it is revealing to consider the case of Ernestine Rose (1810-92). Here was another international woman who made early transatlantic connections with both abolition and women's rights groups.[24] But her origins were far different from those of Mott or Bodichon. Leaving her childhood home in Poland in 1827 (her father was a rabbi), Ernestine Potowsky made her way to England, where—supporting herself by inventing and marketing a kitchen deodorant—she embraced free thought and atheism and became a follower of Robert Owen. She met and married a fellow Owenite, William E. Rose, and emigrated to the United States in 1836, quickly becoming active in the abolitionist movement and later in women's rights.

Friends with Mott, Lydia Maria Child, and the Grimkés and widely known on the lecture circuit, Rose spoke for women's rights, free thought, and abolition. In New York in 1853 she was a major speaker on the anniversary of West Indian emancipation. As an atheist and freethinker, however, she did not fit in with the Christian Protestant background of most of the Americans in the movement, and ultimately she returned to England. But her connectedness throughout the Atlantic community made her a signally important source of later developments.[25] In London in 1888, for example, she met and talked with Aleksandra Gripenberg, who called her "an old, ill, bitter Polish woman, but interesting with grey curls and black eyes. One of the first suffrage pioneers in America."[26] Rose gave Gripenberg a book and told her stories of revolutionary heroes—Lafayette, Lajos Kossuth, Thomas Paine—thus tightening the multiplying bonds of nearly three generations.

Ernestine Rose, from a postcard published by Helaine Victoria Press. A different pose is published in *History of Woman Suffrage*, vol. 1, 1881.

Third Stage:
Aleksandra Gripenberg and Sophia Sturge,
Spiritual Granddaughters

Was the network I am beginning here to describe the precondition for the development of organized, international feminism? Although "direct causation" is not finally a useful concept in historical explanation, it seems clear from the plethora of evidence available that something important happened as the result of this multiplex scheme of interweavings. A strong hint of development in this direction can be gained by pondering what seems to have been a third stage or zone of connectedness—manifest in the relation of Sophia Sturge and Aleksandra Gripenberg.

Sophia Sturge (1849–1936) was the daughter of Joseph Sturge, an English Quaker activist who, with Thomas Harvey, visited Finland in 1854—after the Crimean War—to help bring relief following the British shelling of the Finnish coast. A letter about their visit was published in the *Friends' Review* and read by American poet John Greenleaf Whittier, who then wrote and published, "The Conquest of Finland." In about 1890, Sophia Sturge, by then a prominent Quaker feminist reformer and

Sophia Sturge, from William R. Hughes's *Sophia Sturge: A Memoir* (London: George Allen and Unwin, 1940).

peace activist, wrote to Aleksandra Gripenberg, inviting her to visit because Sophia had "always felt as if we had some special interest in Finland" since her father's visit so many years before. She included a copy of
Whittier's poem about Finland, saying that she had learned it as a little
girl.[27]

Gripenberg had just returned to Finland from more than a year in
England and America, where she attended the founding convention of the
International Council of Women (1888), organized by Elizabeth Cady
Stanton. It seems clear that Sturge was motivated to write Gripenberg because of the latter's involvement in the women's movement. It is likely that
Sturge had met Stanton in England during the latter's 1882–83 sojourn
(see Chapter 7), but she may have missed meeting Gripenberg in 1888
because by that time Sturge was in Ireland, having begun a project to teach
poor Irish peasants to make and sell baskets.[28] Sturge concluded her letter
with this assertion about the importance of women's international connections: "It has been a great help, and pleasure, to have been brought into
contact with so many women from different nations and I do hope that we
shall all be better friends in the future, and that we may be able to do
something, by knowing each other better, to prevent war between the
nations of Europe ever being possible again."[29] This call for women's continued international organizing to prevent war reiterated Fredrika
Bremer's 1854 proposal for a Women's Peace Alliance (see Chapter 8).[30]

Sophia Sturge's letter established a relationship with Gripenberg
that continued for twenty years, with visits in both directions, until
Gripenberg's death in 1913. Sturge traveled to Boston in 1904 for an international conference on peace and arbitration in Boston, meeting,
among others, Bertha von Suttner (see Chapter 6) and Jane Addams. She
also visited a school for black children in Philadelphia, named for her
father, Joseph Sturge, because of his abolitionist work.[31] From the United
States to England and back, from England to Finland and back to the
United States, one strand of an already strong network of like-minded
women grew more definite. The continuity of the relationships is more
than striking when one recalls something about Sophia's father. Joseph
Sturge had made himself well known at the 1840 London Anti-Slavery
Convention by being the British delegate who spoke most vociferously
against allowing women to participate publicly.[32] A prominent Quaker
abolitionist and temperance worker, he was opposed to women's rights.
Mott therefore was one of his great opponents. Yet fifty years later we
find his daughter negotiating an international network that had begun

with Lucretia Mott's London journey. Sophia Sturge had, in her wisdom, become one of Mott's spiritual granddaughters, and like her "grandmother" she had interests and friendships throughout the Atlantic community.

Paving the Way

The "Miraculous Era" in Communication and the "Unprotected Female"

Uncle Tom is not only a miracle of itself, but it announces the commencement of a miraculous Era in the literary world. A dozen years ago, Uncle Tom would have been a comparative failure—there might not have been more than a million copies sold in the first year of its publication. Such a phenomenon as its present popularity could have happened only in the present wondrous age. It required all the aid of our new machinery to produce the phenomenon; our steam-presses, steam-ships, steam-carriages, iron roads, electric telegraphs, and universal peace among the reading nations of the earth. But beyond all, it required readers to consume the books, and these have never before been so numerous; the next year, they will be more numerous still, and Uncle Tom may be eclipsed by the shadow of a new comer in the reading world. It is not Uncle Tom alone who has made the way for himself; . . . he has only proclaimed the fact that the great avenues of literature are all open, wide, and well paved, and free to all who have the strength to travel in them. Hereafter, the book which does not circulate to the extent of a million of copies, will be regarded as a failure. What the first edition of a popular novel will be by-and-by, when the telegraphic wires will be printing it simultaneously, in New-York, St. Petersburgh, San Francisco, Pekin and the intermediate cities, it is not easy to estimate.

—"Uncle Tomitudes," *Putnam's Monthly Magazine,* 1853

Harriet Beecher Stowe's remarkable literary fame and her frequent presence on the European continent made her a powerful agent for bringing women together internationally. Along with George Sand, she personified the unifying power of literary celebrity. Stowe is also important, though, as a *traveling* author whose experience reflects the myriad transformations that made up the great communications revolution of the nineteenth century. In 1853 she toured Europe, escorted by her brother, Charles Beecher, and her husband, Calvin Stowe. Their reports of the material conditions of their travel—their conveyances, lodgings, monetary arrangements, bureaucratic problems and solutions—give a lively sense of the brave new world of geographical mobility then in the making. Without grasping the key elements of this transformation, one can neither fully account for nor appreciate many of the developments described in this volume. Not the least of these was the unexpected—and, for many contemporaries, scandalous—emergence of a figure we now more or less take for granted in the West: "the unprotected female."

Wind, Steam, Speed—and Readers

The 1853 *Putnam's* excerpt above reminds us that the success—critical, political, and commercial—of *Uncle Tom's Cabin* not only offers testament to Harriet Beecher Stowe's talent and to the timeliness of her novel; it also gives historians evidence of the social and intellectual changes made possible by the extremely rapid growth of communications and travel technology and infrastructure. Not only were novels markedly easier to publish and distribute in 1850 than in 1840 or 1830, but all other communication—in business, science, diplomacy, education—was also conducted with much more speed and efficiency. Fast mail coaches (soon replaced by railroads) and steamships moved travelers at ever increasing speeds. Literacy and readership rates rose in the United States and in much of Europe. Relative peace and stability also enhanced international communication, all allowing *Uncle Tom's Cabin* to be distributed more widely than any novel before it.

Increasing literacy, a product of the Industrial Revolution, was obviously a huge component of the success of *Uncle Tom's Cabin*. A generation earlier the level of literacy might have been insufficient to supply that critical mass necessary to generate new philosophical, theological, and political curiosity. There were far fewer Mary Wollstonecrafts than Elizabeth Cady Stantons. Readership and literacy are notoriously difficult to measure, but *Putnam's* was certainly correct in noting that readers, in the United States and internationally, had never been so numerous or so diverse.

In England, readership was not only growing—in the 1830s, middle-class journals such as *Fraser's, Edinburgh Review, Blackwood's,* and *Athenaeum* had circulations over 200,000—but broadening. In some cases, new readers were both poor and politicized; "cheap [leftist] periodicals like *The Mirror of Literature, Amusement and Instruction,* and *The Hive* flooded British bookstalls and coffeehouses in the 1820s with circulations of 50,000 or more," alarming middle-class observers who worried about "'mischievous, profligate, insane' radical writers."[1] *Uncle Tom's Cabin* actually sold 650,000 more copies in Great Britain than in the more populous United States, but for both countries the figures were considered the widest possible circulation of a book.[2]

The development of the telegraph is a good example of the speed with which communication was improving. Samuel Morse sent the first intercity telegraphic message (Baltimore to Washington, D.C.) in 1844, and the first transatlantic cable was laid only fourteen years later. That line lasted only a few weeks, but, as we have seen, permanent transatlantic telegraph service began in 1866. Telegrams are virtually instantaneous, much faster than the mails, and they were important strands in the web of communication. When Harriet Beecher Stowe toured Europe in 1853, many of her travel arrangements were made by telegram, including a series of frantic messages sent by Charles Beecher in trying to track down Harriet's lost trunk.[3] Charles and the other members of the entourage also used telegrams, although none of these were yet transatlantic, to communicate with their banks and to arrange passage from England back to the United States (323, 377). Interestingly, at one French location Charles was not allowed to send a message to England in English, but had to translate it into French (325).

It is difficult to exaggerate the power of the telegraph for easing travel and business, but as a means of exchanging ideas or disseminating information it was much too expensive. For those purposes, the primary method was the post. Governments in Europe and the United States enthusiastically supported and subsidized the mails; doing so made government and business more efficient, and in democracies the mails were considered essential for maintaining an educated, informed populace. The U.S. mail was considered such an instrument of democracy that the government went so far as to allow newspaper editors to send and receive other newspapers without charge, and periodicals and books at low rates (this practice survives today in reduced postage for printed material).[4] Without distant correspondents as well as wire services, editors could not have made their readers into citizens after the Jeffersonian ideal. In 1843, noted the *Universal Yankee Nation,* "there is scarcely a hamlet in New England which the *Daily Mail* does not reach . . . dispensing information, instruction, and amusement almost as cheaply as free gifts amongst every class in society."[5]

The money order system through the post office began in the United States in 1864, partly to accommodate Union soldiers sending money or receiving it from home. In England, postal money orders had begun in 1837. The advent of the telegraph and transatlantic cables, therefore, instituted a safe, convenient, and international system for transmitting money.[6]

Governments were also eager to subsidize mails internationally, especially when there was diplomatic or imperial business to conduct. In the first half of the nineteenth century, transatlantic passage was expensive and risky for shipping companies, particularly during December and January, when few passengers cared to brave the cold and storms, and merchants were reluctant to ship goods that might be damaged by freezing or moisture. So it was government shipping subsidies that kept the mails moving during the worst eight or ten weeks of winter.[7] Starting in 1846 a series of international postal conventions between the United States and the countries of Western Europe standardized postage and mail routes, and in 1874 those countries formed the International Postal Union, which created a single postal territory.[8]

Developments in moving the mails were simultaneous with developments in moving people. For most of the first half of the nineteenth century, mail coaches were the fastest and most reliable means of land transportation. In the mid-1830s, they could average ten miles per hour throughout England; fast and frequent horse changes meant that mail could move from London to the most distant counties in two days. Early in the century in England these diligences were crowded and uncomfortable, with only four passengers enduring a bumpy ride.[9] But in 1853 Charles Beecher, riding in a French diligence, described a six-horse vehicle that carried sixteen passengers and baggage at a "prodigious pace along the smooth macadamized way," changing horses in only ten seconds; he told Harriet that he had never been so comfortable traveling (194-96).

In Beecher's experience, overseas mail was less reliable. By the 1840s, according to one historian, correspondents could expect mail to reach London from Boston or New York in two weeks.[10] But Charles complained that a letter from his wife, Sarah, took nineteen days to reach

him in Dundee—a week longer than he calculated it should take (53)—
and throughout his diary and letters home he recorded disappointment
at not hearing from his family. He even sent mailing instructions and
advice, prepaid letters, specified ships on his envelopes, and repeated his
London address over and over (177). None of this worked, apparently;
mail never did reach him as regularly as he wanted. Yet his complaints
are probably negative evidence of the general reliability of the postal system; after all, if the mails had been regarded as uncertain, he would not
have expected to hear from his family twice a week, and he did have
enough confidence in the mail to send home completed volumes of his
diary.

Charles Beecher's praise aside, mail coaches were doomed even
before his 1853 diary entry from France. As in the case of the telegraph,
the time span between the invention of the railroad and its prevalence
was minute. The first English railway line (using all mechanical power
and a reserved track) started serving the London-to-Manchester route
in 1830, and rail transport rapidly replaced mail coaches; the last one left
London in 1846. In a scant forty years, Britain built virtually all the track
mileage it would need throughout the twentieth century. The superiority of railroads is obvious: fares were cheaper and there was more room
not only for mail but for freight and passengers. And as railroads improved, rates fell; in 1870 British passengers paid 40 percent less for tickets than they had in 1845.[11]

Railroads were an especially democratizing institution, making
transport and travel cheap enough for everyone (of course, there were
two or three classes of seats and prices on most routes). European trains
in 1853, however, were highly various. Beecher complained about the
extreme cold of the Scottish railway cars (56) and the arrangement of
the seats, "like three coaches fastened, end to end, into one" as a compartment with seats facing each other (31). Separate compartments continue today to delineate the difference between European and American
passenger coaches, a difference that also suggests the more democratic
nature of American society. The Beecher-Stowe party found the German
second-class cars as comfortable as the French first-class ones, but the
lack of padding in the cars for Antwerp caused much consternation (286,
312).

Steamships advanced almost as quickly and as dramatically as the
railroads. The first regular steamship service was on the St. Lawrence
River in 1809, and regular mail service on the Cunard Line between Nova

Scotia and Liverpool began in 1830.[12] Sailing ships had made regular crossings between the United States and England since 1816, but with the development of iron ships and screw propellers in the 1830s and 1840s, sails were no longer the most reliable means. By 1839 the Cunard Line's *Great Western* was averaging fifteen days per passage.[13] In 1853 the Cunard steamer *Canada* took only ten days to carry Harriet and Charles to Liverpool, a typical passage for midcentury.

As transatlantic crossings became shorter, cheaper, and more efficient, immigration took on a new dimension: return trips were now much more feasible. In fact, after 1880, between one-fourth and one-third of all European immigrants to the United States returned home permanently—as many as four million before 1930.[14]

Of Thomas Cook, Passports, and the Grand Tour

While some travelers continued to conduct their own research, read guidebooks and even get themselves and their luggage lost, others were entering an era of planned travel. The world's first travel agent, Thomas Cook, was a product of new developments in transportation, but interestingly, his roots were in the social reform movements. As a Baptist lay worker, in 1841 he organized a temperance meeting in Loughborough. To increase attendance, he persuaded the railroad company to provide a special train for his audience from Leicester, twelve miles away. Five hundred seventy people paid a shilling each for the tour, astonishing Cook and the railroads, who were suddenly selling tickets to a whole new class of travelers. So Cook became a travel agent, specializing at first in sending people to temperance meetings. But by 1845 he was conducting weekend tours of Scotland, and by 1850 he was beginning to arrange tours of the Holy Land and the United States. When travelers booked a Cook's tour, they received railroad and ship tickets and coupons to cover hotel accommodations reserved for them.[15] Thus the complicated business of making arrangements was simplified, though finding the right train compartment or asking for directions in a foreign tongue continued to vex travelers.

Language was a problem for the Stowe-Beecher party. Beecher's French was adequate, and he functioned as translator for the group in France, but in Germany his language chauvinism was obvious. Knowing no German, he could not even read a menu and often expressed disgust at conditions there: "I am sick of Germany. The language is harsh, guttural, and unmusical. The hotels are not neat. The fare is bad. And the money is inconvenient. And as to the historical associations they may be cherished more vividly elsewhere" (303). Beecher made fun of the French accent as well, noting that *Uncle Tom* was said to be written by "Madame Henriette Bisshair Stove" (197).

Sometimes they were at a loss in new areas where they lacked a guidebook, worrying about what they had missed. The passports and visas required of Americans traveling on the Continent in the 1850s were another problem; according to an *Oxford English Dictionary* citation, as late as 1840 "the only civilized countries" not requiring passports were the British Isles and the United States. Charles Beecher was horrified at the day-long bureaucratic hassle he went through in Paris to get visas for the rest of their trip, noting that Louis Napoleon had proposed abolishing passports altogether; in Beecher's view, such a move would strengthen his position and popularity more than any other action (182–83).

Such irritations aside, the "wondrous age," the "miraculous Era," of the mid-nineteenth-century Atlantic community referred to by *Putnam's* contributed both to Harriet Beecher Stowe's fame and to the possibility of a network of like-minded women. Without the international peace and relative prosperity that increased the possibility of private travel, without reliable mails, without cheap and plentiful periodicals and books, those connections, once made, would have likely been broken and lost. Instead, by the process of spinning web-like connections, the density of communication grew apace. To be sure, the web was skewed to fit the preoccupations of the privileged classes, yet its existence and importance were undeniable. In 1848 Marx described the general transformation that made this flourishing possible: "In place of the old local and national seclusion and self-sufficiency, we have intercourse in every direction, a universal interdependency of nations. . . . National one-sidedness and narrow-mindedness become more and more impossible, and from the numerous national and local literatures, there arises a world literature."[16] Rousseau, Goethe, and Madame de Staël were of course early authors of an influential world literature, but Marx was pointing to a later flowering. *Uncle Tom's Cabin* was an early volume of the library he was describing.

Travel by women (and their accounts of their travel) became increasingly important in the nineteenth century. Consciously or unconsciously, the aristocratic or middle-class nineteenth-century woman increasingly felt the need for physical and mental space of her own, an environment in which the limitations imposed on her by society were, at the very least, less binding. The rise of the travel industry can be attributed not only to the rise of the middle class, but also to the need of escorts for women travelers, who were journeying in ever greater numbers. By the end of the century most tourists to the obligatory spots on the Continent were women.[17]

International travel for European women often included visits to the "American experiment." This was certainly an important component in the internationalizing of "the woman question." Many of the European travelers whose reflections became famous were women—key figures such as Harriet Martineau, Frances Trollope, and Frances Wright from England and Fredrika Bremer from Sweden. Further, male travelers such as Alexis de Tocqueville and Gustave Beaumont took pains to examine the special condition of women in the United States, and their writing created interest in the subject. Aristocratic and upper-middle-class women traveled to meet the wealthy and famous elsewhere, to "do" the tourist spots on the Continent and in the Holy Land. As it had been for young men in the eighteenth century, "the Grand Tour" quickly became part of a young woman's education in the nineteenth.

Later there were many other international influences traceable to travel. Margaret Fuller journeyed to Europe in the late 1840s and participated in the Italian struggle with Giuseppe Mazzini. During a sojourn in Paris, M.L. Mikhailov was much swayed by Jenny P. d'Héricourt's arguments against Jules Michelet's anti-feminist views on women; returning to Russia, he published reflections for Russian readers (see Chapter 5). Popular entertainers, social reformers, artists, diplomats, the nouveaux riches—all traveled back and forth across the Atlantic and throughout Europe and the Middle East.

"Unprotected Females": A New Species

The Beecher/Stowe party's way of traveling presupposed that Harriet required several kinds of help. Her overwhelming celebrity created a need for insured privacy and controlled access, and the importance of her work as a social reformer suggested a division of labor: she would continue to speak, write, and advocate, while others would take care of more mundane arrangements. Even had she been a male and as famous, similar needs would presumably have emerged. But since Harriet was not only a person of considerable position but also a woman, it was beyond question that men would handle the trying negotiation and bartering that extended travel involved. In short, both gender and class privilege required that Harriet enter the international public sphere as a creature under protection. Accordingly, when her husband returned to the United States, brother Charles remained to spare Harriet not only the distractions of detail work but the "danger" and dishonor it was presumed to entail. In all this, the Beechers and Stowes manifested the conventional wisdom about women and travel. But the communications revolution was already extending to women the possibility of a radically different mode of self-definition and action.

In nineteenth-century parlance, women who traveled alone or in the company of other women were "unprotected females." This terminology appeared in midcentury, although the phenomenon had existed earlier (for example, Frances Wright and her sister Camilla traveled to the United States unescorted in 1819).[18] The *Oxford English Dictionary* documents the use of "unprotected *woman*" in Samuel Richardson's *Clarissa* (1748) and "unprotected *family*" in Ann Radcliffe's *The Romance of the Forest* (1791), but the phrase applied to women travelers is a nineteenth-century artifact. By the late 1850s there were enough "unprotected females" to call forth a series of books, as well as much discussion in the press and satires by the likes of Anthony Trollope, E.M. Forster, and, later on, Henry James.[19]

Trollope's travel essay "The Unprotected Female Tourist," first published in the *Pall Mall Gazette*, describes and satirizes this "species" of traveler. He reveals all his male antagonism to "strong-minded" women in a nevertheless delightful sketch. While pretending to admire his subject, Sabrina Dawkins, he is yet scathing in his characterization, exploring the question of *why* she is traveling alone at all and assuming that it is because, unconsciously, she is really looking for a man. She may say she loves independence, but deep down, insists Trollope, she is trying for a way *not* to be independent. "She cannot unsex herself or rid herself of the feeling that admiration is accorded to her as a pretty woman"; she may have decided on celibacy, but she cannot banish hope. "Such a woman," Trollope continues cattily, "cannot talk to men without a consciousness that intimacy may lead to love, or the pretence of love, or the dangers of love. . . . And therefore it is that they do not go about the world unprotected, either at home or abroad." For, he concludes, "let a woman once be an unprotected female, so she must remain to the end," since no man wants this sort of woman. What would his friends say?[20]

The phenomenon of the unprotected female precipitated a succession of books by women as well.[21] Flora Tristan's first published work was on the subject, and the anonymous author of two such books (presumably Emily Lowe) begins her account (1857) of travel to Norway with a discussion of why traveling *without men* is so advantageous:

> Ladies *alone* get on in travelling much better than with gentlemen: they set about things in a quieter manner, and always have their own way; while men are sure to go into passions and make rows, if things are not right immediately. Should ladies have no escort with them, then every one is so civil, and trying of what use they can be; while, when there is a gentleman of the party, no one thinks of interfering, but all take it for granted they are well provided for. The only use of a gentleman in travelling is to look after the luggage, and we take care to have no luggage. "The Unprotected" should never go beyond one portable carpetbag.[22]

The American writer Caroline Kirkland, traveling with other women, worried only initially about going out in Paris without a male escort: "One feels at first as if it were a transgression, but after a while this subsides into a feeling of agreeable abandon, unalloyed by any sense of naughtiness."[23]

One wonders how much of this bravado was a cover-up for the inherent terror at what they were doing.[24] Certainly, most travel writers were far less sanguine about the advantages of solitary tourism for women. General guides included special advice for women, warning in particular against cultivating intimacies. John Murray's *Handbook for Southern Italy*, under the arresting heading "Italian Adventurers. (A Caution to English Ladies)," admonishes prudishly: "Too much care cannot be taken in forming acquaintances with southern Italians, and especially with that class of them which frequents Pensions. One of their chief aims is to marry for money, and keep their families and themselves in idleness. It is a common complaint among them that English wives do not take a beating kindly."[25] But for some of those who had experienced it, the unprotected way seemed highly palatable. How else can one account for the fact that Lucie Duff Gordon in 1863 remarked favorably on an eighteen-year-old Arab woman in Egypt who was fond of men's society and traveled alone, on her own camel. When Gordon asked about the phenomenon, she was told, "Why not? . . . She is a virgin, and free."[26]

"The Chief Delight Was Not to Be Afraid"

Although it is impossible to determine how widespread the phenomenon of the unprotected female was, Trollope and Lowe were clearly commenting on a discernible change in travel norms for women. Where statistics are absent, the stories of Frances Power Cobbe, Fredrika Bremer, and several adventurous "explorers" fill the picture.

Anglo-Irish Frances Power Cobbe (1822–1904) is more fully studied in Chapter 8 as a "mother of the matrix," but her solitary travel deserves noting here. Like many another eldest or only daughter, she could not pursue her own career or think of marrying while caring for her father; when he died in 1857, she, at thirty-five, inherited a small annual allowance of £200 and immediately went abroad, traveling alone. She reflected later on the advantages: "Of course men do not meet—because they do not want—such services [kindnesses]; and women, who travel with men, or even two or three together, seldom invite them. But for viewing human nature *en beau*, commend me to a long journey by a woman of middle age, of no beauty, and travelling as cheaply as possible, alone."[27]

She traveled for a year on £400 but had to economize everywhere; indeed, she could not even afford the £5 to get into Hagia Sophia in Istanbul. Her attitude to mass tourism was the superior one many adventurous women took: "I rejoice to think that I saw those holy and wonderful lands of Palestine and Egypt while Cook's tourists were yet unborn, and Cairo had only one small English hotel and one solitary wheel carriage; and the solemn gaze of the Sphinx encountered no Golf-games on the desert sands" (1:197–98). In Italy, she was critical of those who visited only what the guidebooks (especially Murray's) labeled worthwhile, never stopping to *look*: "Hurry-scurry is bad enough, but Hurry-Murray decidedly worse."[28] Cobbe's travels helped her to become more independent, more conscious of her need for physical and mental "room," and more aware of women as a group, as she met many notable women of her day.

Born in Åbo (present-day Turku, Finland), Fredrika Bremer (1801–65) became one of the most celebrated persons of her time, as a novelist, travel writer, and religious writer. In her travels—to the United States, Italy, the Holy Land, and Greece—she always looked at two areas: evidence of Christianity and religion, and the position of women. So vigorously did she labor to establish enduring bonds among women in the

Atlantic community that she receives extended attention later (Chapter 8). For now, it is her intrepidity as a solitary voyager that commands our interest.

Like many other Scandinavian women, Fredrika was a world citizen more than a patriot. She always traveled "unprotected," but she had contacts and introductions wherever she went and therefore deflected some of the criticism of being unescorted. As a single person she was used to solitude and was, in fact, made physically ill at times by the numbers of people "protecting" her. In the United States her stay (1849–51) included visits with Indian women in Wisconsin, slave women and slaveowners in the South, and abolitionist women in the North. She even spent several days with fellow countrywoman Jenny Lind in Cuba.[29] During a five-year European and Mediterranean sojourn beginning in 1856, Bremer traveled and met people from Belgium to Turkey, Syria, Palestine, Greece, and Italy. Everywhere, she called on the important women, sought out information on the "average" woman, resurrected women's history, and worried about the state of the souls of her interlocutors or why more was not done for the poor and the sick. She visited schools, convents, hospitals, orphanages, harems, villages—and, as well, was entertained by royalty and the aristocratic expatriate community wherever she went.

The extremists among the "unprotected females" were the explorers and derring-do travelers, remarkable figures who present an interesting challenge to the student of women's internationality. Isabella Bird (1831–1904) and Ida Pfeiffer (d. 1858) each spent half her life traversing the globe on various journeys, usually alone, *craving* solitude, and hiring guides and helpers who were native to the country. In fact, Isabella Bird and Marianne North (1830–90) actively discouraged family members from joining them. Other adventurers—for example, the twins Margaret Smith and Agnes Smith Lewis, who discovered a Syriac manuscript of the Gospels at St. Catherine's Monastery in the Sinai[30]—traveled in sister or mother-daughter pairs.

For a notorious example of the latter, consider Alexine Tinne (1835–69) and her mother Harriet Tinne. Traveling first around Europe, Scandinavia, and Russia and later making three voyages up the Nile, they encountered much criticism and antagonism from society, not because of the extraordinary difficulties of the expeditions but because they were ladies unescorted. Their first trip was to the wild country of Norway, considered in 1854 "unsuitable for ladies," though "gentlemen tourists" could find excellent fishing and shooting there. "The roads were so narrow and rough that it was impossible to go by carriage, and the inns were few and far between," says Alexine's biographer, Penelope Gladstone. But Harriet and Alexine were undaunted; they used Murray's handbook on Scandinavia to plan their trip and traveled in open pony carts, carrying most of their provisions with them. When they traveled in the Middle East—first to Egypt, then to the Holy Land, and back to Cairo—Alexine became determined to continue south up the Nile past Khartoum. As they planned their third voyage in 1861, people were very critical. It was shocking, according to their friends and family in the Netherlands. In Cairo, where they were much involved in the expatriate community, even those who had themselves traveled in the areas the Tinnes were contemplating—the English consul to Ethiopia, a German missionary to East Africa, Linant Pasha of Egypt, and a Dr. Suquet—all advised that "for women, the country was unsafe, impossible."[31] (So intriguing is the Tinne case that I include more about it in Appendix C.)

True to the *Zeitgeist,* Bird and Pfeiffer wanted to go only where no one else had ever gone; they saw themselves as explorers and were pleased to be among the first female members of the Royal Geographical Society. Alexine Tinne too became a loner after first traveling with her mother. Mary Kingsley, Freya Stark, and Mary Somerville all eschewed male escorts. Stark, the great Arabian explorer, captured the spirit of this group of women: "Perhaps . . . it was this unavowed timidity which made me seek out dangerous things and made me find—even in mountaineering—that the chief delight was not to be afraid. Only a person both adventurous and timid can feel this."[32] She thus expressed the view, held by many women, that exploration and adventure could turn passive "feminine" characteristics into psychological assets.

Of Boundaries and (Again) Social Classes

The adventurers in particular provide an arresting example of the difficulties in limiting the boundaries and purview of a study in communicative action among women. Most adventurers evinced scant interest in forging links between women; in fact, they probably actively discouraged any such efforts. Nevertheless, they demonstrate perhaps better than any other examples the possibilities for women which the communication revolution opened up. That they wrote about their feats—and were in turn the subject of others' writing—is of course of signal importance, for in doing so they planted ideas in the minds of female readers. While few such readers ended up searching for the sources of the Nile (as did Tinne), they might well have been emboldened to undertake (for them) significant ventures in the now imaginable new horizons of the nineteenth century. More than likely they would alight in Switzerland or Italy instead of Khartoum. But there too they would be positioned to inaugurate or strengthen Atlantic community linkages.

The majority of women travelers were from the upper middle class and middle-aged; some were aristocratic, and most were well-to-do—a point that can hardly be overemphasized. Their sense of class, social status, and social hierarchy enabled them to do what they did. Comments historian Philippa Levine, "The wealthy women travellers of this era put considerable trust in their ability to maintain a social distance from those with whom they came into contact on their journeys. . . . Much of their undeniable bravery and sense of adventure rested on the hierarchical assurances lent them by age, social class and a modicum of traditional English superiority."[33] The travel plans of these elite women, especially in the Middle East and the Western Hemisphere, often were occasioned by the imperialist ideology of the nineteenth century. These women did not represent "the Other as female" when they traveled in Egypt or Palestine or Saudia Arabia. They "transcended" their femaleness and represented the imperial power; their attitudes were much the same as those of their governments; they helped to protect male powers abroad by their very presence. This may be one reason so many Victorian women liked to travel; they were powerful by virtue of their class, which was more important than their sex.[34]

Mervat Hatem has insightfully analyzed the images that European and Egyptian women had of each other through their writings in this period. Why was it, she asks, that European women avoided finding commonalities between themselves and Egyptian women but, instead, described differences? Why did European women usually participate in Egyptian *male*, not female, society? "They avoided," she says, "asking themselves why they felt powerful in the Orient and less so in their own societies. Here, the need for symbiosis (identification with the power of their culture) contributed to an exaggerated stress on the differences between the Orient and the West."[35]

One does find some accounts of travel by working women of the middle or lower classes, especially immigrants and governesses (see Appendix D). Emmeline Lott was governess to the Egyptian pasha; Anna

Leonowens (of *The King and I* fame) was governess to the children of the king of Siam (see Chapter 4); Rosalie Roos of Sweden was a governess in South Carolina—and all three wrote about their experiences and travels.[36] Women made connections in the course of their business dealings as well, and there were international women entrepreneurs in the nineteenth century, most often between colony and mother country (see Appendix E). One of the most fascinating is Mary Seacole, a Jamaican Creole who sailed to London as an adolescent and sold pickles and preserves for two years before returning to Jamaica.[37]

Alyson Cunningham, who traveled as a nurse or nanny with the young Robert Louis Stevenson and his family, kept a diary and wrote home about her interactions with others "in service" wherever they stayed. Cummy, a devout Scotch Presbyterian, attended a "Scotch" church wherever she could; English (Anglican) church was second best; Catholic services were a last resort. Many of her ingenuous observations were occasioned by differences in religion: she was appalled by the "gross superstition" of the Roman Catholics in France and Italy and horrified that shops remained open on Sunday. Her account of Maria, a maid in Mentone, showed her astonishment on learning about fasting during Lent and on Fridays, as well as about confession. Maria, in turn, learned from Cummy about reading the Bible, about Sabbatarianism, and about the Catholic persecution of Protestants during the Reformation.[38] But although international connections between women were certainly being made, and although they fostered cross-cultural learning, it is not certain that these furthered a "network." It is clear that most lower-class travel was occasioned by upper-class travel: working-class women usually only traveled only as employees, slaves, or entrepreneurs.

Of all scholars, historians are the best situated to appreciate the ironies and bizarre consequences of "purposeful" human action. The communications revolution of the nineteenth century furnishes more than its share of unforeseen and unintended consequences. Its architects were privileged males, the driven, rambunctious bourgeois daredevils whom Marx both celebrates and excoriates in his midcentury writings. Their steamers, railroads, mail systems, and telegraph lines were constructed for commercial benefit and for the advancement of class and gender advantage. But steam presses could thunder with the message of Simon Legree's cruelties and railroads deliver a Mrs. Stowe to a waiting audience in Scotland or Italy, where she (or her amanuensis) would denounce a slave system that had furnished capitalism with some of its greatest benefits. Captains of industry hoped for safe marriages for their daughters and contentment for their wives. But their devices brought forth the lady explorer and the socially threatening unprotected female. So, too, would another unforeseen consequence arise from this material basis: a vital Atlantic-world scheme of female cooperation, communication, and mutual support.

The Ironies of Pentecost

Women Religious and Evangelistic Outreach

Unite England and America in energetic and resolved co-operation for the world's salvation, and the world is saved.
—Andrew Reed and James Matheson, *Narrative of the Visit to the American Churches, by the Deputation from the Congregational Union of England and Wales*, 1835

[At the Keswick revival conference in England], no one acted as though I was a black woman. . . . I struck in to sing the Old Coronation the way we sang it in America, "All Hail the Power of Jesus' Name," but no one joined, and I thought it was so strange. . . . I turned to [the Wesleyan brother] and said "Why don't they sing?" He says, "They don't know the tune." Then I said, "You start it to the tune they all know." . . . My! how they sung it! . . . Of course it don't beat the American tune, but still it is grand. . . . I don't know just the number that professed to receive peace that night, but I know it was a goodly number. To God be all the glory. That was my first work in England.
—Amanda Smith, *The Story of the Lord's Dealings with Mrs. Amanda Smith, the Colored Evangelist*, 1893

Evangelism brought Britain and America together in ways that transcended political nationalism. Its "brisk traffic across the Atlantic," Frank Thistlethwaite claims, "was concerned with nothing less than world salvation." Here, he asserts, was "a genuine Atlantic community."[1] Since female evangelists were very much a part of the movement for world salvation, connections they built helped form the basis for an international feminist network.[2]

Both Catholic and Protestant Christians expanded the "proper" sphere for women by fostering international contacts and debating so-cial issues—though most of the women involved would have been hor-rified to think that they were transforming accepted roles. Distributing holy tracts and ministering to the poor (at home and as foreign mission-aries) would have been considered spiritual activities, not occasions for enlarging women's influence.

Transatlantic Christianity

Roman Catholic missionary nuns were sent to serve immigrant groups in North America as early as 1727, first to New Orleans and then to Mary-land; by the beginning of the nineteenth century, orders of nuns were being assigned to work with the Indians. Earlier, of course, women reli-gious had been sent to various parts of the New World Spanish empire, including present-day New Mexico. Between 1820 and 1890 there were no fewer than 202 different Catholic orders of women religious located in the United States, most of which had their origins in Europe (usually France, Italy, Germany, or Ireland).[3] According to Mary Ewens, during the nineteenth century the number of Catholic sisters in the United States grew from forty to more than forty thousand; there were nearly four times as many nuns as priests by the end of the century.[4]

Education and nursing were important occupations the nuns en-gaged in, and in both capacities they were capable of having a profound effect on the women and men of their communities. During epidemics and wars (particularly the Civil War, when they were called "the Florence Nightingales of America"), nursing sisters did heroic work. As teachers, the influence of nuns upon generations of students, male and female, was incalculable; in some remote areas the Catholic school became rec-ognized as the public school of the community. Since many of the sisters were well educated, there is a wealth of documentation of their experi-ences in the New World: their journeys across the Atlantic and North America; their views on manners, customs, and food; their attitude to-ward their vocation.

A vivid example of Catholic internationality is provided by Cornelia Connelly (1809–79). Born a Protestant in Philadelphia, she married an Episcopal priest in 1832. Within four years, while living in Natchez, Mis-sissippi, both Cornelia and her husband converted to Catholicism. A pro-longed stay abroad and then teaching positions at Catholic institutions in St. Charles, Louisiana, brought them in contact with many different groups. When her husband decided to become a priest, church doctrine decreed that she become a nun and give up her four children. This she did, at first reluctantly. But soon she took her final vows and was made superior of the Society of the Holy Child Jesus in England, as she had foreseen in a vision. She did not renounce her vows and her vocation even when her former husband changed his mind and went to court to get her back.[5] She and the Society of the Holy Child Jesus established schools for girls and convents in England and the United States, including Rosemont College in Philadelphia; in this work she made numerous international contacts by letter and in person.[6]

Connelly was far from exceptional in this regard. Many other Catholic women, such as Mother Theodore Guérin of the Sisters of Providence from Lemans, France, founder of St. Mary-of-the-Woods, Indiana, in 1840, endured the privations of frontier living in order to provide education and religious example to women and girls in the expanding United States.[7] There was also Mother Philippine Duchesne (1769–1852), of the Religious of the Sacred Heart, sent from France; in 1818 she opened the first free school west of the Mississippi (Florissant, Missouri), and in 1841 she established a mission to Potawatomi Indians in Sugar Creek, Kansas. She was canonized in 1988.[8]

These women religious found and participated in opportunities not open to most women in the nineteenth century. They enjoyed "involvement in meaningful work, access to administrative positions, freedom from the responsibilities of marriage and motherhood, opportunities to live in sisterhood, and egalitarian friendships," as Mary Ewens puts it.[9] But they probably would not have interpreted their vocation in this way, and thus their importance in internationalizing women's experience and connectedness is still a negative or ironic one—as is that of most of their Protestant counterparts.

Like the Catholics, Protestants sent missionaries to North America in the eighteenth century, and those missions were strengthened by voluntary societies, which often followed the paths of empire all over the world. Early in the nineteenth century, Bible societies were formed in most European and North American countries, and many were aided in fund raising and distribution by auxiliary or autonomous societies such as Philadelphia's Female Bible Society, founded in 1814. Such groups came to be considered well within the proper sphere for women. The Women's Bible Society of Stockholm, for example, founded in 1819 "to contribute to the dissemination of the Holy Word," fended off possible criticism of women doing this public work: "It has been recognized that women, who are called to work within 'private' life and only through [dissemination of the Bible] in the 'public' sphere, far from abandoning their mission, understand it in its correct sense."[10]

There were many female evangelists during the first half of the nineteenth century in both Britain and the United States, and several who undertook international preaching missions. Elizabeth Atkinson Finney (the second wife of successful evangelist Charles Finney) is an example of those who were very effective on both sides of the Atlantic but careful never to step outside the bounds of prayer meeting or women's Bible class. Earlier, English women preachers had come to America, such as Ruth Watkins, a Primitive Methodist missionary who arrived in the late 1820s. And English female preachers such as Hester Ann Rogers often traveled from England to Wales or Ireland for revivals.[11] Fanny Newell (1790–1824) sublimated her own call to be a preacher by marrying a preacher and becoming an equal part of a team ministry in early Maine. She spoke before and after his sermons and organized women-only groups.[12]

As observed above, most of those involved would have been appalled to be told they were fostering internationality or enlarging and transforming women's role and place. Yet the Old Testament prophet Joel (2:28) had foretold, and the Book of Acts (2:17–18) had repeated, that both sons and daughters would prophesy and that both sexes could receive the Holy Spirit. Of course, that activity had to take place in the very narrow framework of spreading the gospel; expansions in women's leadership and influence were not to be the goal. Nevertheless, the impact of such apocalyptic texts cannot be overestimated.

Female Evangelists on Women

What was it that enabled Protestant women to move so forcefully onto the international stage? The answer lies mainly in the realm of ideation, as secular and theological modes of thought interacted. Women evangelists were often embroiled in the controversy about women's right to preach, even though they did not often speak or testify on that subject per se. Their justification included two kinds of argument, both strands common in other nineteenth-century discussions on the woman question. Nancy Cott has summarized these two opposing general arguments for women's advancement. On the one hand, she says, women claimed that they had the same intellectual and spiritual endowment as men—were human beings equally with men—and therefore deserved equal or the same opportunities men had, to advance and develop themselves. On the other hand women argued that their sex differed from the male—that whether through natural endowment, environment or training, human females were moral, nurturant, pacific and philosophically disinterested, where males were competitive, aggrandizing, belligerent and self-interested; and that it therefore served the best interests of both sexes for women to have equal access to education, work and citizenship in order to represent themselves and to balance society with their characteristic contribution.[13]

These two positions—called variously "equality" and "difference," or "minimizers" and "maximizers," or "equal rights" and "women's rights"—can be detected in the two main arguments used to justify women's preaching. Biblical and theological reasoning drove the discussion forward, and its centrality must shape the historical account.

The view that women evangelists had talents and gifts different from those of men was usually tied to some kind of premillennialist view. Premillennialists believed that the millennium, a thousand-year period of peace and plenty, would be *preceded* by the second coming and the fulfillment of the prophecies regarding "the last days." The very fact that many women were testifying showed, according to premillennialists, that this time was approaching. Women preachers were in fact a *sign* of an imminent second coming. This attitude toward the spread of female preaching is based on a reading of the prophecy in Joel 2:28–29 ("Your sons and your daughters shall prophesy . . . and upon the handmaids in those days will I pour out my spirit"). Olive Anderson discusses several British women evangelists who preached on "the last days," including Elizabeth Foster, Geraldine Hooper, and Octavia Jary.[14] Phoebe Palmer used precisely this argument in *Promise of the Father; or, A Neglected Speciality of the Last Days* (1859), and one of her last publications was a pamphlet titled *The Tongue of Fire on the Daughters of the Lord* (1869).

The other position is a variation on the "sameness" or "equality" perspective: women and men are both human, and their rights and duties should be based on their common humanity. The often used Pentecostal argument—the Holy Spirit was and is no respecter of sex—

enunciates this position. Anyone can be visited by the Spirit's tongues of fire; women therefore are the same as men in this context. Many who held this view were postmillennialists, who argued, in Anderson's helpful summary,

> that Joel's prophecy had already been fulfilled at Pentecost, that "the last days" were to be understood broadly as the whole post-Christian dispensation, and that therefore one of the characteristics of the dispensation of grace was intended to be female ministry on equal terms with men. After apostolic times, however, it became "the lost ministry" (a favourite phrase), with disastrous results for the Church; only in their own age, which was witnessing the progressive triumph of truth and the revival of religion was this lost ministry evidently being recovered as the Kingdom of God was ushered in.[15]

This was Catherine Booth's position in her pamphlet *Female Ministry* (1859) and elsewhere; she continued adamant in her belief that one's sex was irrelevant in Christianity. That belief was enshrined in Salvation Army doctrine from its beginning (as the Christian Mission) and became the "Women's Charter" in its constitution.[16]

An interesting take on the position comes from the Quakers and Lucretia Mott. "One day after half the world had been voted out" of the World's Anti-Slavery Convention, while Joseph Sturge was chairing the proceedings, Elizabeth Cady Stanton asked Mott, "Suppose in spite of the vote of excommunication the Spirit should move you to speak, what could the chairman do, and which would you obey? the Spirit or the Convention?" Mott replied, "Where the Spirit of God is, there is liberty."[17] Thus she invoked the "higher law" doctrine as well as the view that one must obey the voice of the Spirit.

As was true in other contexts in the nineteenth century, Protestant women could and did argue both ways for women. They used the text from Galatians 3:28 to argue "we are all one in Christ," neither Jew nor Greek, male nor female, slave nor free, and they used other texts to argue woman's particular competence for receiving the "second blessing" that was part of Holiness doctrine (see below on Phoebe Palmer).

The model that female evangelists established was clearly exceptional, not one they might counsel other women to follow. But all would say that if "total surrender to God's will" led in the direction of the call to preach, the woman *must* follow it. John Wesley, interpreting St. Paul, wrote in 1771 to one of his female preachers, Mary Bosanquet, that "the strength of the cause rests there, on your having an *extraordinary* call."[18] Phoebe Palmer, in the preface to *Promise of the Father,* posed the dilemma in terms of the "higher law" doctrine: "The will of the church and the will of Christ in conflict!"[19] Women *must* speak when the Spirit commands even though church order forbids it. Obviously, preaching or testifying to "promiscuous" (mixed-sex) groups was only the most unconventional action of several that women evangelists engaged in. Traveling across the Atlantic, organizing large gatherings, soliciting speaking invitations, managing administrative detail, arranging for child care, publicizing revivals—all these and more were entailed in the position of female evangelist. These were not traditional female tasks.

The spiritual pilgrimages of evangelical women, as often evidenced in their autobiographical "memoirs," helped them to a sense of self-empowerment even as they followed "the clear leadings of Providence." As Joanna Gillespie shows in her study of such early nineteenth-century works, it was "women in revivalistic religious groups [who] were among the first to erode [the] powerful taboo" against women speaking in public.[20] In both the equality and difference positions, I would argue, the words and actions of evangelical women helped to create structures of expanded possibilities for women both inside and outside the church, on both sides of the Atlantic. For what female hearers of this new kind of preaching could help but imagine such a role for themselves, one that involved an unimaginable but intensely exciting emancipation from grim local geographies?

Amanda Berry Smith and Catherine Booth

The case of Amanda Berry Smith (1837–1915) provides a good example of one whose spiritual path led inadvertently to extending women's domain of action in the last quarter of the nineteenth century. Internationally known as "the colored evangelist," Smith had been born a slave in Maryland in 1837 and moved to Pennsylvania when her father purchased her family's freedom. By the time she was thirty she had been married twice, had given birth to at least five children (all of whom died young), and had worked continually as a maid and washerwoman. In 1868 she attended the Tuesday Meetings at Phoebe Palmer's house in New York

and there experienced "entire sanctification" at a service led by Methodist minister John Inskip. Soon she was preaching for the A.M.E. Church
in Philadelphia, New Jersey, and New York.

She became involved in the Holiness movement, participating in
camp meetings as far away as Tennessee and Maine. An invitation to go
to England began her international ministry, which lasted some ten years
and took her to the British Isles, India, and West Africa, working with
Methodist missions, preaching and teaching. *An Autobiography: The Story
of the Lord's Dealings with Mrs. Amanda Smith, the Colored Evangelist* is
her wonderfully ingenuous account of her experiences, told with great
detail and fervor. In Perth, Scotland, for example, she was informed that
she could preach only to women's groups, since speaking in a mixed group
would be embarrassing to her as a woman. She protested that she was
used to speaking before men, but those in charge wanted to "protect"
her. Here is part of her account, detailed in her inimitable style:

> When we got to the hall there were seven or eight men. I saw
> these ladies looked very sharp and surprised. I went on and
> opened the meeting with a lively hymn; and the Scotch can
> sing, depend upon it. Then I asked some one to lead in prayer;
> and one of the lady workers did so, but it was very faint. Poor
> thing, I knew it was a struggle; fortunately it was not lengthy.
> So we rose, and I gave out the next hymn.
>
> While they sang I noticed a great deal of quiet whisper-
> ing and uneasiness: these good ladies were very nervous; I
> was greatly amused. Just before I began my address, one of
> them said to me, "Now, Mrs. Smith, there are those men; and
> they know quite well this is a meeting for women only; and
> they know they should not be in here. If you would like, I will
> speak to them, and have them go out." "Oh, no," I said, "I don't
> mind; I think they came with their wives; I saw one man bring
> the baby and give it to the mother, and if they behave them-
> selves it's all right; I want to talk to the women about their
> souls, and their salvation; and that is what the men need as
> well."
>
> "Then it don't embarrass you to have the men present?"
>
> "Not in the least," I said. And she sat down, comfortably
> surprised; and I had no further trouble about the men com-
> ing to meeting with the women. They did seem glad. They

Amanda Smith, from *An Autobiography: The Story of the Lord's Dealings with Mrs. Amanda Smith, the Colored Evangelist* (Chicago: Meyer and Brothers, 1893).

would shake hands with me, and say, "Lord bless you," and
they smiled, and I suppose they thought I had given them the
best chance they had ever had to get into a mixed meeting.[21]

For Amanda Smith, certainly, witnessing about the state of one's soul
had nothing to do with one's sex. She was on a quest for souls, not a
quest to improve the influence and standing of women or black people,
yet in this historical context she clearly was something of a revolutionary.

Catherine Booth (1829–90), cofounder of the Salvation Army, was
not particularly interested in promoting connections among women either, but as a preacher she saved souls and made fruitful friendships simultaneously. When Phoebe Palmer was attacked in England for
preaching as a woman, she was defended by Catherine Booth. Booth's
Female Ministry; or, Woman's Right to Preach the Gospel (1859) has ever
since been a cornerstone of Salvation Army doctrine on women's role in
religion. Another connection between the two women was Palmer's gift
of her home on East 15th Street in New York City to the Salvation Army;
it became the Army's first hospital in the United States.

The Salvation Army quickly became an international movement,
and since women were made officers equally with men, they had a great
influence. Although women's emancipation per se was far from Booth's
intention, her magnetism was felt far and wide. One example of her power
is told in the story of a young Finn, the aristocratic Hedwig von Haartman
(1862–1902) of Åbo. Traveling in France and Switzerland when she was
seventeen years old, she had been much taken by two other international
Finnish women, Louise af Forselles and Mathilde Wrede. Louise af
Forselles had studied with the Salvation Army in England, Germany,
France, and Switzerland, and she inspired Haartman to attend the Salvation Army War College in London in 1884.[22] There she lived for a time
with Catherine Booth, who advocated a woman's right not only to preach
but also to participate in public life. Commissioned in the Salvation Army,
Lieutenant von Haartman returned to Finland and founded the Salvation Army in that country. She served mainly in working-class areas of
Helsinki, but also in Tampere and Åbo until her untimely death at the
age of forty.[23]

Among female evangelists, the lines of influence run from England's
Wesleyan preacher, Hester Ann Roe Rogers (who also preached success-
fully in Dublin), to Phoebe Palmer in New York, back to England (via

Palmer's significance as a woman preacher) to Booth. And Booth, as a
founder of the Salvation Army, made a worldwide impact on women.
Frances Willard, Amanda Berry Smith, and Catherine Booth all traced
their own "calls" or "second blessings" to Phoebe Palmer's revivals. Frances
Willard (1839–98), well-known for her national and international work
with the Woman's Christian Temperance Union and her strategy for supporting woman suffrage from the Christian evangelistic perspective,
speaks in her autobiography about having received the "second blessing"
in 1866 at a revival in Evanston, Illinois, led by "Dr. and Mrs. Phoebe
Palmer."[24] Later she too wrote about women's right to preach in *Woman
in the Pulpit* (1888). But again, Phoebe Palmer herself would not have
seen her role in public life as a secular matter of adding to earthly opportunities for women. Like Amanda Berry Smith and Catherine Booth, she
would have understood her influence over women as spiritual and in no
way practical or political.[25]

Phoebe Palmer

As I have already indicated, Phoebe Palmer (1807–74) is the best example of a woman evangelist who attained great renown on both sides
of the Atlantic. A lifelong Methodist, she married Walter Palmer, a ho-
meopathic doctor, when she was twenty. She began her devotional career
by participating in the Tuesday Meeting, a female prayer group begun by
her sister Sara Lankford in the New York home where they and their
husbands lived together. Her conversion, facilitated by Sara, took place
after she suffered the third death of a child (only one of her four children
survived childhood). Palmer wrote later of finally understanding their
deaths as a way of binding her to God: "God takes our treasure to heaven
that our hearts may be there also."[26] Hester Ann Roe Rogers (1756–94),
one of John Wesley's preachers and a profound influence on Palmer, dealt
with the near-death of one of her own children in a similar way,[27] and
Amanda Berry Smith and Hannah Whitall Smith also witnessed the deaths
of their children.

By 1840 "the Tuesday Meeting for the Promotion of Holiness" was
sexually integrated, interdenominational, and nationally known (by
means of Holiness periodicals such as *Guide to Holiness*). All were wel-
come, and everyone, male or female, was encouraged to speak. Palmer
became widely known as a revival speaker. She developed her "altar
phraseology" by which anyone could receive the "second blessing" by

Phoebe Palmer, from *Four Years in the Old World* (New York: Foster and Palmer, 1866).

"laying all upon the altar" and willing a new life (the first blessing was of course baptism). It demanded not an instantaneous change but a gradual learning of the new way. Her works, especially *Way of Holiness* and the periodical *Guide to Holiness,* brought her message to thousands. *Way of Holiness* was translated into French and German.

Remarkably, for the first twenty years of her ministry she traveled and preached alone; Walter stayed in New York and supervised the house and servants. Only when she began to evangelize abroad did Walter travel with her and they develop their partnership as revivalists. In 1853 Phoebe undertook her first Canadian tour; in Ontario she made over 500 conversions and nearly as many experienced "entire sanctification" or the "second blessing."

They decided to carry their message to England in 1859, since her Tuesday Meeting was well known, and her Holiness works were selling well enough to demand English editions.[28] *Four Years in the Old World* is Phoebe Palmer's account of that journey. It is a huge book, a compendium of journal entries over four years, letters, and newspaper clippings from both the religious and secular press. Both a travelogue and a spiritual diary, it records the Palmers' visits to various pilgrimage places (such as Wesley's home and grave, and "sacred" sites for Hester Ann Rogers, George Whitefield, Mary Bosanquet Fletcher), as well as more usual tourist centers. The book is also a spiritual record, telling what the revival was like in each town—how many were saved, what was preached, what kind of testimonials were given—and explaining, over and again, Palmer's theology of entire sanctification. It gives her position on moral issues: her opposition to drinking (and to receiving publicans at her services), gambling, theater (President Lincoln was shot, she later wrote, because he went to the theater), and Sabbath work (she refused to hire a carriage to go to church).[29]

A typical Palmer revival had a recognizable format and planned structure, the arrangements having been worked out carefully in advance with the host minister. Usually, staying in one town for several weeks, the Palmers held nightly services, but sometimes there were as many as five in one day, including prayer meetings at 5:00 and 6:00 A.M. Richard Carwardine describes a Newcastle service, using contemporary quotations from the local press:

A circuit preacher opened the service with singing and prayer; Dr. Palmer then read and expounded on a chapter of Scripture. This was followed by "a brief and appropriate address" from the minister, after which Dr. Palmer announced the hymn and invited intending leavers to depart. Few did so, for the peculiar attraction of the service was yet to come. "Mrs. Palmer now modestly walks within the rails of the communion, not to preach according to the modern acceptance of that term, but simply to talk to the people. . . . She speaks deliberately. . . . Her voice is clear and musical." Her address (not a sermon) "on the duty of Christians to be holy, and to exert all their powers to bring sinners to Christ," was in style emphatically anecdotal and very heavily flavored with sentimentality. On completion of her address, her husband "in a very affectionate manner" invited penitents to walk forward to the communion rails while the rest of the congregation continued to sing hymns. Prayer and the recording of penitents' names brought the service to a close.[30]

Who came to these meetings? Phoebe Palmer liked to talk about how democratic their services were, with a social mix of old and young, rich and poor in attendance. In fact, most people who attended were employed working class, artisans, and lower-middle-class. There were other revivals that attracted the bourgeoisie and aristocracy in England, the most famous being at Broadlands, the country estate of Lord Mount Temple.

What Palmer achieved in her preaching was a theological breakthrough, called the "altar phraseology": the view that holiness or "the second blessing" is dependent on the individual, not on "grace" alone. It is a process, not an instantaneous change. The individual makes a personal decision; this enables her to act and to will a new life.

It is important for my purposes that this doctrine also functioned as a reinterpretation of woman's role in nineteenth-century middle-class life.[31] In the "altar transaction" a woman could lay all the details of house and children on the altar, and thus be freed from worldly attachments and responsibilities. It was not that the woman should "neglect" her domestic responsibilities but that they "should cease to be absorbing." At several points in *Promise of the Father,* Palmer castigates those who silence women called to witness, noting that resisting the divine call was following man's law, not God's. She narrates various examples of women who were first persecuted and silenced, but later in a different community brought many souls to God. Additionally, the altar phraseology encouraged the individual woman to be less emotionally dependent on husband and children, to become spiritually independent and to consecrate the domestic sphere to the inner life of "heart holiness." Thus, she gains a kind of freedom, not of "self-dependence" but of "situation" (to follow Theodore Hovet in using Charles Taylor's analysis of liberal values).[32] As Palmer says in *Promise of the Father*, "The female part of the church have the advantage. Retired from the turmoil and perplexities of business life, the mind is, or may be, free from the anxiety and distraction of debts, or business competitions, with a reputation and religious influence that have not been scathed and trammeled by exposure to the storms and combative elements of business or political life, they are free to throw their whole souls most effectively into the work of God."[33]

One wonders how much of this is wishful thinking on Palmer's part—with her full schedule of lectures, writing deadlines, and travel. Again, Palmer was modeling a very different role from the one she was recommending. Nevertheless, her theological formulations clearly represented a refocusing or recentering of women's conception of their activities and place. The implication was that if the work of God called one to unusual and unexpected ventures, one had to follow, regardless of the dictates of tradition. Thus, in the end, it is Palmer's *theology* that one must look to as the source of her very startling challenge to male prerogatives in church and society. Her international ventures derive from the same source.

Hannah Whitall Smith

An important transitional figure is Hannah Whitall Smith (1832–1911). Although a lifelong Quaker and a generation younger than Phoebe Palmer, she had many of the same affiliations (including a deep friendship with Frances Willard). Also, like many of her predecessors, she became involved in the Holiness movement after the death of a child. She gained fame on both sides of the Atlantic as an international Holiness evangelist and religious author who combined Quaker quietism with the doctrine of sanctification. Important in the "Higher Life" movement, she participated in revival meetings at Broadlands and at Keswick in the Lake District. Eventually she moved to England and was a great influence on both secular and religious feminists, such as M. Carey Thomas, Lady Henry Somerset, and various British suffragists. There she met Amanda Berry Smith when the latter returned from Africa.[34]

Hannah advocated a "gospel of submissiveness" in the writing that gained her the greatest audience, *The Christian's Secret of a Happy Life* (1875). The work was translated into many languages, sold thousands of copies, and is still in print. One of her many biographers says of her fame in evangelical circles, "The signature H.W.S., attached to tract after tract, was in Hannah's own lifetime known not only throughout the European world but wherever there were missionaries capable of translating her works into native languages. Her Bible readings were in perpetual demand, whether she was in England or America, and she received thousands of letters clamoring for spiritual and temporal advice."[35]

According to Debra Campbell, *The Christian's Secret* is "a practical guide to the annihilation of the will."[36] One should note, however, that this work and most of her articles for the Holiness movement journal *The Christian's Pathway to Power*, edited by her husband, Robert, were written at his insistence. Although the book detailed Smith's own position, at least publicly, during the years when her children were young, within a year after its publication she was already moving in different directions, straying emotionally away from her husband and the Holiness doctrines she had espoused earlier. Now spending increasingly more time in England (her daughter had moved there when she married in 1875), Smith became involved in the women's temperance movement and other feminist causes. In England she renewed her friendships with wealthy women made in her evangelistic Higher Life campaigns, introducing Frances Willard to Lady Somerset, the leader of the British women's temperance movement.

At first, Smith felt alienated from politics and wrote as an antinationalist feminist: "I do not feel myself to be any different as an English subject than as an American. I have not the vote in either place, as I am not a citizen of either and have no call to be patriotic. In fact, I do not see how *women* can ever feel like anything but aliens in whatever country they may live, for they have no part or lot in any, except the part and lot of being taxed and legislated for by men."[37] In 1885, however, she published *The Maiden Tribute to Modern Babylon: The Report of the Pall Mall Gazette's Secret Committee* in England. It described the international prostitution trade—or "white slavery," as it was called—an issue on which Josephine Butler and Frances Willard, among others, began to organize internationally. The campaign against "the traffic in women" was but one of many in which Hannah Whitall Smith participated.

The difference between Smith and Phoebe Palmer is that although the actions of both were in opposition to what they wrote and preached to women about women's roles, Palmer was much less conscious of the inherent contradiction. Smith understood this contradiction, and in her autobiography, *The Unselfishness of God and How I Discovered It* (1903), was able to shift her focus from annihilation of the will to "a purification that comes from service to humanity."[38] By the last three decades of her life her public self and her private self were no longer at odds; she was both committed and conscious. Her work in the international network had been thoroughgoing; she joked that her epitaph would have to be "Died of too many Meetings."[39] She attended the 1888 International Council of Women in Washington, representing and reporting on the World's Woman's Christian Temperance Union.[40]

In a lovely letter to her granddaughter Ray (Rachel) Strachey, Smith talked of the next generation of women's rights advocates:

> March 1, 1908
> Thy account, Ray, of your enthusiasm over the suffrage victory (second reading passed) thrilled me through and through, and I actually wept some tears of joy to think that you girls have embraced the cause of Women's Liberty with such enthusiasm. I feel now that I can die in peace, and leave the Cause to your fresh and eager young hands.[41]

A network on which women could later build was set in place in the nineteenth century by the personal connections of evangelists, institutions such as camp meetings and revivals, the religious press (there was an astonishing number of both denominational and thematic religious periodicals available in this period), and organizations such as world mission societies and Holiness groups. Whether Roman Catholic women added importantly to such a network is a complicated question. The unrelenting internationality of the system of female orders—as well as the actual work of women religious—must necessarily have suggested alternative modalities of women's experience. This is clearly an area demanding more careful attention by historians, theologians, and historical sociologists.

Even if, as the "equality" doctrine argues, evangelistic women did not see themselves as different and separate from men, the fact remains that structures and models were being built for eventual institutions that would more equally integrate the two sexes. Does Cott's thesis, that the "sameness" and "difference" positions were often argued at the same time, hold true here?[42] Were women evangelists arguing both, even though the two views are logically contradictory? Palmer's stated position on women was always on the side of the "difference" advocates, but her professional life, ironically, was more like a model for the "equality" advocates, as it seemed to differ little from that of a man.

4

Unwitting Allies

Harriet Beecher Stowe, George Sand, and the Power of Literary Celebrity

Mrs. Stowe, who was before unknown, is as familiar a name in all parts
of the civilized world as that of Homer or Shakespeare.
　　　　—"Uncle Tomitudes," *Putnam's Monthly Magazine,* 1853

What a brave man [George Sand] was, and what a good woman.
　　　　—Ivan Turgenev, 1876, quoted in Ellen Moers, "George Sand"

The woman-genius, known under the name of George Sand,
is indisputably the foremost poetic glory of the contemporary world.
　　　　—Vissarion Belinsky, 1842, quoted in Isabelle Naginski, *George Sand*

Historians and literary scholars who take the trouble to look cross-nationally at the Atlantic community in the nineteenth century almost inevitably stumble upon an odd fact. Two writers—Harriet Beecher Stowe (1811–96) and George Sand (1804–76)—exerted an astonishingly massive influence in a variety of national settings, an influence that bore no real relation to the intrinsic literary merits of their works. Furthermore, although an important effect of their popularity was the promotion of the cause of female emancipation, neither author was gripped by a sense of the overriding importance of this cause. Indeed, as noted in Chapter 2, Harriet Beecher Stowe operated in most respects as a deeply conventional upper-class female. I thus describe Stowe and Sand as "unwitting allies," women whose writings and lives advanced a process of which they were largely unaware and a campaign to which they were not really dedicated. Yet the importance of their contribution to the fostering of international exchange, friendship, recognition, and identification cannot be overestimated.

In focusing on the impact of the literary celebrity of these two women, I am betraying an allegiance to certain assumptions. At least three underlie the analysis. (1) A community of devoted readers constitutes something real, despite the notorious difficulty of defining and measuring its reality. (2) Some members of a community of readers can be transformed into "author-focused enthusiasts"—that is, "fans"—who model elements of their lives on the bearing, style, personality, or perceived individuality of the author. (3) Members of a community of readers are, by virtue of their reading, rendered open to appeals and strategies of mobilization to which they may hitherto have been closed. This last assumption is important, for it relates directly to the notion of a pre-organizational matrix of associations, affinities, affiliations, and connections upon which a mature women's movement could build. If such writer-heroes as Stowe and Sand somehow made women (and men) more disposed to entertain novel claims about the proper place of women, they were doing something very substantial indeed. Further, if their readers either developed actual international contacts with one another or were prepared by their literary involvement for such contacts, then an important structuring power was haunting the Atlantic community.

The popularity enjoyed by Stowe and Sand—attributable in part to the "advanced" ideas they represented—awakened into existence what might be called "virtual communities" of readers. These communities often became genuine, when their members began to respond to the presence of the authors in various places in Europe.[1]

Tomitudes and Siamese Audiences:
The Popularity of *Uncle Tom's Cabin*

Three thousand copies of *Uncle Tom's Cabin* were sold on the first day of its publication in 1852. Within a year more than 300,000 copies had been sold in the United States and 1.5 million copies in Great Britain. As Harriet Beecher Stowe's son says in his biography of his mother, "Almost in a day the poor professor's wife had become the most talked-of woman in the world, her influence for good was spreading to its remotest corners, and henceforth she was to be a public character, whose every movement would be watched with interest, and whose every word would be quoted."[2] Four rival editions were selling faster than any other book in Paris in January 1853; the Augsburg *Allgemeine Zeitung* gave Stowe's work pride of place over all other modern novels, including those of Dickens and George Sand; *Uncle Tom's Cabin* was also immediately popular in Italy.[3] The novel was staged as early as August 1852 in the United States and in September 1852 in England; in 1853 there were popular productions at the National Theatre of New York and at the Boston Museum.

Favorable reviews, letters, and translations were published throughout the world. Within a year *Uncle Tom's Cabin* was translated into fifteen European languages and ultimately into more than thirty languages. The National Union Catalog lists twenty-two pages of citations, with nearly seven hundred separate editions of the work. Entrepreneurs were quick to capitalize on the book's popularity by marketing all kinds of antislavery merchandise, including English Staffordshire figurines of the principal characters in the novel (called "Tomitudes"), toy theaters, even wallpaper.[4] There were also paintings, pantomimes, panoramas, and exhibits, such as the panoramas of Henry Box Brown mentioned in Charles Beecher's journal.[5]

The worldwide popularity of Stowe's novel was fabulous. The famous dramatization at the court of the King of Siam, "The Small House of Uncle Thomas," was probably a fabrication of Oscar Hammerstein for *The King and I,*[6] but the actual events interestingly expose the dynamics of increasing internationality, literary celebrity, and the emerging "woman question." Historically, it was Lady Son Klin (not Tuptim) who became the scholar of *Uncle Tom's Cabin*. Anna Leonowens, the English governess, had been given the book (along with other books by American authors) when she was a grieving widow in Singapore in 1861; she became a staunch abolitionist. Lady Son Klin, in the course of her studies with Anna, discovered *Uncle Tom's Cabin* and read the book over and over, talking about the characters as if she knew them. She adopted the name Harriet Beecher Stowe Son Klin and signed all her letters that way. She translated the book into the Siamese language. In 1867, Anna's last year in Siam, Lady Son Klin invited Anna to a ceremony during which she freed her own 132 slaves, saying "I am wishful to be good like Harriet Beecher Stowe. I want never to buy human bodies again, but only to let go free once and for all. So from this moment I have no more slaves, but hired servants."[7] In 1872 Anna Leonowens met Harriet Beecher Stowe, who "embraced her as if she had known her for a lifetime."[8]

Renown and Ridicule

Invited to Scotland by the Anti-Slavery Society of Glasgow, Harriet— with her husband, Calvin Stowe (1802–86), and her brother Charles Beecher (1815–1900), and her widowed sister-in-law Sarah Beecher, plus Sarah's young son and Sarah's brother William Buckingham—sailed for Europe in April 1853. Harriet was asked to appear at numerous large and small gatherings; some were women-only discussions, but as pointed out earlier most were "promiscuous" assemblies at which her speeches were read by her husband or her position on abolition "represented" in speeches by Calvin Stowe or Charles Beecher. When she returned to the United States, she wrote and published her travel memoirs, *Sunny Memories of Foreign Lands* (1854), basing them on the journal that Charles kept of the trip, noting whom she met and where; they continued and strength- ened the connections that she made abroad, as people she met read about themselves in her work. Charles was adamant that excerpts from his jour- nals and letters were not to be published until after the trip, when he and Harriet could work on editing together (Beecher, 48).[9] The result was that his more fascinating impressions were not contemporaneously pub- lished at all. Some of the most interesting detail in Charles's journal is missing from Harriet's published work, nor does her book recapture the immediacy of the moment—from Charles's frustration over Harriet's lost trunk to his disgust over excessive European drinking to his sexist wonder at female clutter.

Even though she was greeted with enthusiastic crowds everywhere, there was much criticism of her visit both from the American South and from class-conscious Scotland (because of a reception hosted by the Duchess of Sutherland and the continuing antagonism against the Sutherlands for their part in the Highland clearances).[10] There was even a reply to her memoirs, published in Toronto in 1857: *Donald M'Leod's Gloomy Memories in the Highlands of Scotland versus Mrs. Harriet Beecher Stowe's Sunny Memories in (England) a foreign land; or, A faithful picture of the extirpation of the Celtic Race from the Highlands of Scotland.*[11] The tour ultimately succeeded, however, in making the antislavery movement more respectable in the American South and in the British Isles.

It was as the most famous (nonroyal) woman in the world that many were interested in Stowe, and she was subjected to the stereotyped notions of what a woman should be. Her lack of beauty was widely re- ported in the press, especially by those opposed to her (as in the Ameri-

Harriet Beecher Stowe, courtesy of the Harriet Beecher Stowe Center, Hartford, Connecticut.

can South). Since photography was not yet widely available, unflattering line drawings and caricatures took her likeness around the world. When she began traveling, people were almost more interested in her supposed ugliness than in her writing. In Edinburgh in 1853 she wrote in her diary about young boys who recognized her by her hair style: "Some boys amused me very much by their pertinacious attempts to keep up with the carriage. 'Heck,' says one of them, 'that's her; see the courls!'" (*Life*, 217). Later, she remarked that most people were glad to see that she was not so "bad-looking as they were afraid I was." Her ironic self-deprecation lightened what must have been a daily trial: "May 7: . . . I do assure you that when I have seen the things that are put up in the shop windows here with my name under them, I have been in wondering admiration at the boundless loving-kindness of my English and Scottish friends in keeping up such a warm heart for such a Gorgon. I should think that the Sphinx in the London Museum might have sat for most of them" (*Life*, 231).

On her second voyage to Europe, in 1856, she was still plagued by body-image discussions, writing to her husband from Paris on November 7: "As usual, my horrid pictures do me a service, and people seem relieved when they see me; think me even handsome 'in a manner.' Kingsley, in his relief, expressed as much to his wife, and as beauty has never been one of my strong points I am open to flattery upon it" (*Life*, 288). Even Frances Power Cobbe, when they met in Italy, commented that Stowe "struck me as a woman who had been completely stared out of countenance. . . .[She] seems to have been looked at till she could no longer venture to open her eyelids quite comfortably."[12]

In Paris the Beecher-Stowe party not only sat for portraits by Hilaire Belloc (husband of Stowe's translator) but also took advantage of the new daguerreotype technology to have impressions made (Beecher, 322–23). Had photography been slightly more advanced at the time *Uncle Tom's Cabin* was published, Harriet might not have had so many curious onlookers.

Stowe and the International Reformist Network

A significant international network of reform-minded persons predated Stowe's journeys, but she added immensely to its density and strength. Ideas of female emancipation were already part of the manifold conversations out of which the network was formed, and even though she herself was no champion of women's rights, Stowe nevertheless contributed to that cause. The crusading vision that had produced *Uncle Tom's Cabin,* her willingness to travel the world on behalf of antislavery, and her way of magnetically drawing a variety of influential people to herself and her movement—these ineluctably created a new image of what was possible for females. Stowe's capacity as a networker was thus a key contribution to the communications revolution.

With the popularity of her book, Stowe quickly became the spokesperson for abolitionists; as such, she met aristocrats, famous writers, and royalty (including Queen Victoria), and in each group she paid special attention to women. In England she was guest of honor at Stafford House (home of the Duke and Duchess of Sutherland) at a meeting arranged to present her with a letter and petition "in behalf of the ladies of England" on antislavery. This document, "The affectionate and Christian Address of many thousands of Women of Great Britain and Ireland to their Sisters, the Women of the United States of America," was signed by over 500,000 British women and presented in twenty-six folio volumes. In Stowe's later description, signatures of "wives of cabinet ministers appear on the same page with the names of wives of humble laborers— names of duchesses and countesses, of wives of generals, ambassadors, savants, and men of letters, mingled with names traced in trembling characters by hands evidently unused to hold the pen, and stiffened by lowly toil" (*Life,* 377). Signatures had been obtained from British residents abroad as well, as far away as Paris and even Jerusalem.

The petition appealed to the women of the United States "as sisters, as wives, and as mothers, to raise your voices to your fellow-citizens, and your prayers to God, for the removal of this affliction and disgrace from the Christian world." It acknowledged British complicity and sharing in "this great sin" and asked for help in ridding the world of "our common crime and our common dishonor" (*Life,* 376). Stowe was also presented with a gold bracelet "made in the form of a slave's shackle, bearing the inscription: 'We trust it is a memorial of a chain that is soon to be broken'" (*Life,* 234). On two of the links were inscribed the dates of the abolition of the slave trade and of slavery in British territory. She also received donations (a minimum of one penny from every woman signing the petition) for use in the abolition campaign.

Many of the speeches made in her honor (some of which are reprinted in *Sunny Memories*) alluded to the importance to the abolitionist struggle of Stowe's being a woman. For example, at the public meeting in Dundee on April 22, 1853, a Mr. Gilfillan lauded Stowe's book and asserted, "None but a woman could have written it. . . . Who but a female could have created the gentle Eva, painted the capricious and selfish Marie St. Clair, or turned loose a Topsy upon the wondering world? [Loud and continued cheering.] And it is to my mind exceedingly delightful, and it must be humiliating to our opponents, to remember that the severest stroke to American slavery has been given by a woman's hand." He went on to compare Stowe to two Old Testament heroes: the young David who slew Goliath, and the woman who killed the murderer Abimelech with a stone.[13] Calvin Stowe, speaking on behalf of Harriet at the April 13, 1853, public meeting in Liverpool, alluded to sisterhood between slave and free women everywhere: "For in slavery it is woman that suffers most intensely, and the suffering woman has a claim upon the sympathy of her sisters in other lands."[14] The Rev. Dr. Wardlaw, at the public meeting in Glasgow, April 15, 1853, claimed Stowe as a world citizen: "It may sound strangely, that, when assembled for the very purpose of denouncing 'property in man,' we should be putting in our claims for a share of property in woman. So, however, it is. We claim Mrs. Stowe as ours— [renewed cheers]—not ours only, but still ours. She is British and European property as well as American. She is the property of the whole world of literature and the whole world of humanity [cheers]."[15] The ironic analogy to property in slaves was not noted.

Met in Paris by fellow American and abolitionist Maria Weston Chapman, Stowe became a tourist, visiting the obligatory sights. She also met important people there, especially in the emigré and expatriate community—Polish, Russian, British, and Italian. Mary Clark Mohl (1793–1883), British wife of Julius von Mohl (1800–1876, Orientalist and translator of Persian poets) and hostess of an important salon, served tea to Stowe and Chapman. In Dresden the travelers were invited to an expatriate gathering by a Belgian American couple (Beecher 298).

In Paris she stayed at the home of her translator, Louise Belloc.[16] Always interested in the differences in living arrangements and sex roles between America and other cultures, Stowe noted the cool, waxed floors of French houses, wondering if they could be introduced in the United States. "Not," said her companion, "while the mistress of the house has every thing to do, as in America; I think I see myself, in addition to all my cares, on my knees, waxing up one of these floors." The French had male servants who came in early in the morning with brushes on their feet, dancing and polishing the floor; American women, she averred, would have to do it themselves. Stowe herself, though not remarking the class bias here, referred to Fourier's utopian socialist communities: "Here is Fourrier's [sic] system in one particular. We enjoy the floors, and the man enjoys the dancing."[17]

Although Stowe had gone to France to get some rest from the rigors of celebrity travel, she continued to be lionized there. In Paris the party was met by a deputation from Belfast, Ireland, with gifts and speeches, asking Stowe to use her influence on behalf of Irish home rule. Even in rural areas, such as the Jura Mountains, the common people (especially women) all knew of Harriet Beecher Stowe and her Uncle Tom. Says Charles Beecher, "The good hostess, even the servant maids, hung about Harriet, expressing such tender interest for the slave. All had read 'Uncle Tom'; and it had apparently been an era in their life's monotony, for they said, 'Oh, madam, do write another! Remember, our winter nights here are very long!'" (Life, 244).

Fredrika Bremer, whose own American journey was taken partly to see slavery for herself, lauded Stowe and her work for bringing the details of slavery horrors to the world. Stowe has, said Bremer, "stood forth . . . as no other woman in the realms of literature has yet done . . . with a power which has won for her the whole ear of humanity."[18]

On her second voyage to Europe three years later, Stowe's fame had not lessened. She received letters from Harriet Martineau and Elizabeth Gaskell and subsequently visited Gaskell in Manchester. Her reaction reflected her "separate spheres" beliefs: "Mrs. Gaskell seems lovely at home, where besides being a writer she proves herself to be a first-class housekeeper, and performs all the duties of a minister's wife" (Life, 312). Stowe's third voyage (1859–60) included a winter in Florence, where she entertained visitors and began her only work with a setting outside of the United States, Agnes of Sorrento, a novel set in the time of Savonarola. In the last three decades of her life she continued her voluminous correspondence and entertained guests at both her homes—in Florida on the St. John's River and in Hartford, Connecticut, at Nook Farm.

Stowe and International Female Solidarity

Stowe was famous partly because she was a woman. Her celebrity status brought people together who were otherwise isolated; indeed, she may have been the cause of the invention of the "fan"—male or female. At each of many public meetings in Scotland there were over two thousand in attendance; people waited six or seven hours to see her. Charles Beecher compared her fame to that of singer Jenny Lind or exiled Hungarian political leader Louis Kossuth but called her reception more "genuine" and "spiritual" (Beecher, 36). The fact that she had written a political novel from a woman's perspective was often remarked. Ironically, although a "separate spheres" woman, she did not take her twin daughters with her to England but left them at home with a caregiver. Again ironically, she was thrust into the role of abolitionist leader, although she had never been a public figure in the movement before writing *Uncle Tom*. Women like Lydia Maria Child and Lucretia Mott had been outspoken abolition-ist leaders for decades, but newcomer Harriet Beecher Stowe became the spokesperson.

A networker she was in her own person, there is no doubt. Yet it was her very celebrity that most effectively drew together different and, at times, partially overlapping groups of enthusiasts. One can only specu-late about what happened in such groups once Stowe was no longer present and her popularity had diminished. But having celebrated both her literary achievement and her personal example, her loyalists must certainly have entertained new conceptions and images of what women were capable of and the causes to which their gender called them. In her later life, even when she was old and senile, Stowe herself stayed aloof from women's rights struggles and continued her belief in woman's sepa-rate sphere. Making connections based on gender was not important to her, for abolitionist conversion among both sexes was her overriding con-sideration. Unwittingly, however, she furthered both female-to-female relationships and a form of womanist political advocacy.

"So Corrupt a Woman": The Scandalous Mrs. Sand

On leaving Paris for Switzerland and Germany in 1853, the Beecher-Stowe party spent much of the travel time reading aloud from contemporary works by women writers: *Mary Barton* by Elizabeth Gaskell, Fredrika Bremer's *Homes of the New World* (mistakenly called *Homes in the West* in Charles Beecher's journal: Beecher, 340), and *Consuelo* by George Sand.[19] Stowe liked Sand's work but not the author, worrying because newspaper accounts had compared her to Madame Sand and the Paris bluestockings. Said Charles on Saturday, July 2, 1853, Génève: "I read aloud much of the way from *Consuelo*. Hatty said it was amazing that so corrupt a woman could describe so beautiful a character" (Beecher, 216).

Stowe admired Gaskell and Bremer, but Sand was anathema; she was echoing the conservative Anglo-American reviewers who for years had been castigating Sand's morals even as they lauded her style.[20]

George Sand was very different from Harriet Beecher Stowe, but both were powerfully influential with women. Stowe traveled and people clamored to see her. Sand did not travel much internationally (except to Italy and Majorca), but people vied to wangle introductions to meet her, and she was constantly mentioned in the press, in letters, in conversations. Her work, although never achieving best-seller status, was in some ways more popular than Stowe's—partly because she wrote more, but mostly because people were both fascinated and repelled by her conduct. Many reviews gave far more space to her personal life than to her novels, and like Stowe she was judged by her looks. Her books were translated quickly (often by women) and frequently referred to. Although in her lifetime she was read, reviewed, and revered by critics and other writers, within twenty-five years of her death she was quickly forgotten. Typical perhaps is the fact that although her portrait appears in the chapter on Continental Europe (written by Theodore Stanton) in the *History of Woman Suffrage,* the text of the chapter makes no mention of her work.[21] Was her writing neglected because of her unconventionality? One thinks of the similar antagonism expressed toward the life styles of Mary Wollstonecraft and Frances Wright, such that their works and ideas were nearly forgotten for generations.

Sand as a Concept

Beginning in 1836, George Sand's novels were widely available in Russia, and in the 1840s and 1850s her romantic ideas of complete freedom in love—"whether before, after, or outside of marriage"—were known by all literate Russians. Indeed, various terms were coined: *zhorshsandshchina,* female individualistic and "free feeling" (usually sexually adulterous) acts; and the *zhorzhsandistka,* a comic type. Actually, Sand's ideas were not only about love but also about spiritual and moral purity, "emotional honesty," and independence for women. Given the strict patriarchal system of the Russian family, many educated Russian women, such as Nadezhda Stasova and Elena Gan, noted that they first awakened to ideas of self-definition in reading Sand's novels.[22]

Sand also advocated socialism and "associationism" and was acquainted with the Saint-Simonians and Fourierists. Many early Russian

George Sand, from a postcard published by the Helaine Victoria Press.

revolutionary men (such as Aleksandr Herzen and Vissarion Belinsky) traced the kindling of their conscious understanding to reading her works.[23] It is important to note that from the time of the Decembrist uprising in 1825, most foreign books of political import (economics, philosophy, history, social thought) were banned in Russia; novels were the only medium by which ideas from the West could enter Russia.[24] All the Russian literary giants refer to Sand, and her influence on women writers such as novelist Elena Gan is incalculable.[25] (Her connection to nineteenth-century Russian revolutionary women such as Natalie Herzen is discussed in Chapter 5.)

Sand's influence in Russia continued into the revolutionary years of the twentieth century, long after she was no longer regarded as an important novelist in the West. Lenin referred to her obliquely by criticizing the "emancipation of the heart," and right-wing prudes such as Polina Vinogradskaya excoriated Alexandra Kollontai by calling her "a twentieth-century George Sand."[26]

Outside of Russia as well, as a writer and as a person, Sand was an international sensation. Parts of *Consuelo* were translated for publication in the first number of the American Brook Farm periodical, *The Harbinger* (1845), by Francis G. Shaw.[27] Eliza Ashurst, one of the radical Ashurst sisters in England, translated Sand for British readers.[28] American journalist Margaret Fuller met her hero, Sand, when she was in Paris, carrying a letter of introduction from Joseph Mazzini in London.[29] In 1839 Paris the British salonnière Mary Clarke Mohl wrote to Elizabeth Reid of two French men who told her that George Sand was the best French writer (not the best woman writer) and "had a better right to be a member of the Academy than any man."[30] Sarah Grimké filled four pages of a notebook with Sand quotations and wrote a fan letter in 1867 asking Sand for help in locating a picture of Jeanne d'Arc to be published in her translation of Lamartine's work.[31]

These international linkages branched out endlessly. Lydia Maria Child called Sand her "twin" because of the similarity of their ideas.[32] Marie Zebrikoff, author of the "Russia" section for Theodore Stanton's *The Woman Question in Europe* (1884), reviewed and translated George Sand, the Brontës, and George Eliot into Russian.[33] Fredrika Runeberg (novelist, translator, and wife of the Finnish national poet), influenced by Sand, wrote articles on women's rights as early as 1850.[34] French artist Rosa Bonheur's famous painting *Ploughing in the Nivernais* (1849) was based on Sand's novel *La mare au diable* (1846).[35] The list of British women writers influenced by Sand is long: Eliot, Elizabeth Barrett Browning, Charlotte Brontë, Gaskell, and many others.[36] Sand herself read Stowe's book and wrote about it favorably immediately after its 1852 publication.[37]

Sand too, like Stowe, declined to be made into a spokesperson for feminist causes. Nominated to run for the French Assembly in 1848 by some former Saint-Simonian women, she refused the honor, citing the inequality of women in law: "For the condition of women to be changed, society must first be changed radically.... Social conditions are such that women could not honorably and honestly exercise a political mandate."[38] When she did write about women, it was most often against French marriage law as enshrined in the Napoleonic Code, which gave husbands complete rights over their wives and denied divorce. Still, any discussion of "the woman question" in the nineteenth century would invariably bring her name, as well as Stowe's, to mind.[39]

Results

We can point to at least four different kinds of connections made between women because of Stowe or Sand—or both. The fact that such connections were not intended or consciously sought by these celebrities does not negate their existence.

First, that so many women read and found themselves or their convictions reflected in the works of these authors created a bond. Especially clear for Sand is the production of an identifying community among Russian women, for whom novels were the only allowable reading. Stowe's novel probably evoked less identification than collective indignation and interest in a cause. Significantly, although Lydia Maria Child saw her own situation as similar to that of Sand, calling Sand her "double" or "twin," she noted that American society was less oppressive than French: "She [Sand] has lived in a very artificial and corrupt state of society; while I, thank God, was born in New England." Sand's strength, said Child, was her intellectual honesty, which Child attempted to emulate:

> She is under the *necessity* of speaking the *truth*. She sees society promenading and waltzing over an infernal pit, from which ... it is separated by the thinnest coating of conventional respectability. Others may put finger on lip, if they please, but *she* knows, and *they* know, that the pit is there, and thousands

are continually tumbling into it, and God has made *her* so
sincere and direct, that she *must* describe the pit, in all its
horrible and disgusting details. With a kind of moral despera-
tion, she says, In God's name, let the truth come out, be the
consequences what they may, to myself, to others.[40]

An additional and very intriguing point of comparison between
Child and Sand was in dress. Although Child did not go to the extreme
of wearing trousers and top hat, she did refuse to dress stylishly. Instead,
she wore threadbare, old-fashioned, comfortable dresses and was therefore rarely recognized as she went everywhere in New York, later writing
about tenements, immigrant areas, and wharves in her column "Letters
from New York." Such freedom of movement was not usually available to
upper-class women, and it was for this reason too that Sand first adopted
masculine dress, which allowed her to observe and be anonymous in
ways a woman could not: "I went out whatever the weather. I came home
at all hours. I sat in orchestra seats in all the theaters. No one paid attention to me or suspected my disguise. Not only did I wear it with ease, but
the absence of coquettishness in my attire and in my face removed all
suspicion. I was too poorly dressed and I looked too unsophisticated . . .
to attract or hold anyone's stares."[41] Other women must surely have identified with Sand in their frustration over expensive and cumbersome female garments. We might remember that in the 1820s Frances Wright
wore the full-trousered New Harmony costume later named for Amelia
Bloomer, who instigated a dress reform movement in the United States
in the 1850s. Nordic women artists Fanny Churberg, Victoria Åberg, and
Ida Silfverberg were part of a similar reform movement in 1850s Berlin
and Düsseldorf, refusing to wear crinolines in order to free themselves
for their painting.[42] Innovative style traveled—and that included both
fashion and greater comfort.

Cross-dressing itself is far older than George Sand. Early modern
Europe saw a plethora of well-documented cases, especially in the Netherlands and England. Economic motivation, particularly the option of
joining the army or navy as an alternative to prostitution, seems to have
been a common reason.[43] Marjorie Garber, in her book *Vested Interests:
Cross-Dressing and Cultural Anxiety,* argues that cross-dressing both historically and at present questions rigid classifications of gender, as well
as race and class, and ultimately "category itself."[44] The profound dis-
comfort that greeted Sand's cross-dressing (and that of her contempo-

raries Daniel Stern [Marie d'Agout], Rosa Bonheur, and Louisa Aston) tends to support Garber's view of its cultural importance.

The fact that both Sand and Stowe were writing at a time when many women used male pseudonyms to get a fair reading was significant in providing a second kind of connection for aspiring female writers. There was, of course, a distinct difference between the two women in this matter. Harriet Beecher Stowe would never have used a male pseudonym, as she believed strongly in her position as a wife, but she began publishing fully two decades after Sand, when women writers were more common. George Sand's birth name was Aurore Dupin, and upon marriage, Dudevant. She began writing as J. Sand, then G. Sand, then Georges Sand, and finally George Sand, without the *s*. This idiosyncratic spelling gives a strange androgynous look to the name in French and suggests Sand's generic ambivalence. She was conscious of making her own identity, writing, "In Paris, Mme Dudevant is dead. But Georges Sand is known to be a vigorous fellow."[45] Stowe, on the other hand, continued to be "the preacher's wife" for her entire literary career. Despite this difference, the strong public personae fashioned by these women, together with the intense appeal of their advocacy writing, necessarily provided inspiration to ambitious female artists.

We may speculate that a third kind of "bonding power" sprang from the antagonism occasioned by both writers—though greater in the case of Sand. Most of the negativity Stowe confronted had to do with male critics' attitude toward women writers in general—especially popular ones—typified by Nathaniel Hawthorne's infamous remark about "those damned scribbling women." Plenty of women as well, including Stowe, were antagonistic to Sand because of her numerous affairs and male attire. Yet even dislike could create ties between these authors and like-minded women.

A fourth kind of connection—applicable only to Stowe—is the invocation of sisterhood, first used in evangelical religious contexts, then continued in the abolitionist struggle to bind slave and nonslave women, when women insisted on the analogy between the slave situation and their own. The figure of the kneeling female slave with the motto, "Am I Not a Woman and a Sister?" was first used by the Ladies Negro's Friend Society of Birmingham, England, in 1826; it was discussed in *The Ladies' Repository* in 1830 by editor Elizabeth Margaret Chandler and then used as cover illustration for L. Maria Child's *Authentic Anecdotes of American Slavery* in 1838.[46] Since the idea of sisterhood had already been applied in these contexts, it was easy to extend its use to connect women internationally—as in the petition of 500,000 British women to "their Sisters, the Women of the United States of America," presented to Stowe in 1853.

In short, the literary celebrity of such women as Stowe and Sand, even though they were neutral or negative toward women's causes, unwittingly helped women meet one another across national, linguistic, and even class boundaries. Working in political and communal settings gave them both opportunity and an egalitarian philosophy; conscious awareness of women's goals and the efficacy of cooperation broadened the web of connections. By 1888, the acquaintances, the associations, the knowledge of others' situations were already there. What was then necessary was the impetus of a few women activated by the intuition that out of this environment of preexisting relatedness they might possibly generate an organized international movement.

A Developing Consciousness

Revolutionaries, Refugees, and Expatriates

Sisters of America! your socialist sisters of France are united with you in
the vindication of the right of woman to civil and political equality.
—Jeanne Deroin and Pauline Roland, letter to
Worcester (Mass.) Women's Rights Convention,
from Paris, Prison of St. Lazare, June 15, 1851

In the nineteenth century Europe functioned as a powerful demographic
engine, more than doubling its population even while sending its sons
and daughters abroad in unprecedented numbers. Between 1815 and 1932
more than 60 million persons migrated from the old countries, swelling
especially the populations of North and South America, Australia, New
Zealand, and Siberia. Population pressure—the result of medical progress
and the rising standard of living—accounts for much of this outmigration,
but political factors were far from negligible. The enormous movement
of Russian Jews after 1881 was a response to savage pogroms and official
discrimination. Scandinavian young people reacted against the stifling
control of social and economic life by a privileged ecclesiastical and gov-
ernmental class. In Ireland, little land remained open for purchase, controlled as it was by wealthy landlords, many of whom resided in England;
additionally, the disastrous potato famine of 1846–47 sent more thousands across the Atlantic. The great upheavals surrounding the revolutionary events of 1848 also produced a significant migratory movement.
As a result, not only did the New World receive new residents, but Europe itself witnessed a churning and stirring of peoples. With the failure
of dramatic campaigns for republican constitutions, national unification, universal manhood suffrage, parliamentary authority, civil liber-

ties, the end of serfdom, and (in France) socialist strategies for improving the lot of workers, repression followed, and radicals of all sorts had to find safe havens. Various cities—especially Paris, Geneva, Zurich, and London—sheltered wave after wave of emigrés. London eventually became the main center for refugees from the failed revolutions, although large numbers also made their way to the United States.

Disastrous though they proved to be for liberal and radical aims, the thwarted revolutions in France, Italy, the Austrian Empire, and the German Confederation did provide a certain ironic dividend for some women. In their home countries feminist exponents of perhaps the most heretical doctrines in the liberal camp could easily become isolated. But in dislocation they found like-minded souls, male as well as female, of their own nationalities and others, and these contacts quickened the general ferment of ideas and communication. As usual, writing was the best and commonest means of expression, and it took many forms: expatriate women wrote memoirs, travelogues, diaries; they produced autobiographies and thinly disguised autobiographical novels; they wrote letters and journalistic reports; they published newspapers expressly for women and in their mother-tongues. They also communicated in salons, performed charitable and political work together, and became friends and lovers. All these activities placed revolutionary women squarely in the increasingly cosmopolitan cadre of individuals strengthening the web of internationality.

The 1848 Revolutionaries

Malwida von Meysenbug, Johanna Kinkel, Jenny Marx, Agnes Ruge, and Amalie Struve were among the women from the "Generation of '48" who went to England in exile.[1] Struve later went to the United States, where, according to historian Rosemary Ashton, she participated in the American women's rights movement.[2]

Johanna Kinkel (1810–58) and Malwida von Meysenbug (1816–1903) became acquainted with liberal English women such as Barbara Leigh Smith Bodichon and Mrs. Gaskell, as well as with other revolutionary exiles: Jeanne Deroin from France and the circles around Mazzini, Kossuth, and Russian revolutionary Aleksandr Herzen. After the death of Herzen's wife, Natalie, Meysenbug became the governess for his children and earlier had accompanied English families to Paris. In 1858 she began a study group for emigré workers, both men and women, but was disillusioned both by the acquisitiveness of the members and by the "communist ideas" of some.[3] Both Kinkel and Meysenbug, with their liberal-radical political views, stressed the importance of education for women. Meysenbug also worked on campaigns for women's medical education and the rights of married women.[4] Although they were critical of England's legal and social strictures for women, they were impressed with individual English women who provided models for emulation, describing them in both private letters and published writings. Kinkel also wrote favorably about the open, international atmosphere in London at the time:"The best from all parts of the world meets together here in this great country. People travel with amazing ease to all corners of the globe; one man has a brother in the Australian colonies, another sends his daughter to be married in India, there is constant interaction with those parts of the world. The women are acquainted with the dangers of journeying by land and sea, and become, as a result, indifferent to trivial problems."[5]

Meysenbug became well known with her autobiography, *Memoiren einer Idealistic*.[6] In Johanna Kinkel's autobiographical novel about the life of exiles in London—*Hans Ibeles in London. Ein Familienbild aus dem Flüchtlingsleben* (Hans Ibeles in London: A family picture of refugee life; Stuttgart, 1860)—the character of the governess Meta, a professional single woman, is probably based on Malwida von Meysenbug.[7] More important, Kinkel portrays sympathetically several women characters and their difficulties as women in exile.[8] For her part, Bodichon wrote favorably about Johanna Kinkel in her *English Woman's Journal*.[9] Nevertheless, according to historian Christine Lattek, the interaction of the exiles with the liberal-feminist English community was minimal; most of their contacts were with other emigrés.[10] Malwida von Meysenbug continued her cosmopolitan life by accompanying Herzen's daughters to Italy in 1861.[11] She remained in Italy until her death in 1903, maintaining constant communication with her many comrades-in-arms.

Other revolutionary women joined the exiles in London by choice, among them Baroness Marie von Bruiningk of Vienna. She established an emigré salon near the Kinkels' residence, although both Kinkel in her novel and Meysenbug in her memoirs imply that von Bruiningk's motives were more sexual than political. Another self-exile to London was Amely Bölte, a governess who knew Jane Carlyle, among others.[12]

Women '48ers went also to Paris (Emma Herwegh and Fanny Lewald) or Switzerland (Claire von Glümer). Still others remained in Germany and organized women to help those in exile. Kathinka Zitz-

Halein founded the Humania Association for Patriotic Interests in Mainz in 1849 to help patriots and their families both in Germany and abroad. She herself traveled to Switzerland and Strasbourg to distribute money and clothing to needy exiles. She also raised money especially for Johanna Kinkel and her husband, Gottfried, who were personal friends.[13] As one of the first women's organizations in Germany, the Humania Association gave women needed experience in a public sphere, and it was a forerunner of many later international philanthropic efforts.

Interestingly, it was a man, exiled Captain A.D. Korn, who helped draw together women's international contacts in Austria. Returning from exile in England and the United States, he and his wife founded a women's newspaper, the *Allgemeine Frauen Zeitung,* and the General Society for Popular Education and the Amelioration of Women's Condition (Allgemeine Verein für Volkserziehung und Verbesserung des Frauenloses). The organization sponsored German women's conventions at Leipzig, Stuttgart, and, in 1872, Vienna. The resolutions offered were modeled on those at American women's rights conventions.[14]

The remarkable saga of Mathilde Franziska Anneke (1817–84) illustrates some of the dynamics at work in this volatile political environment.[15] Born to a wealthy family in Westphalia in Germany, she became a journalist, educator, and women's rights advocate. She was connected to the mid-century European revolutionary movements through her husband, Fritz Anneke, and knew Marx, Michael Bakunin, and other revolutionaries. Her experience clearly illustrates the way the Atlantic had long since ceased to be a barrier separating women from one another; rather, for Anneke (as for Marx), the Atlantic had become a busy bridge joining different centers of the same revolutionary activity.

Married at nineteen to a French wine merchant, she divorced after only a year and a half. Her political life began with her struggle for custody of daughter Fanny and the return of her maiden name. By law at that time the child belonged to the father, and Mathilde Giesler had to appeal at several judicial levels to gain custody. She began her literary career by writing books of religious verse and almanacs but was further radicalized after meeting Fritz Anneke and his freethinking, socialist circle in the ferment of European revolutionary movements. In 1847 she married Anneke and published her controversial pamphlet *Das Weib im Konflikt mit den sozialen Verhältnissen* (Woman in conflict with social conditions), beginning a turbulent decade of struggle on two continents. She began to publish *Neue Kölnische Zeitung* in revolutionary Cologne under the name of her husband but after his imprisonment changed the title to *Frauenzeitung*, the first feminist paper in Germany.[16] In the revolutionary battles in Baden the next spring she rode with her husband, dressed in trousers and with her hair cut short, serving as adjutant.[17] When the revolution collapsed, she escaped with her children and husband to Switzerland and then to the United States.

First in Newark, New Jersey and then in Milwaukee (where the family settled in 1852), she published a German-language feminist paper, *Deutsche Frauenzeitung*, and lectured on socialism, women's rights, and women's education while attacking nativism, organized religion, and temperance. Including the daughter from her first marriage, Mathilde gave birth to seven children, but only two outlived her (three died of smallpox because Fritz did not believe in vaccinations). An ardent abolitionist, she spent the Civil War period back in Europe as a freelance journalist, interpreting and translating the American conflict for the German press. Her husband had returned to Europe as a correspondent for American papers, but when the Civil War began, he came back to the United States to fight, while Mathilde remained in Europe with the children and her good friend Mary Booth, wife of antislavery agitator Sherman Booth. She never again lived with Fritz but depended on female friendships, not only with Mary Booth but also with Cecilie Kapp, whom she met in Switzerland.

Mathilde and her children returned to the United States with Cecilie Kapp. Together in 1865 they founded a girls' school in Milwaukee, "Madam Anneke's German-French-English Academy," and continued their close friendship after Kapp became a professor of German at Vassar College.[18] The school was known for its progressive teaching methods; Anneke's aim was to educate and free her young pupils. Thus, discussions about bobbed hair or women speaking in public were part of the curriculum, along with lessons in French, art, and music.[19] Anneke went on writing as well: journalistic pieces (especially theater reviews), poetry, and short fiction. But she made her main impact as a lecturer and organizer for working women (especially German immigrants; she continued to lecture in German) and women's rights. She was a lifelong friend of Susan Anthony and Elizabeth Cady Stanton, even though she as a good German disagreed with the emphasis put on temperance by the suffrage movement. She worked particularly hard in her home state of Wisconsin and with various groups in Milwaukee.[20] Her philosophy, so shaped by European movements and values, was transformed in the

American environment of moral reform and the possibility of peaceful change.

Veterans of earlier struggles for women, Jeanne Deroin and Pauline Roland were jailed in St. Lazare prison in Paris for six months in 1850 for breaking the new rules against political association in the aftermath of the 1848 revolution. From prison they wrote an open letter in 1851 to the Women's Rights Convention in Worcester, Massachusetts. Their letter reiterates women's demands from 1848, proclaims solidarity with the "Sisters of America," and uses the phrase "one half of humanity" to call for solidarity of all women with the working classes.[21] "One half of humanity" is a phrase reminiscent of William Thompson and Anna Wheeler's 1825 work (see Chapter 7), as well as that of both the Marquis de Condorcet and Mary Wollstonecraft during the French revolutionary period. Both Deroin and Roland were classed as dangerous to the state in Louis Napoleon's consolidation of power in 1852. Pauline Roland was sent to a penal colony in Algeria and died shortly after her return; Jeanne Deroin went into exile in London, where she continued to make international linkages, building on connections with Anna Wheeler's old Owenite group. She published *Almanack des femmes* (1854), as well as Pauline Roland's last letters from prison in Algeria, and articles about feminist developments in England and the United States.[22] As the first woman candidate for election to the National Assembly in 1849, Deroin had been well publicized in England by Anne Knight, who was in Paris during the 1848 revolutions and after.[23] Knight wrote to Lord Brougham and others, praising Deroin's brave candidacy and describing it in sacrificial terms: "[She] comes forward to offer herself on the altar of her country, with her living heart of woman, to speak peace and concord to the stormy heads of that company called legislators."[24]

Emma Willard—founder of the important girls' school, Troy Academy, where Elizabeth Cady Stanton was educated—wrote French politician Jacques-Charles DuPont de l'Eure in April 1848 to argue that a Council of Women should be established in the new government. Universal manhood suffrage had been established briefly in 1848, specifically excluding women, and the repercussions of that decision were felt across the Atlantic.[25]

The Hungarian revolutionary patriot Louis (Lajos) Kossuth (1802–94) and his wife escaped from Hungary in the aftermath of the failed 1848 revolution and in 1851 sought asylum in England for their children.[26] There they spent a triumphant month, speaking and winning adherents to the cause. At the end of November they sailed for the United States, accompanied by Francis and Theresa Pulszky. The Pulszkys' two-volume work, *White, Red, Black: Sketches of American Society* (1853) is mostly Theresa's diary of that trip. She met women of various political views, from Lucretia Mott to the slave-holding southern aristocrat Madame Octavia LeVert. The American War of Independence had given hope and inspiration to the revolutionaries of Central Europe, and Pulszky took pains to discuss the position of women and the differences she noted between the class society of Europe and the classless democracy of the United States.

Still, she was not uncritical: the long account ended with three letters dated July 1852, received from an unnamed New England woman, which critiqued the problems that the "classless" society had created, especially the domestic work that it required all women to do. In fact, much of the discussion about American women in *White, Red, Black* detailed regrets that their workload was heavier because of the democratic nature of society and the lack of servants (except in the South). Like Tocqueville twenty years earlier, Pulszky lamented Americans' rising expectations and unfulfilled desires—which, she said, redound particularly on women, who are always tempted to spend: "The American has no fixed limit of what is essential to his happiness or to filling well his station" because "his station is always moving." The last letter was taken up with the problem of the high cost of labor and a plea for Americans to live more simply so that women would not have to fill their whole lives with household duties.[27] Of course, the assumption that only women should do this work remained unexamined.

Pulszky's Christmas Day visit to Lucretia Mott was mostly taken up with discussion of the abolition question. Afterward, however, Pulszky was criticized by southern conservatives for having talked with Mott at all, since Mott was a female Quaker preacher of "powerfully inciting" sermons. Pulszky was moved to read some of her sermons and was impressed by "that fervent desire to seek truth."[28]

Pulszky had long conversations with Robert Dale Owen, son of Robert Owen, who described his successful efforts at getting women's property rights accepted into the constitution of the new state of Indiana. He had been intimately involved with the communal experiments and efforts at egalitarianism for women and former slaves first at New Harmony, Indiana, with his father and then with Frances Wright at the Nashoba community in Tennessee and at the Workingmen's Institute in

New York. Pulszky remarked that Hungary had never accepted the Roman law which treats wives as minors and that women there managed their own inheritance. She was quite surprised at the racism of the new Indiana constitution, which Owen espoused despite his radical egalitarian background; it forbade any Negro to come into the state and recommended adoption of the recolonization scheme to transport free blacks to Liberia because "public opinion disapproved" of free blacks owning property.[29]

Theresa Pulszky and Madame Kossuth also met Octavia LeVert of Mobile, Alabama. LeVert, herself an inveterate traveler who had met Fredrika Bremer, was gracious in her hospitality, made effortless by the institution of slavery. Indeed, many southerners welcomed Europeans in their efforts to defend slavery, and some visitors (such as Amelia Murray) did subsequently advocate the southern position.

Vojta Fingerhut-Náprstek, son of Anna Fingerhutová, took part in the March revolution of 1848 in Vienna and then in October, along with other political refugees, sailed from Hamburg for the United States. Settling in Milwaukee, he opened a bookstore and library, helped to organize a German school, became a lawyer and notary public for the state of Wisconsin. He also collected and sent books, periodicals, and animal and insect specimens to the Bohemian National Museum in Prague. After the general amnesty in 1857 he returned to Prague in February 1858. What happened next is indeed remarkable: he became a champion of new ideas from America, especially egalitarian ideas on women, noting their opportunities for equal education and their movement for legal equality. He organized, lectured, and preached on women's position in England, the United States, and France.

Fingerhut-Náprstek's efforts were taken up by Princess Jenny Taxisová, author Sofie Podlipská and her sister Bozena Nemcová, and the writer Karolina Svêtlá, a "Sandian"; in 1863 they organized an open letter, signed by three hundred Czech women. Then in 1865 they formed the "Club américain de dames," or the "Americky klub," dedicated to new technology, to women abroad and their activities and enterprises, and to *travail ménager* (housework). Náprstek became known as *l'avocat des femmes* and although men made fun of him, he kept working. He gave all the decision-making power in the Americky klub to the women, opening his library to them twice a week.[30] Marie Riegrová-Palacká (1833–91) helped Náprstek and became acquainted with the work of Hortense Cornu in Paris and V.H. Suringar in the Netherlands, among others. She later traveled all over Europe for the women's committee's philanthropic work, and wrote many articles and books about different systems of child care, defending the French *école maternelle* against the German kindergarten system of Friedrich Fröbel.[31]

The connections continued in the next generation when American Charlotte Garrigue, studying piano in Leipzig, met and in 1878 married the Czech hero Tomás Masaryk. She became a Czech nationalist and a feminist, participated in the Americky klub, and even translated into Czech John Stuart Mill's *On the Subjection of Women*.[32]

The Italian Risorgimento

The Italian nationalist movement took longer than others to unify the country, and numerous foreigners, including many women, were involved in the half-century-long effort. For these women, Italy was a beloved place in their education and travel. As they participated in the revolutionary struggle, the Risorgimento both radicalized and solidified the views of many non-Italian women about women. Jessie White Mario of England and Margaret Fuller of the United States are the two best-known examples, but many others were involved, either while residing there or by raising money and consciousness abroad: the British mathematician Mary Somerville, the poet Elizabeth Barrett Browning, the reformer Frances Power Cobbe, even American novelist Harriet Beecher Stowe. Italian women in exile also helped to publicize the issues, raise funds, and connect with women in other countries. One of the most intriguing of these Italian women is Cristina Belgiojoso.

Aristocrat Cristina Belgiojoso (1808–71) was a colorful figure in the struggle for Italian unification and independence. From her exile in Paris she wrote articles and books on the Italian situation and Italian history. Later she began writing on the condition of women, her nationalism having led to work for women's education and equal treatment in addition to her struggle for a unified Italy.[33] In Paris in the 1830s she hosted a salon to which artists and intellectuals, exiles and revolutionaries flocked. Historian Beth Brombert describes the world of exiles in Paris in the 1830s: "To French dreamers [such as Fourier and Saint-Simon] were added the tens of thousands proscripted in Italy, Portugal, Spain, Germany, Hungary, Poland, Russia—liberal noblemen, idealistic warriors, censored writers—for whom France was a paradise after the tyrannies they had left, and who came to find the torch lit by Napoleon. It was they who fanned the flame after it went out in France, for each group was fired by its national mission which was brought to the new Parisian salons in the search for converts to the faith."[34] Italy was the darling of the decade, and Italophilia raged.

Cristina Belgiojoso had come to Paris just at this time. As Brombert describes it, "Her unusual beauty, her titles, her frozen assets, her heroic stance against husband and emperor, her mission to liberate Italian prisoners held by Austria, all titillated the imagination. Rossini was an old friend, Bellini her protégé; by 1833 her salon was the center of Italian thought and art."[35] She became known throughout Europe as the Romantic heroine par excellence. Returning to Italy in 1848, she was put in charge of hospitals in Naples, Milan, and Rome. There she came to know Margaret Fuller.

After the failure of the Italian efforts against Austria, Belgiojoso escaped to Malta and then traveled on to Greece and Constantinople. Finding affordable property at Ciaq-Maq-Oglou in the hill country north of Ankara, Turkey, she and her daughter and two servants began a kind of Fourierist community, providing employment and education in agriculture and husbandry for the local people. She became well known for her medical knowledge and miraculous cures. Traveling through Turkey and Syria to Jerusalem, she described the landscape and the local people in travel articles (later books) for French, Italian, and American periodicals.[36] Always she noted the situation of women, worrying most about the lack of education, even as she criticized the oppression of women in harems (being one of the first Western women to stay in one overnight). Returning to Paris and then Italy in 1855, she continued to spend half her time in each country, writing and publishing. She was finally repatriated and her property in Lombardy restored.[37]

There were no American or English revolutions at midcentury, but those countries did produce revolutionaries for export, especially to Italy: Jessie White Mario (1832–1906), the Ashurst sisters, and Margaret Fuller (1810–50). A child of Dissent in England, Jessie White was an early believer in such causes as abolition, factory reform, and women's education. Educated in Paris, she quickly became involved in Continental liberal politics. She met Garibaldi in 1854 and brought his son Ricciotti back to England for orthopedic treatment. There she began her long involvement with the Friends of Italy and Giuseppe Mazzini's republican struggle for a unified Italy. It was through the Friends of Italy that Jessie White met the Ashurst family, Barbara Leigh Smith Bodichon, the American

Cristina Belgiojoso, from a print of an 1836 pastel by Vincent Vidal, courtesy of
Beth Archer Brombert.

Margaret Fuller, and others of the radical-liberal Italophile group in England. Mazzini's headquarters by that time was in England, and all four Ashurst daughters devoted inordinate amounts of time and money to "the cause." Emilie had married early but divorced when she became infatuated with Mazzini. She spent countless hours translating, editing, and polishing his work for publication. Like Jessie White later on, she also became involved in various plots and plans: providing him with a false passport, undertaking Continental trips on his behalf, inserting false notices of his whereabouts in the newspapers.[38]

Jessie White had attempted to study medicine in order to treat the wounded in the Italian struggle. But when her desire was thwarted by the ban on women in British medical schools, she turned to journalism. Her first project was a translation of Felice Orsini's *The Austrian Dungeons in Italy* (1856). Soon she was not only translating but fund raising and lecturing in England and Scotland for Mazzini's cause, as well as writing articles on Italy for newspapers. In May 1857 she went to Italy, ostensibly as a journalist. Imprisoned for four months in July 1857, she received love-letters from Alberto Mario, a compatriot and fellow prisoner.[39] After their release and her marriage to Mario, she continued her work in the struggle for Italian unification. In 1858–59 she and her husband made a lecture and fund-raising tour in the United States, where she met William Lloyd Garrison, Lucretia Mott, and other antislavery activists. Interestingly, a controversy surrounding her use of Elizabeth Barrett Browning's name as a "recommender" caused an angry exchange of newspaper letters, since Browning had come to disagree with the Marios politically and no longer wanted her name connected with theirs.[40] The Marios returned to Italy during Garibaldi's campaign in 1860, arriving ostensibly as correspondents, but Jessie expended heroic efforts in nursing (she was soon the director of nursing) and in procuring food for officers on the march.[41] Sent to England in 1877 for treatment and complete rest at the St. Vies home of Barbara Bodichon, a lifelong friend, she ended up nursing Bodichon through an attack of aphasia and "nervous weakness."[42]

Bodichon and George Eliot remained her correspondents and friends, but White Mario did not build upon female relationships for the benefit of women per se. Indeed, although she obviously had countless international ties and functioned as both a courier and minor diplomat, most of the connections she made were not to women but to men. She did write some journalistic pieces about Italian women, but relative to

Jessie White Mario, from Elizabeth Adams Daniels's *Jessie White Mario: Risorgimento Revolutionary* (Athens: Ohio Univ. Press, 1972); Museo Centrale del Risorgimento, Rome.

her total output, these were few. She never saw her work in the Italian nationalist movement as that of a *female* revolutionary, unlike many German and French women revolutionaries and Margaret Fuller, who emphasized their status as female members of the oppressed class. Yet Jessie White Mario vividly demonstrates the growing density of international exchanges between revolutionaries and the way that a distinctive communicative milieu was forming.

Margaret Fuller's Italian sojourn is finally being given the attention by scholars that it deserves. She too went to Europe and Italy ostensibly as a journalist (for Horace Greeley and the *New York Tribune*), and she too found in Italy a political cause and marriage. But there the resemblance to Jessie White Mario ends. For Margaret Fuller was always interested in women's position, and her political belief—a kind of utopian socialism, based on Fourier and "associationism" (which, at Brook Farm, she had earlier rejected)—became solidified by the Italian struggle. Thus, "the personal is political" could have been her motto, as she came to feel her personal life and her politics meshing.

Fuller went to Europe in 1846, meeting reformers, radicals, and revolutionaries.[43] In England she visited Harriet Martineau, whom she had known since Martineau's visit to the United States. In fact, she had hoped to travel to Europe with Eliza Farrar in 1836, accompanying Martineau on her return home. But the death of her father in 1835 had left Fuller in charge of the care of her mother and younger siblings, and she had to postpone her planned trip by ten years.[44] She was finally enabled to go when her communalist friends Marcus and Rebecca Spring invited her to travel with them to care for their son. Rebecca Spring later became the primary hostess and confidante of Fredrika Bremer in her subsequent journey to the United States in 1849 (see Chapter 8). Fuller met W.J. Fox, editor of the *Monthly Repository,* which published many articles on women's rights, and William and Mary Howitt, Quaker reformers and writers. She met Mazzini in London and Adam Mickiewicz, the Polish patriot, in Paris. Everywhere she concerned herself with the suffering of the poor, especially women, such as Glasgow laborers (79) and Lyons weavers (127). In Paris in 1846–47 she met George Sand, Pauline Roland, and Charles Fourier. Of Sand she said, "She has that purity in her soul, for she knows well how to love and prize its beauty; but she herself is quite another sort of person. She needs no defence, but only to be understood, for she has bravely acted out her nature, and always with good intentions."[45] Communal laundries, Parisian *crèches* for

Margaret Fuller, from a postcard published by the Helaine Victoria Press.

children and deaconess institutions for poor women all impressed her greatly. Europe was, in fact, Fuller's natural element, shaped as she was by a classical education and a philosophical bent. As a child, she had imagined herself "a European princess being raised among common- ers"(3). A true cosmopolitan, she was able to bring to her journalism a historical and cultural context that were unique in American letters. In Italy at the height of the revolution she became involved with the Prin- cess Cristina Belgiojoso's hospital work and was made director of the Hospital of the Fate Bene Fratelli (280).

It is clear that Fuller was both radicalized and made more feminist by her participation in the Italian Risorgimento and her own experience of single motherhood. Had she lived she would undoubtedly have ex- panded the radical and feminist connections made during her four years abroad and participated in various campaigns for abolition and women's rights in the United States.

Revolutionary Stirrings in the Russian Empire

George Sand's novels were widely available in Russia from the 1830s on (see Chapter 4), and her ideas of complete freedom in love were known and often imitated by literate Russians. Sand's ideas became political as well, read as paeans to freedom and individualism in the repressive cli- mate of nearly complete censorship of writings from the West. Educated Russian women often alluded to the influence of Sand in their own com- ing-of-age.

Natalie Herzen (1817–52), the illegitimate daughter of wealthy Aleksandr Iakovlev, was raised by Princess Maria Khovanskaia and en- amored of George Sand. When her cousin Aleksandr Herzen (also ille- gitimate) was exiled, she was just seventeen. They corresponded and she helped him "to life again."[46] They eloped and spent his final year of exile in Vladimir together. In 1847 they left Russia for the West and by March were in Paris, where they were able to witness the 1848 revolutions and their defeat. Natalie was lonely and developed a passionate friendship with a younger Russian woman, both of them influenced by George Sand. She called Natalie Tuchkova "Consuelo," after Sand's character in the novel of that name. Later she became involved with George Herwegh, a Ger- man poet exiled from 1848, also living in Paris with his wife Emma Siegmund, a wealthy Jew from Berlin. This affair, beginning in a passion- ate triangle friendship with Aleksandr, lasted for several years. The three of them saw themselves as the characters in Sand's novel *La petite Fadette*, concerning twin country boys—Landry and Sylvinet—and Landry's fiancée, Fadette.

Natalie died in childbirth in 1852, having previously miscarried a child from her romance with Herwegh. Hundreds of her letters have survived, as has her diary, in which the influence of George Sand's religion of love can be clearly seen. Even before leaving Russia in 1847, she wrote:

> Oh great Sand! How profoundly she has penetrated human nature, boldly carried the living soul through sin and debauchery and brought it unscathed out of this all-devouring flame! Four years ago Botkin remarked of her that she was a female Christ. It sounded comical, but there is much truth in it. What would you have done without *her* to poor Lucrezia Floriana, who at twenty-five already had four children by different fathers whom she had forgotten and about whom she had no desire to know even where they were? Even to speak of her would have seemed a sin; but now you are ready to fall on your knees before this woman. . . . Oh, if there were no other way I would rather a thousand times that a daughter of mine should fall, I would receive her with the same love, the same respect, if only her soul remained alive. Then everything passes through the fire, all uncleanness is burned away, and what is left is pure gold.[47]

"The woman question," *Zhenskii vopros* in Russia—frequently attributed to the influence of George Sand—was debated in all intellectual circles and journals and came to stand for the more general liberation of the individual.[48] People like Herzen talked about the "emancipation of the heart" advocated by Sand. Thus, a literary text could operate almost as a magnetic force, drawing women together in contexts already prepared by the great revolutionary movements of midcentury.

Outside of Mother Russia itself, revolutionary women from the empire also participated in the international commerce in ideas. Born at Bucharest as Helena Ghika, by the time she was eleven Dora d'Istria (1829–88) had translated the *Iliad*. A linguist who spoke and wrote six languages fluently, she traveled widely, especially in the Russian empire during the years 1849–55 after her marriage at the age of twenty, when she became the Princess Koltoff Massaltsky. Ostracized by the Russian court when she toasted "the Allied Armies" during the Crimean War, she was exiled to Switzerland, where she wrote *La Suisse Allemande* and then several histories of women and women's position—*Les femmes de l'Orient* (1858), *Les femmes d'Occident* (1865), and *Des femmes, par une Femme* (Of women, by a woman: 1865)—under the pseudonym Countess Dora d'Istria. The last named surveys women's situation and prominent women writers and professionals; the first volume deals with "Latin" countries (including France, Italy, Spain, and Greece) and the second, "Germanic" countries (including Austria-Hungary, Germany, Britain, and Scandinavia). D'Istria's encyclopedic knowledge in the second volume covers everyone from Ida Pfeiffer, the inveterate Viennese adventurer, and Johanna Kinkel—her career during and after the 1848 revolution— to English novelists Brontë, Gaskell, Eliot, Rosina Bulwer-Lytton; Mary Somerville, and Harriet Martineau. Though living for the most part in Switzerland as a recluse, d'Istria seemed to know everyone and everything. She wrote also for Paris periodicals.

Fredrika Bremer (see Chapter 8) had already corresponded with Dora d'Istria in Sweden and finally met her in Greece. Bremer called her "unquestionably one of the most important authors of the present day," "a noble and gifted woman, in whom a man's head and a woman's heart are united with singular harmony." "Study and work seem to be her only passion," Bremer says. "In Athens she is for the present celebrated as a new Corinne," showing the continuing influence of Madame de Staël.[49]

Said to be both the most beautiful and the richest woman in Finland, Aurora Karamzin (1808–1902) grew up in upper-class circles. Invited to the czar's court in St. Petersburg in 1832 after the death of her fiancé, a Russian officer, she there met and married the wealthy Paul Demidov and bore a son, also named Paul. Widowed at thirty-two, Aurora became wealthy through inheriting Russian gold and platinum mines, which she managed throughout her life. Married to Karamzin and then widowed again, she lived in Paris and Vienna with her crazy and wasteful son, who was attached to the Russian embassy. She corresponded voluminously with both aristocrats and bourgeoisie throughout Europe, writing mostly in French but also in German, Russian, English, and Swedish. Letters arrived regularly from Paris, Mulhouse, Florence, Berlin, Minsk, St. Petersburg, Helsinki, Vladikavkas, Spain, Switzerland.[50] The last third of her life was spent in philanthropic work; she founded a deaconess institute (1867) and a hospital (1896) and gave vast sums to charity work.

Aurora Karamzin and son Paul, from Ingrid Qvarnström's *Tarunhohteinen elama: Aurora Karamzin ja hanen aikakautensa* (Helsinki: Otava, 1938).

Marie Linder (c. 1830–70) was Aurora Karamzin's niece. She grew up in Russia; her mother tongue was French; she learned Swedish when she moved to Finland. After the early death of both parents (her father, Count Vladimir Musin-Pushkin, was exiled after the Decembrist rebellion), she was raised by Karamzin, her mother's sister. Traveling often on the Continent, Linder became knowledgeable in all intellectual matters, including the woman question. In 1868 she published *En Qvinna af vår Tid* (A woman of our time), a journalistic account of her own life. Although neither woman traveled transatlantically, their business dealings did extend to Alaska, then owned by Russia.

Many revolutionary youths in Russia were influenced both by M.L. Mikhailov's writings on women and by Nikolai Chernyshevskii's novel *What Is to Be Done?* (1863), which focused on a young woman's search for a meaningful life and her escape into a phony marriage. The sham or phony marriage freed women from patriarchal control in order that they might go abroad for education. Sofia Kovalevsky (1850–91), the first woman doctor in mathematics and the first woman professor in Stockholm, was one who escaped her father's control in this way. After many years of poverty she became internationally known, involved in the new Swedish women's movement, and committed to an intimate friendship with Swedish playwright and novelist Anne-Charlotte Edgren-Leffler (1849–93); both women had married for convenience.[51] M.L. Mikhailov, in Paris with his lover and her husband, was much influenced by Jenny P. d'Héricourt's arguments against Michelet's famous diatribe against women, which he then summarized for Russian readers.[52] Jenny d'Héricourt subsequently lived in Chicago for ten years, 1863–73, meeting with American women's rights activists and writing for their periodicals.[53]

Russian women exiled for their political position were usually sent to Siberia—a somewhat uncertain place for international contacts. Only if they were able to go into "self-exile" were they able to meet like-minded people, usually in Switzerland or Paris. Vera Zasulich, one of the five women revolutionaries whose first-person accounts are published in *Five Sisters: Women against the Tsar*, went to Switzerland. Many other Russian women went abroad to study, especially after the liberalization in education was reversed in 1864. The first three Russian women admitted to medical school in Zürich were Maria Knjaznina, Nadezhda Suslova, and Maria Bokova. Knjaznina dropped out in 1867, but Suslova defended her thesis in December of that year and was awarded the first medical degree bestowed on a woman in Europe. Suslova and Bokova both returned to practice medicine and research in Russia; Bokova in particular, a researcher in ophthalmology, was touted as a real-life example of the main character in Chernyshevskii's famous novel.[54] According to Barbara Engel and Clifford Rosenthal, "by 1873 there were over a hundred Russian women in medical school in Switzerland."[55] In fact, medical schools in Paris, London, Berlin, and Edinburgh, as well as Zürich, all admitted Russian women during this period—before they admitted women from their own countries. The influence of the Russian women on European universities, and the spread of Western ideas about women to Russia when these students wrote or returned home added more strands to the increasingly tangled web of connections.

In several ways, then, the political upheavals of the nineteenth century were vitally and ironically instrumental in bringing women together, often in the most unlikely circumstances. New ideas were imported into traditional systems, and, thanks to emigration, women and men already adept at organizing and speaking met and listened to one another, corresponded, and published journalistic reports—all as a result of their failed political movements. Another irony is that the motives of these revolutionaries were so various. Jeanne Deroin and Theresa Pulszky seemed to have had only the highest altruistic aims for their countries or their people or for women; others had more convoluted motivations, joining the movements for love and adventure; the Ashursts come to mind immediately, as do Anneke (who revolted partially for sexual freedom) and Herzen (who lived unconventionally, moving from one passionate relationship to another). Some aristocrats became active in order to protect property (Belgiojoso) or to gain access to a profession (Russian women doctors).

The ferment surrounding the midcentury revolutions propelled different groups of people together and enabled them to learn from or struggle against one another. Both activities served to thicken the matrix. Thus, when Elizabeth Cady Stanton and Susan B. Anthony persuaded the English women to join them in a call for an international congess of women to take place in 1888, there had already occurred much cross-fertilization of ideas, through relationships already well-established. The webs of connectedness had grown many thousands of kilometers wide and several layers or generations deep. These webs, and women's consciousness of their importance for women, had been adding strands throughout the century also by means of the various reform organizations; these connected women as surely as the growing number of undersea cables.

Higher Consciousness

Reformers and Utopians

Until women assume the place in society which good sense and good
feeling alike assign to them, human improvement must advance but
feebly.

—Frances Wright, "Of Free Inquiry," 1829

The world does grievously need the aid of one half of the human race to
mitigate the evils which oppress it.

—Frances Power Cobbe, "Social Science Congresses
and Women's Part in Them," 1861

All the reform movements of the nineteenth century—abolitionism, temperance, antiprostitution, peace, utopianism—served as practice arenas
for creating the matrix. Early in the century, abolitionists were extremely
vocal and active in the United States and abroad, and they were in constant contact: collecting signatures on petitions, writing letters and articles, organizing conferences. Temperance, antiprostitution, and peace
organizations also became increasingly international in scope, and the
various utopian groups (secular and religious) transplanted members
and ideas throughout the world. Frances Wright was especially well connected to the various reforms around her and very international in her
thought and action as well. Wright was also adept at meeting other reformers; she was active in abolitionist circles, knew Robert Owen and
Thomas Jefferson and General Lafayette, was influential as a writer and
speaker who advocated free thought, and created her own utopian community. Her considerable efforts and talents were directed less at women
than at problems of race and class, however: she did not organize women;
she organized people. Because she did not especially target "the woman

question," I see her as a model of a developing (rather than full-fledged) matrix-maker.

Reform is perhaps the most obvious of the various categories of women's internationality, since the reform movements were transatlantic in scope and regarded by some, especially the utopian socialists, as the potential stimulus for worldwide change. More active and change-oriented than philanthropy, reform often began with the Christian dictum of "charity" or "good works," then shifted to reform as the belief in the possibility—indeed, the inevitability—of universal improvement gradually took hold. The ideas undergirding reform efforts drew great strength from the Enlightenment. The rhetoric of the American and French Revolutions, with their emphasis on natural rights and the efficacy of constitutional mechanisms, played a crucial motivating role. By midcentury a fully developed ideology of progress—substantiated by scientific advance and the Industrial Revolution—was exerting a powerful influence on opinion-makers in the Atlantic community.

Many reformers worked on several fronts and thus built up dense local, national, and international relationships with like-minded people. The connection between abolitionism and women's rights is well-known; other reform movements too helped women join with other women.[1] Susan B. Anthony began her social reform work in the temperance movement; Phoebe Palmer (see Chapter 3) embarked on her public career by attacking prostitution in the Five Points area of New York; Suzanne Voilquin began as a Saint-Simonienne and later served as a midwife in St. Petersburg. That reform was gradually becoming a "practice"— whether the relatively simple step of participating in a petition campaign or discussing an issue with close friends, or a more ambitious step like writing an article or letter to the editor, or even joining a utopian society—should not be forgotten.[2] All of this has been studied in various national historical contexts.[3] What has not been much looked at, however, is the extent to which reform ideas and associations became internationalized within the Atlantic community and on the European continent.[4]

Women were working on "the woman question" throughout the nineteenth century, well before the late-century formation of international women's organizations. Many began their political work with participation in one or more reform organizations—abolition (Lucretia Mott, Elizabeth Cady Stanton), moral reform (Josephine Butler, Barbara Bodichon), temperance (Susan B. Anthony), peace (Fredrika Bremer,

Bertha van Suttner)—but quickly saw the connection to women's situation generally and the importance of organizing with other women for women's rights. Even before the groundbreaking 1848 Seneca Falls Convention with its "Declaration of Sentiments," women such as Sarah and Angelina Grimké, Maria Weston Chapman, Lydia Maria Child, Anne Knight (who wrote a pamphlet advocating female suffrage in 1847), Anna Doyle Wheeler, and the French Saint-Simonians were writing and organizing for women. Of course, once women's rights conventions began to be held in the United States (e.g., Seneca Falls and Rochester, N.Y., 1848; Akron, Ohio, 1851; Worcester, Mass., 1850 and 1851; Syracuse, N.Y., 1852), preexisting connections became even stronger; there were letters of support and congratulations, discussions in the foreign press, resolutions in favor of or opposed to the American sisters.

Abolition

Abolition was the oldest and best known of the specific reform movements. The ideas undergirding it predated the Enlightenment with religious beliefs on the sanctity of the individual person and the inherent evil of owning a person. Quaker beliefs and practices were especially important; Quakers in Germantown, Pennsylvania, articulated their disagreement with slavery as early as 1688.[5] Slavery was abolished in England in 1772 and in various northern American states in the early nineteenth century; the international slave-trade was outlawed in 1807. Yet as long as there was a European market for cotton, sugar, and other slave-produced goods, the U.S. domestic traffic continued to flourish. The abolition movement was of interest to women from the beginning, and, predictably, Quaker women took an early lead in organizing in both England and the United States.

British abolitionist women, campaigning to abolish slavery in the colonies (accomplished for the Caribbean in 1834), inspired the Americans. Amelie Opie (1769–1853) helped appeal to Parliament with anti-slavery petitions; Elizabeth Coltman Heyrick (1769–1831) from Leicester published a proposal in Manchester and London, *Immediate Not Gradual Abolition* (1824), advocating a boycott of West Indian sugar.[6] This inspired William Lloyd Garrison's immediate abolition campaign and prompted Lydia Maria Child to say, "Has not the one idea that rose silently in Elizabeth Heyrick's mind spread until it has almost become a world's idea?"[7] In Birmingham, women were organized as early as 1826 when they began using the "Am I Not a Woman and a Sister?" emblem and motto (which then traveled to the United States).[8] Elizabeth Pease (1807–97) organized a Woman's Abolition Society in Darlington, England, in 1836.[9] Maria Weston Chapman, who was educated in England, became a leader in the Boston antislavery movement; her *Right and Wrong in Boston* was the source and inspiration for Harriet Martineau's "The Martyr Age in the United States," published in the *Westminster Review*.[10] Additionally, Martineau's *Society in America* critiqued both slavery and women's position and provoked much antagonism in the United States.

Shock waves from the 1840 World Anti-Slavery Convention in London generated many such alliances. Lucretia Mott, Ann Green Phillips, Elizabeth Cady Stanton, Sarah Pugh, and other American women who were in attendance became acquainted with British women. Marion Kirkland Reid of Edinburgh attributed her own heightened consciousness about the woman question to the furor aroused by the attempt of American women delegates to be credentialed at the conference. As already pointed out, her *A Plea for Woman* is a model of the synthesis possible as these reformers engaged in the debate; the book combined utilitarian, natural rights, and Owenite socialist arguments.[11] Abolition was also one of Frances Wright's key interests, and she was one of the earliest to consider its practical and economic complexities, complexities that she attempted to remedy in her utopian commune.

Clare Taylor's huge collection of transatlantic abolitionist letters, *British and American Abolitionists: An Episode in Transatlantic Understanding, 1832–1870*, gives a wealth of evidence of the buildup of a transatlantic female network. Of the 493 letters reprinted, 110 (22.3 percent) were written by women, and of those 88 were from one woman to another. In the collection, 201 letters (40.7 percent) were either written by or sent to a woman. Since these letters are all on a public topic, the abolition of slavery, it is astonishing how many women were involved. Many of the letters concern organizing for the Boston Anti-Slavery Fairs, the prime method of fund raising used by the women's abolitionist groups.

One who was thwarted in her attempts at internationalism (at least in person) was Lydia Maria Child, who kept up a steady stream of letters on all phases of abolitionism. In the spring of 1835 the Garrisonian antislavery group decided to send David and Maria Child to England to lecture, write, and organize, for Maria's books were selling better in England than in the United States, and David was an effective speaker. Friends gave them a farewell party in August, and they sold their household ef-

Lydia Maria Child, from *Letters of Lydia Maria Child* (Boston: Houghton, Mifflin, 1883).

fects, anticipating a lengthy stay. But on the day they were to sail David was arrested on the dock in New York for nonpayment of debts. Ultimately they did not go at all, although for eighteen months they kept rescheduling their passage.[12]

In 1841 Lydia Maria Child was named editor of the *National Anti-Slavery Standard* and moved alone to New York. She edited and wrote columns and articles, tried to get the publication out of debt, and was "determined to avoid controversy." As editor and sole staffer of the *Standard*, she wrote ceaselessly. Her "Letters from New York" columns for the paper, later collected in two quite popular volumes, discussed her ramblings in the city and issues such as poverty, capital punishment, women's rights, and religious toleration. Her desperate desire to travel is reflected in her correspondence: "I wish you would bear it in mind that I will go abroad *anywhere*, in *any* capacity with well-educated people, who may choose to take me. I am serious. For the first time in my life, I have set my heart upon travelling, and *must* compass it."[13] Because of financial pressures, she was never able to do so. Nevertheless, her pen, the international post, and her international perspective combined to make her singularly effective. In London in 1840, Mott read letters from Child aloud to her abolitionist audience.[14] Her body stayed home, but her ideas traveled.

Like Child, the Grimké sisters of South Carolina, who became abolitionist lecturers in 1836 on the Garrisonian circuit, never traveled abroad, but their fame and their works did.[15] They were both well aware of transatlantic currents and ideas on women and abolition. Kathryn Kish Sklar points out that Angelina Grimké's *Appeal to the Christian Women of the South* (1836) recalls Elizabeth Heyrick and other British women who led the petition movement to Parliament for the emancipation bill of 1833.[16] And Sarah Grimké's *Letters on the Equality of the Sexes* (1837) cites both Harriet Martineau and Madame de Staël. Angelina's marriage to Theodore Weld led to the sisters' retirement from public life, but they continued to write letters on behalf of abolition and women's rights, both to individuals and for periodical publication; many were sent across the Atlantic.[17] Sarah wrote to (among others) Jeanne Deroin in 1856 and to George Sand, probably in 1867.[18]

Sarah Remond (1826–94), a "free person of color" from Salem, Massachusetts, was also part of the web of abolitionists. In 1858 she traveled to the British Isles for an antislavery lecture tour, following the path of her brother Charles, who had been a delegate to the 1840 convention in London. Her sister Caroline Remond Putnam also traveled to England and, although a first-class passenger, was refused service in the ship's dining room. The incident created a stir in both the British Parliament and the press, and on the return journey, she was permitted to be seated—even though there were still American slaveowners on board.[19] Sarah remained in England throughout the Civil War period and was active in British organizations helping newly freed slaves. In 1867, after attending Bedford College in London, she enrolled in medical school in Florence, Italy. Receiving her diploma in 1871, she practiced medicine for twenty years in Florence, married an Italian from Sardinia, and never returned to the United States; she is buried in the Protestant Cemetery in Rome.[20]

Frederick Douglass visited the Remond sisters (Caroline, Sarah, and a third sister) in Rome at the Palazzo Moroni on his European trip in 1886. By that time, the Palazzo had become a center for international and interracial artists, including Edmonia Lewis, the renowned Afro–Native American sculptor.[21] Other women of color who made international contacts through their abolitionist work include Mary Ann Shadd Cary, who emigrated to Canada and became a journalist and publicist for the emigration movement; in 1852 she wrote *A Plea for Emigration; or, Notes of Canada West, in Its Moral, Social, and Political Aspect.*[22]

Temperance

The temperance movement (in which "temperance" quickly came to mean total abstinence from all alcoholic beverages) developed out of the Second Great Awakening and evangelical Christianity. Temperance societies also provided many interlocking circles of contact for women and, like abolitionism, spread to many countries and were knit to moral reform at every level. Many women got their first public experience in the temperance movement. Although men were involved early on (in the Sons of Temperance, for example), given women's later almost total hold on the movement, it is astonishing to remember that the World's Temperance Convention in New York in 1853—like the abolitionists a decade earlier in London—refused to seat women delegates or give them a public voice.[23]

The temperance cause is spoken of often in Mott's diary, since leaders in that movement were part of her network of abolitionists and British Quakers.[24] Later in the century Frances Willard, future president of the Woman's Christian Temperance Union, did the Grand Tour of Europe and the Middle East (1868–70). In her diary, she explicitly depicted the United States as the source of Christian imperialism, which she was later at pains to relate to the female sex: "Oh! native land—the world's hope, the Gospel's triumph, the Millenium's [sic] dawn 'are all with thee, are all with thee.'"[25] (One may rightly wonder about the sort of internationalism Willard's view might have entailed!)

WCTU internationalism had its roots in Methodist culture, John Wesley's command that "the world is your parish." According to Ian Tyrrell, the sources of WCTU's internationalizing bent were three: first, American involvement with temperance reform; second, the experience of women in the temperance movement; and third, the development of the American missionary movement (including evangelicalism and the Holiness movement) from the 1820s on, as a training ground for reformers. The millennial tradition also helped internationalism. "Good and evil knew no geographic boundaries, and pollutants anywhere threatened evangelical integrity everywhere," in the apt phraseology of Tyrrell. The WCTU's "Do Everything" motto and policy dovetailed nicely, deriving from the theological tradition that "saw earthly purification as a sign of regeneration already in process that would culminate in the Second Advent."[26]

In 1876 the first Woman's International Temperance Convention was held in Philadelphia, designed to coincide with the American Centennial Exposition. It was planned largely by Frances Willard before she became president of the WCTU. Grandly, Annie Wittenmyer, then the national president, proclaimed that this was "the first . . . international convention . . . for women the world has ever known."[27]

Early international women missionaries for temperance included Mary Coffin Johnson, who traveled three times to England in the 1870s, where she organized very successful drawing room meetings with women of the British upper classes. She also organized in northern Ireland. Mary Bannister Willard, Amelia Quinton, and Mary Livermore sailed to Britain in 1878 for the World WCTU. Mary Livermore, Maria Treadwell, Mary B. Willard, and Charlotte Gray went to France, Belgium, Sweden, and Germany in 1885–87. Other temperance missionaries traveled to Asia and Australia.[28]

Although there was obviously great difficulty in persuading European beer- and wine-drinking cultures to give up alcohol, it is astonishing how successful the "White Ribboners" (so called for their symbol, a white ribbon) were, especially in Protestant areas of northern Europe,

LONDON, 1893.

Frances Willard, from Anna A. Gordon's *The Beautiful Life of Frances E. Willard* (Chicago: Women's Temperance Publ., 1898).

including Scandinavia. Temperance advocates were always clear about making the economic connection between the dependency of women and children on men and the cost of alcohol, as well as pointing out the rising rate of violence against women. These arguments were used world-wide.

Moral Reform

"Moral reform" was the nineteenth-century euphemism for the movement to do something about prostitution, first focusing on getting the women off the streets. By the last third of the century, however, the protest targeted not the women prostitutes but government regulation of prostitution under which males suffered no blame or penalty, while the prostitutes themselves were prosecuted. Borrowing the rhetoric of abolitionism (as had the labor movement with "wage slavery"), reformists at the turn of the century organized an international outcry against "white slavery," or international prostitution, and the virtual imprisonment of immigrant women, usually from Southern or Eastern Europe. Other campaigns related to moral reform were also international in scope, by necessity—such as opposition to the opium trade, and efforts to solve the dual international citizenship problem (the fact that when a woman married and was assigned the nationality of her husband, she lost legal and civil rights).[29]

By the end of the century, when "the traffic in women" and "white slavery" became international issues, there was already in place a wealth of experience and relationships among people who had worked in various facets of the movement for more than fifty years. Lucretia Mott, for example, spoke with British moral reformers when she was in England for the Anti-Slavery Convention in 1840.[30] And when Phoebe Palmer took her experience as a temperance and anti-prostitution reformer abroad, she found that her efforts and good works had already made international contacts. Carroll Smith-Rosenberg, Christine Stansell, and Judith Walkowitz document much of this work in their pioneering studies.[31]

Josephine Butler (1828–1906), daughter of the abolitionist John Grey, is the most famous name in this movement.[32] Like several of the women evangelists, she dated her spiritual awakening to the death of a child, her daughter, in 1866. Her campaign was in opposition to the Contagious Diseases Acts of 1864, 1866, and 1869 in England, which attempted to regulate prostitution by forcibly examining those suspected of being prostitutes and locking them in hospital until certified clean of venereal disease. Butler argued that the acts debased all women and certified in law the sexual double standard: after all, the men who patronized prostitutes were not forcibly examined or incarcerated. As the founder and leader of the Ladies' National Association against the Contagious Diseases Acts, Butler at first confined her work to Great Britain but was soon seeking international support, even in such countries as Germany that already had state-controlled prostitution (and in which venereal disease had increased). She toured the Continent, beginning with the St. Lazare prison and hospital for prostitutes in Paris. She made contacts and lectured in Lyons, Naples, Rome, and Geneva and then founded the International Society against State-Regulated Vice; its first congress was held in Liverpool in 1875. Continuing to travel and organize on the Continent, Butler spent some time in Geneva in 1877 mobilizing the Protestant bourgeoisie against state-run brothels.[33] Everywhere her charismatic figure won converts, so that when Hannah Whitall Smith's report on the international traffic in women, "The Maiden Tribute to Modern Babylon," was published by W.H. Stead in the *Pall Mall Gazette* in 1885, the public outcry easily could be transformed into an organized movement that included many American and European women, especially those already involved in temperance work.[34]

Peace

Peace movements began to develop early in the nineteenth century, and in these too women reached out to other women. According to David Barash, peace societies were organized in New York and Massachusetts in 1815; in 1816 "the Society for the Promotion of a Permanent and Universal Peace" was formed by the Quakers; and in the next decades "other organizations were founded, on both sides of the Atlantic, including the American Peace Society and the Universal Peace Union in 1866." In midcentury, international peace gatherings were held in London (1843), Brussels (1848), Paris (1849), and Frankfurt (1850).[35]

When Fredrika Bremer proposed an alliance that would ask each country to organize all its female societies and send out a newsletter describing their work to a central committee, she demonstrated an understanding of the necessity of establishing and maintaining ties between groups and individuals. Her proposal, made in the form of a letter to the

Times (London), appeared on August 28, 1854, during the buildup to the Crimean War; it was, according to Harriet Clayhills, met with ridicule.[36] A lengthy editorial response explained that such a scheme would be not only expensive but useless. "Besides," the editors continued, "if universal woman-hood is to turn itself to the organization of charitable associations, what is to become of our *homes*?"[37] Bremer had written that "these associations have acted mostly without connexion with each other, scarcely knowing of each other's existence." But we know "the power of association," she continued: "United exertions to promote a common acknowledged aim strengthens the individual and increases the general amount of energy. It exercises a powerful attraction on those who stand indifferent, or otherwise isolated from the general movement, which thus grows in power and influence to an extent not to be calculated."[38] (Chapter 8 narrates further Bremer's talents as an organizer fully aware of the implications of her web-weaving activities.)

Marie Goegg (1826–99) of Geneva founded the International Association of Women in 1868 as an outgrowth of the International League of Peace and Freedom. It lasted until the outbreak of the Franco-Prussian war in 1870. In 1872 the organization was reinstituted as "Solidarity" and continued until 1880. Connected especially to Josephine Butler's International Society against State-Regulated Vice and to the peace movement, Marie Goegg's efforts put her in touch with women all over the Atlantic community. She had come to know Barbara Bodichon and others when she was in exile in London after the failed 1848 revolutions, and she kept up those contacts in the next decades. She mentioned the work of scores of women in her *Journal des Femmes* (1869): Elizabeth Cady Stanton, Suzanne [*sic*] Anthony, Olympia Brown, Barbara Leigh Smith Bodichon, Lydia Becker, Louise Otto-Peters, Maria Deraismes, Paule Mink, Maria Mozzoni.[39]

A less formal organizer than Bremer, Austrian writer Bertha von Suttner (1843–1914) is perhaps the best known of the women working internationally for peace in the nineteenth century.[40] Although most of her work was done after 1890 and is therefore beyond the boundaries of this study, her formative years were spent all over Europe, which helped to develop her international perspective and her aversion to war. Born in Prague as Bertha von Kinsky, she was educated in Vienna, Paris, Baden-Baden and Italy by private tutors. Meanwhile, her widowed mother gambled away the girl's inheritance; when her mother ran out of money, Bertha began working as a governess and personal secretary, first in Aus-

Bertha Von Suttner, from Brigitte Hamann's *Bertha von Suttner: ein Leben für den Frieden* (Munich: Piper, 1986).

tria, and then for Alfred Nobel in Paris. A nineteenth-century cosmopolitan, Bertha was fluent in German, French, Italian, and English. She
spent nine years living and working in the Caucasus, learning Russian
and Ossetian with her husband during the time of the last Russian-Turkish
War. (Younger than she, he had married her secretly, a fact that antago-
nized his upper-class family.)

It was in the Caucasus that she began to write first short stories,
then novels. By 1883 her novels, penned under various pseudonyms, were
beginning to reflect her pacifist views. Her best-selling novel, *Die Waffen
nieder* (No more arms, 1889), was specifically written to argue against
war. Translated into many languages, it became such a cause célèbre that
even the Pope had read it. Leo Tolstoy wrote to her: "I look at the publication of your book as a good token. The book *Uncle Tom's Cabin* by
Harriet Beecher Stowe contributed toward the abolition of slavery. God
give that your book will serve the same purpose when it comes to the
abolition of war."[41]

Von Suttner organized and attended international peace congresses
in Europe and the United States, proposing in 1892 at the Bern Congress
the formation of a European Federation of States. Known as "Friedens-
Bertha" (Peace-Bertha, first used in derision), she became "the most famous woman of the age" according to a poll taken in Germany in the
1890s, ahead of the actresses Sarah Bernhardt and Eleonora Duse.[42] Although she never organized specifically for women, she did remind lis-
teners of the importance for women of the peace movement and often
noted the scarcity of women at international peace conferences, where
she was often the only woman delegate.[43]

The last part of her life was spent in working for world peace, lecturing and writing, continuing her international contacts, and being truly
a *citoyenne du monde*. Scandinavians called her "Conciliatrix."[44] Having
helped to persuade Alfred Nobel to add a Peace Prize to the list provided
for in his will, von Suttner, as the first female Nobel laureate, was herself
awarded the Peace Prize in 1905.[45] She died just before the beginning of
World War I and did not live to see the organization of what was to
become the Women's International League for Peace and Freedom (organized in 1915).[46]

Other details of women's participation in the international peace
movement of the nineteenth century have been laid out by Sandi Cooper and others.[47] It is important to note for our purposes, however, that
most traditional histories of the peace movement do not deal with

women's formative role, let alone the way peace advocacy brought together women from a variety of national settings.[48]

Utopianism

Utopianism is a special case of reform, since it dreamed of a fully transformed social order that would eliminate the specific abuses singled out
for attack by liberal activists. Intentional communities, both religious
and secular, flourished throughout this period. And, since most utopians believed it necessary to withdraw from the rest of society in order to
foster the ideal community—either because the rest of the world was too
sinful and they were a chosen people, or because the rest of the world
needed an example—in many ways religious and secular communities
were similar. To use language already employed in Chapter 3, all the groups
were millennialists (either pre- or post-) in the sense that they looked for
full deliverance and a spectacular new age for humanity. And because
the Second Coming would have global impact, the millennial tradition
sustained internationalism.

The United States was imagined to be a special place for bringing
ideal societies to life. Utopian ideas from Europe found fertile soil here,
and Owenites, St. Simonians, Fourierists, and Cabetians, as well as such
religious groups as the Shakers and Amish, founded communities in
North America. Much has been written about these individual and clusters of communities,[49] but that these groups formed intensely *international* societies of like-minded people has been little remarked. Even before
the nineteenth century, national boundaries mattered little to such sec-
tarians. As Charles Woodmason, the Anglican investigator of heresies in
the Carolinas in 1765, observed: "Africk never more abounded with New
Monsters than Pennsylvania does with New Sects, who are continually
sending their Emissaries around."[50]

Most of the religious radical groups began in Europe, but the United
States became particularly important for many because of its comparative tolerance for bizarre religious trends, the openness of its frontier,
and the possibility of making a comfortable living. Bodies that had grown
out of the Reformation in Germany included Rappite Harmonists, Zoarite
Separatists, and Amana Inspirationists. There were as well the Shakers,
an English Quaker sect; the Oneida Perfectionists, John Humphrey
Noyes's revolt against New England Calvinism; various transcendental-

ist communities such as Brook Farm and Fruitlands, growing out of Unitarian and Universalist beliefs; and perfectionist sects such as the sanctificationists of Belton, Texas. Additionally, the Church of Jesus Christ of Latter-Day Saints (Mormons) was originally communal.[51]

Often these groups believed either in an androgynous god or a dual, gnostic principle of divinity. For instance, those who followed Jakob Boehme (German pietist groups such as Rappites and Zoarites) believed that only with the Fall was there a separation into two sexes and that with redemption there would be no necessity for sex and reproduction, which they construed as evil. Emmanuel Swedenborg, the eighteenth-century mystical philosopher, believed in both male and female principles in all spiritual reality; Brook Farm and Fruitlands were heavily indebted to Swedenborg. The Shakers too believed also in male and female principles, with God as both Father and Mother; hence their famous advocacy of celibacy, since they saw the separation of sexes as the beginning of sin. Indeed, many such groups countenanced celibacy. Only the Mormons, who believed that God has a wife and Jesus had two (Mary and Martha), directed the faithful to practice patriarchal polygyny.

Many religious groups were founded or headed by women: Mother Ann Lee (1736–84) of the Shakers; Mary Baker Eddy (1821–1910), the founder of Christian Science; Barbara Heinemann (1795–1883) of the Amana Inspirationists; Ellen Harmon White (1827–1915) of the Seventh Day Adventists. Of these, however, only Shaker belief ensured that female leadership would continue after the death of the charismatic leader who preached as the Spirit told, and even the Shakers were not interested in changing traditional gender roles; their communal polity ranked the brothers over the sisters.

Utopians both religious and secular tended to be European imports to the United States, but the secular communities fostered more prolonged and regular transatlantic contact; members came and went (as the communities so often rose and fell) bringing new ideas. The French Saint-Simonians and Fourierists maintained considerable international communication: the former across the Channel with the British Owenites, the latter with many American groups, including Brook Farm. Visits, letters, newspapers flowed back and forth; articles were translated from French and English and published in their journals. Suzanne Voilquin, Zoé Gatti de Gamond, and Flora Tristan were three individuals whose activity—writing, meeting, speaking—helped to extend the international reach of the group to which each belonged.

All utopian socialists agreed on the importance of abolishing private property—both within community and within marriage—and living in intentional community. The Fourierists looked to a progressive liberation of women within marriage, tracing out an elaborate theory of evolution based on marriage patterns. The Saint-Simonians anticipated a second coming in the person of a new female messiah (members eventually went to Egypt to find her), and the Owenites postulated a New Moral World in which both men and women would be transformed. All understood that marriage and the nuclear family were economically tied to the patriarchal structure of the present system and must therefore be radically altered. Equality in marriage, economic equality, elimination of personal dependence, nonestablished religion, equal education—these principles show how important a tenet female equality was for these groups. Anna Doyle Wheeler, the Anglo-Irish networker who had first been involved with socialist thought in France, believed that it was her responsibility to do everything she could to bring the various utopian groups together (see Chapter 7).

Fourierism developed the remarkable ideas of Charles Fourier, whose goal was to alter the environment in order to prevent evil from taking hold in humanity. He believed that since people's passions constantly impel them to seek pleasure, an environment that channeled its residents' passions in constructive ways would result in utopia. His ideas were very influential in the United States; even Brook Farm changed its charter in 1844 to become Fourierist. More important for our purposes are the Saint-Simonians, who espoused communal living, a couple-pope hierarchy with a man and a woman in charge, and the "rehabilitation of the flesh" through the synthesizing love of the couple-pope. Incongruously, even as they awaited the female messiah, *La Mère*, the hierarchy of the sect remained male dominated, and women had little power.[52]

In 1832 the Saint-Simonian women began their own newspaper, *Tribune des femmes*. This was the first feminist separatist collective: writings were by and for women only—and not only Saint-Simonian women. Writers used only first names, noting that surnames are male-controlled. Suzanne Voilquin, an embroiderer by trade, was the codirector. Others important to the journal were "Marie-Pauline" (Pauline Roland), "Jeanne-Victoire" (Jeanne Deroin), and Claire Démar. For several years sexual liberty and class issues among women were debated in the *Tribune*'s pages. Many editorials were printed on the necessity of economic self-sufficiency. In later issues the writers spoke more of marriage reform and less of free unions. They also discussed the necessity of divorce and of changing the civil code: "We no longer want this formula: 'woman, submit to your husband.' We want a marriage based on equality. Better celibacy than slavery."[53]

The Saint-Simonian women ultimately rejected doctrine in favor of more pragmatic reform strategies. Many of them, left with the care of illegitimate children, saw that free love was not freedom for women. Suzanne Voilquin's situation illustrates a lifetime of disappointments in the idealistic views she held, but it also shows clearly the opportunities for international experience afforded by the group. In 1834 she traveled to Egypt with the group seeking the female messiah; there she gave birth to a child (the father's name is in dispute, and the baby died within a month). The Grand Pasha of Egypt promised to build a hospital for women in Cairo after the outbreak of plague in 1835, but this was not done. Voilquin had helped Dr. Dussap and studied with Dr. Delong, gaining experience and learning Arabic through her work in Cairo's Coptic quarter.[54] She returned to France in 1836 and completed a diploma in midwifery in November 1837. Meanwhile, the Saint-Simonians who had gone to Louisiana included her estranged husband and her sister, Adrienne Mallard, who founded and directed a French school there; Voilquin officially divorced his wife in 1838.

Having difficulty earning money as a midwife in Paris, Suzanne Voilquin traveled to St. Petersburg, Russia, where she practiced her trade from 1839 to 1846, writing descriptive letters to her sister in Louisiana.[55] On her return to Paris she announced to her mentor, Pierre Enfantin, a central employment project for nurses, one that never materialized. During the 1848 revolution she wrote a petition to the provisional government asking for the establishment of a corps of midwives (in French, *sages-femmes*, or "wise women"), but in September she left for Louisiana, where her sister was gravely ill. She did not return to France until 1860.[56]

Zoé Gatti de Gamond's intellectual career also shows both how international were early socialist ideas and how similar were the systems of Saint-Simonians, Fourierists, and Owenites. Growing up in bourgeois Brussels, she first heard about Saint-Simonian feminism in her parents' salon, from French revolutionary liberals who came to newly independent Belgium after the July Revolution. Her first published writing, in 1832, was on women's subjection in marriage and the need to reform girls' education. After marrying an Italian art teacher and beginning a girls' school in Brussels, she moved to Paris and joined the Fourierist movement, opening a Fourierist bookstore and writing two books: *Fourier et son systèm* (1839) and *Réalisation d'une commune* (1840). With the Englishman Arthur Young she established a phalanstery (a Fourierist community) of 117 people at the cloisters at Cîteaux, but it failed after two years because of insufficient capital and inadequate agricultural knowledge to sustain its economic base. She returned to Brussels, where she became a schools inspector but continued writing on socialism.[57]

Flora Tristan (1803–1844), a self-proclaimed "pariah," was by birth an international person, born of an aristocratic Peruvian Spanish army officer and a French mother and considered illegitimate because their religious marriage ceremony was not recognized by the state. After traveling to Peru to "claim kin" and gain her patrimony, she returned to Paris. Here she wrote and became a socialist. Joan Moon says, "As a result of her travels, Tristan recognized the universality of her own experiences as a woman; in the writings of the utopian socialists she found the formulas to express her feminism."[58] Although not a Fourierist herself, she had contacts with all the early socialist groups, including the Owenites and Chartists in England, and made many international contacts. She visited England in 1826, 1831, 1835, and 1839, and in her *Promenades sur Londres* (1840) she speaks of meeting Anna Wheeler and other Owenites and Saint-Simonians.[59]

Her travel to South America and her published travel diary, *Peregrinations of a Pariah,* show her nascent understanding of women as a group. This idea she enshrined in her *Workers' Union* (1843), in which she detailed her scheme for an ideal society. Her utopia was much influenced by both Fourierist and Owenite schemes. Beginning with the "absolute equality of man and woman" in the working class, and by means of education of children in workers' "palaces," the principles of equality would gradually spread to all women and all society. Women workers' equality was not ancillary but a prerequisite. She called for the internationalization of the working class in a famous footnote that anticipates Marx. She died, however, after only a few months of organizing in France.[60]

Robert Owen, the Manchester manufacturer turned "co-operator," enunciated his principles early on, identifying the three culprits of social malaise as religion, marriage, and private property: "religion because it perpetuated 'ignorant superstitions' about the innate imperfections of the human character and fomented a 'sectarian spirit' within its adherents; marriage because it converted women into male property and established 'single-family interests' which eroded neighborly feelings; and

Flora Tristan, from a postcard published by Ala Verlag in Zürich, Switzerland.

private property because it made individual wealth the basis of social power and transformed all human relationships into competitive contests for individual gain."[61] Both Anna Wheeler (see Chapter 7) and Ernestine Rose (see Chapter 1) were converted to Owenite principles, and both used their ideas in an international setting—Wheeler on the Continent, Rose in the United States. But for the purposes of this study, Owen was most important in his influence on Frances Wright, who met him and became preoccupied with Owenite ideas.

Owen's first attempt at creating a community was in Scotland, the famous New Lanark, which was conceived to solve the social problems of poverty, ignorance, and alcoholism which plagued the new manufacturing centers of Britain. When Owen exported his communal philosophy, in 1825 he purchased the New Harmony community in Indiana, where Frances Wright was involved from the beginning (as were many other Europeans). Lucretia Mott, who had met him on her trip to London, discussed Robert Owen and Frances Wright in the same breath.[62]

Frances Wright as Reformer and Utopian

A radical woman espousing racial integration, free love (i.e., state-sanctioned marriage vows are unnecessary), working-class rights, birth control, and opposition to the stranglehold of organized religion on human freedom and thought, Frances Wright (1795–1852) remains one of the most unusual and enigmatic of early feminists.[63] Throughout her life she advocated complete universal suffrage—for blacks, for women, for the working class—and education as the means for achieving equality between male and female, black and white, rich and poor. The breadth of her energy and interests is staggering, and she was more democratic in her beliefs than any woman for the next hundred years; she also remained faithful to the traditions of the Scottish Enlightenment and to the currents of reform around her. She appears earlier in history than the Fourierists and the Saint-Simonians, but since she was both a reformer and a utopian socialist, it is appropriate to conclude this chapter with her life and transatlantic work.

Born in Scotland, daughter of a devotee of Thomas Paine, Wright was orphaned at the age of two. Thereafter she and her younger sister Camilla were raised by a succession of relatives, both in Scotland and in England. She speaks in her third-person autobiography (*Biography, Notes, and Political Letters of Frances Wright d'Arusmont,* 1844) of first hearing of America in the Italian account of Carlo Botta and of being immediately entranced with the democratic experiment. At age twenty-one she settled in Scotland, where an uncle, James Milne, was professor of moral philosophy at Glasgow College. There she devoured his library and determined to visit America. In 1818 she and Camilla sailed for New York. The letters she wrote home for the next two years to her friend Rabina Millar consisted of accounts of her travels and meetings attended, and observation on American character, institutions, and morals; these were published in 1821 as *Views of Society and Manners in America*. This volume became a sensation in England, and in France it brought Wright to the attention of the aging Marquis de Lafayette, hero of the American Revolution. The essays show a vivid sense of detail and enthusiasm for America as well as insight into such institutions as education, the position of women, and slavery—matters that were to occupy Wright for the rest of her life.

When she returned to the United States with the Marquis de Lafayette (though discreetly traveling separately with Camilla), she quickly began modifying her earlier enthusiasms. In particular she became alarmed over the institution of slavery after seeing a slave ship and auction in Virginia, and, as well, the wretched condition of freed blacks. She advocated a scheme of gradual emancipation, whereby slaves would work off their freedom on productive farms (the land to be set aside by Congress), participate equally with whites in the affairs of the farm, be educated, and eventually earn their freedom. The idea would not pose an economic hardship to southern landowners, because they would be given the profits of the blacks' labor for several years.

In 1825 Wright published this scheme as "A Plan for the Gradual Abolition of Slavery in the United States without Danger of Loss to the Citizens of the South." Various leaders were encouraging, including Thomas Jefferson and Robert Owen, the latter having just purchased the Rappite community of New Harmony, Indiana, for his own communal experiment; the plan was advertised and promoted in the Owenite journal *New Harmony Gazette*.

In December 1825, Wright persuaded several to join with her, purchased 640 acres east of Memphis, Tennessee, bought a number of slaves, and set out to carve a utopia from the mosquito lowlands and pine forests on the Wolf River; she called the community Nashoba, Chickasaw for "wolf." What is remarkable is not that Nashoba ultimately failed but that it lasted as long as it did—four years—largely thanks to Wright's

Frances Wright, from Elizabeth Cady Stanton, Susan B. Anthony, Matilda Joslyn Gage's *History of Woman Suffrage,* vol. 1 (New York: Fowler and Wells, 1881).

persistence, charisma, and optimism. The beginning of the end came when an abolitionist paper published parts of overseer James Richardson's journal, giving the community's views on intermarriage and miscegenation. Wright, at that time on a speaking tour in the British Isles, did not repudiate the group but instead returned and published a manifesto in the *Memphis Advocate* restating her compensated-emancipation plan. She then went on to attack segregation in education and sexual relations, organized religion, and marriage itself. This declaration was the last straw: once supported even by the governor of Tennessee, Wright became anathema even to dedicated abolitionists; southern slaveowners and northern socialites alike considered her beyond the pale. When it became apparent that the community would fail, Wright herself made arrangements for the thirty former slaves to be given land and place in Haiti and in 1830 personally escorted them to President Jean-Pierre Boyer in Port-au-Prince.

Though her foray into practical utopianism had failed, Wright continued to work for various social reforms, and she never stopped traveling or meeting influential people. With Robert Dale Owen, son of Robert Owen, she edited the *Free Enquirer* (successor to the *New Harmony Gazette*), purchased an old church in the Bowery, founded there the Workingmen's Institute, and continued her lecture circuit—all to promote the education of the working class and to agitate on its behalf.

She saw education as the key to equality for all and advocated a system of collective cooperation with a Kantian view of individual rights bounded only by those of other persons. She considered children to be full human beings and advocated the development of all their faculties. She held that it was in the interest of all to enlighten females, for society could never be perfected with half its population remaining uneducated. She was one of the first to equate women with other subjected classes (blacks, workers), and her use of the term "humankind" predated twentieth-century nonsexist language by 150 years.

Wright was so influential in the nascent working-class political movement that the election of 1829 won her group a seat in the New York legislature and the nickname, "the Fanny Wright party." Soon, though, she returned to Europe with her dangerously ill sister, this time settling in Paris near Phiquepal d'Arusmont, an Owenite French doctor and teacher she had known in New Harmony and New York. When Camilla died, d'Arusmont helped the grief-stricken Wright with arrangements. Before the birth of their first child in 1831, Wright and d'Arusmont were married. The baby girl died in her first year, but a second daughter, Sylva, was born in 1832. By 1835 Wright was again lecturing in the United States, d'Arusmont and Sylva sometimes accompanying her and sometimes remaining in Paris.

After Wright inherited the family fortune in Scotland, her relations with d'Arusmont became strained. Divorce proceedings in Cincinnati (where she settled in the last decade of her life) were bitter, but she continued lecturing and writing. Her last work, *England the Civilizer* (1848) presents an apocalyptic vision of a new egalitarian society, the instigators being science, industry, and woman. At the same time, she had become disenchanted with much of the American "experiment," critical of prevailing attitudes toward women, blacks, and the working class and particularly hostile toward the hold that evangelical religion had on the Midwest and South in the time of the Second Great Awakening.

By any standard, Wright's story is remarkable. What accounts for it? One may, I think, begin an answer by comparing her briefly with another exceptional internationalist. Like Frances Wright, Ernestine Rose was far outside the mainstream of her time. Most of the reformers I discuss had their roots in evangelical Christianity, but Wright and Rose were freethinkers; in fact, coming from a Polish Jewish background, Rose was very far from the Protestant tradition. Both were born in regions regarded as the "margins"—Wright in Scotland, Rose in Poland—but traveled widely. After leaving Poland, Rose spent time in England, then the United States; she died in London. In reading Wright's biography one imagines her as a precursor of the twentieth-century jet-setter: her frequent trips between the United States, Britain, France, and even Haiti were almost routine (she also traveled a great deal within the United States in an era when overland journeys were inconvenient and dangerous). Their international travel reflected an internationality of perspective: both women were heavily influenced by the works and ideas of Robert Owen and by socialism, philosophies that expressly denounced nationalism in favor of world cooperation. And in that new world there would be, both hoped, equality among persons regardless of sex and race.

Clearly, methodological questions can be pressed at this point. How durable and fruitful were the woman-to-woman connections made in reform work and utopian struggle? How, for example, can we know that an individual such as Sarah Parker Remond did indeed significantly strengthen international linkages? Did she befriend Italian women? Did she write home to American women? She is noted favorably in the early British feminist periodical, the *English Woman's Journal,* and we know that she participated in British branches of Freedmen's Aid Societies after the Civil War. But with what impact? How to research such questions is obviously very difficult to discern. I am constrained to assume that such contacts and relations were contributory rather than negligible or evanescent. It falls to future researchers to refine or challenge such an assumption.

In this chapter I have attempted to view both reform and utopian movements in terms of their capacity to join women of the Atlantic community in multiple ways. In moving through a number of individual cases, I have tried to display the varieties of international experience and female connectedness. Without such a detailed account, my claims about the "pre-organizational matrix" are bound to seem poorly established and lives like Frances Wright's exceptional. That Wright should not be regarded as an extreme example will become clearer as I move now to those women whose philosophies, outlook, actions, and writings made them the "nodes" of the nascent network of transatlantic connectors of women. Frances Wright, the quintessential international reformer, also serves to introduce Anna Doyle Wheeler: both women were Owenites, both were non-English Britons, and they lived at about the same time. But whereas for Wright women were one complication among problems of class, Wheeler invested her considerable intellectual gifts in writing specifically about women.

Mothers of the Matrix (I)

Anna Doyle Wheeler, Elizabeth Cady Stanton, and Forms of Feminism

[Patriotism is] an ignorant mother whose partiality strained heaven and earth for one child which in her blindness loaded she with a thousand evils.

—Anna Doyle Wheeler, c. 1825, quoted in Michael Galgano, "Anna Doyle Wheeler"

As the nations of the earth emerge from a state of barbarism, the sphere of woman gradually becomes wider, but not even under what is thought to be the full blaze of the sun of civilization is it what God designed it to be. In every country and clime does man assume the responsibility of marking out the path for her to tread.

—Elizabeth Cady Stanton, 1848, at the Seneca Falls Convention

There is a language of universal significance, more subtle than that used in the busy marts of trade, that should be called the mother-tongue, by which with a sign or a tear, a gesture, a glance of the eye, we know the experiences of each other in the varied forms of slavery.

—Elizabeth Cady Stanton, 1888, at the International Council of Women

Chapter 1 described Lucretia Mott as a full-fledged "mother of the matrix," an authentic "webster." In this and the next chapter I celebrate the achievement of four quite different women who rank with Mott as premier contributors to the strength, density, and utility of the international network. Although all the women discussed thus far helped to construct the fertile web of communication, Anna Doyle Wheeler, Elizabeth Cady

Stanton, Fredrika Bremer, and Frances Power Cobbe exhibit in full measure the qualities required to put them foremost among the "matrons" who superintended the conversations about women out of which the network was constituted.

What particularly marks these five women? It is the way they embodied in full measure a number of key characteristics. They faithfully maintained ties with women in different countries; occasionally traveled; and produced sufficient writings about their work to let us gauge the richness of their effort. Moreover, they were quite conscious of their mission in this regard, seeing themselves as "brokers" (the network analysis term) or connection-makers for women *qua* women. They also worked on various campaigns or reforms on behalf of women. Important too was their reputational status: they did their work early enough in their lives to be recognized by later followers as mentors, models, or foremothers. Finally, these "transatlantic Amazons," as one British contemporary called some of them,[1] persistently saw themselves as international figures operating in international contexts.

Mott, Wheeler, Stanton, Bremer, and Cobbe are all "mothers" but not necessarily "sisters": that is, they disagreed on many issues. Conveniently, the metaphor of "matrix" in its mathematical as well as biological meaning suggests a multiplicity of ideological beliefs. We can certainly call them all feminists, but they were different kinds of feminists. But what do we mean by this "feminism"? Current discussions of both historical and contemporary definitions are long and stimulating. At this point, suffice it to say that I am in agreement with Karen Offen's important delineation of the twin historical strands: "relational feminism" and "individualist feminism." I also concur with her general definition of feminism, which (1) acknowledges and values women's distinctness from men; (2) exhibits consciousness of women's inequity as a group problem, not merely an individual one; and (3) advocates elimination of that inequity or injustice.[2]

In the nineteenth century, those arguing from the "relational" perspective (valuing the relational dimensions of selfhood which differentiate males from females) were in the majority; "individualist feminists" (stressing natural rights and the similarity of the sexes) are those most often cited as "early feminists." Still, the early relational-feminist arguments of people like Hannah More, and—in the United States and France—the Republican Motherhood plea for giving women better educations and more equal treatment for the sake of their citizen-sons, were more likely to gain adherents and the majority necessary for any change to occur. Teenagers Caroline Wells Healey (Dall) and Ednah Dow Littlehale (Cheney) debated the issue in 1837–38 in Boston, and even Mary Wollstonecraft used Republican Motherhood in the conclusion to *A Vindication of the Rights of Women* (1792). Both individualists and relationists can be called feminists, since there is no doubt that both wanted to change the status quo for women.[3]

I have divided the discussion of the four women into two chapters on the basis of this distinction, whatever their other differences. Thus Wheeler and Stanton were for the most part individualist or equal-rights feminists, though Stanton was never a socialist, as was Wheeler, and they would have also disagreed vehemently on the place of religion in a woman's life. Likewise, Bremer and Cobbe were "relational" feminists, emphasizing sexual difference; single women themselves, both nevertheless stressed woman's role as daughter and mother. Yet although they would have agreed about the importance of religion and morality, they disagreed strongly on the terms of religious belief, Bremer being a staunch Lutheran Protestant and Cobbe a Unitarian theist who rejected the divinity of Christ.

Anna Doyle Wheeler, an International Woman

Anna Doyle Wheeler (1785–1848) was perhaps the most important single builder of cross-national women's connections during the early period. Like Frances Wright, she seems the epitome of the international woman in the early nineteenth century, but unlike Wright's work, Wheeler's was consciously undertaken for women. That she was Anglo-Irish means that in a narrow but important sense she was already "international" in orientation. Born to an Anglican family of Clonbeg Parish in Tipperary, she was a beautiful and headstrong youngest daughter. Her father, a middle-level Church of Ireland cleric, died when she was not yet two years old. Even though her godfather was the great Irish nationalist Henry Grattan, she did not have his patriotism or nationalistic fervor; in fact, as the epigraph above reveals, she abhorred patriotism. She was brought up mostly by her father's people, the Doyles, a family important in the military and civil service for British colonial government not only in Ireland but also in the American colonies, on the Continent, on the Isle of Guernsey, and in India.[4] She was thus predisposed to an international outlook.

In 1800, when Anna Doyle was only fifteen, she was noticed at the races by nineteen-year-old Francis Massey Wheeler, a young heir to his family's estate at Ballywire, who proposed to her at a ball. Her family opposed the match and tried to divert her with an invitation to London from her uncle, Sir John Doyle. Anna would have none of this and married Wheeler the same year. In twelve years she bore six children, the first four of whom were girls.[5] Unfortunately, the marriage was an unhappy one. Rosina, the second daughter, remembers being told about the wrath of her drunken father on learning that Anna had borne another girl. Later the sons were born, but only Henrietta and Rosina survived infancy. Anna took refuge from her abusive husband in books; Rosina remembers her mother reading the French philosophes and Wollstonecraft on one couch while her mother's maiden sister, Bessie Doyle, read the sentimental novels of the Minerva Press on the other.[6]

Cut off from most of her family and childhood friends, however, and brutalized nightly by a drunken husband, Anna plotted escape, aided by her sister, brother, and uncle—who had all opposed the marriage in the first place. In August 1812 she fled with her children, her sister, and her brother John to the Isle of Guernsey where her uncle Sir John Doyle was governor. Francis Wheeler made no attempt to end the estrangement and refused her any allowance for the rest of his life. She never returned to Ballywire. After her husband's death in 1820,[7] she lived with her brother outside of Dublin for three years while settling the estate. But she was cut off without a penny and was just able to live, precariously, on her own allowance from the Doyles and by judicious moving around from friend to friend. Her daughter Henrietta, who was named principal heir to the Wheeler estate (according to Michael Galgano), died in 1826, but Anna still did not inherit.

In high society on Guernsey, Anna Wheeler was lionized by the aristocratic and wealthy, mostly French royalty; the aging Duc de Bouillon courted her for twelve years, according to Rosina. Four years after Anna arrived, however, Sir John was forced to resign his office because of his debts of £20,000. Anna and her family left at the same time, beginning the peripatetic life she was to lead for the next two decades. London, Dublin, Caen, and Paris—these were her principal stops. At Caen as early as 1818 she became part of a Saint-Simonian group and was known as the "Goddess of Reason."[8]

In France again in 1823, she met Charles Fourier in Paris. She always claimed that his system was essentially the same as that of Robert Owen and Saint-Simon. In all three, cooperation is central; men and

Porter Pinx.   Drawn on Stone by M. Gauci

Anna D. Wheeler

Anna Doyle Wheeler, from *Appeal of One-Half the Human Race, Women, Against the Pretensions of the Other Half, Men, to Retain Them in Political and Thence in Civil and Domestic Slavery* (London, 1825). Courtesy of Goldsmith's Library of Economic Literature, University of London Library.

women are entitled to equal education and employment opportunities; and marriage and divorce laws are changed to abolish the double standard and give women equal rights. For the rest of her life she attempted to bring these three versions of socialism into union. To that end she arranged for Fourier to meet Robert Owen, introduced Saint-Simonian missionaries to Owenites in London and Manchester and elsewhere, translated Fourierist and Saint-Simonian articles for the Owenite press, sent young people to France with letters of introduction to Fourier, persuaded Owenites in England that Saint-Simonian doctrines were similar to theirs, advised Robert Owen on French socialist philosophy, distributed free Saint-Simonian literature in England, and shared her lodgings with young Saint-Simonian women.[9] Jeanne-Désirée Véret lived for a time with Wheeler in England and later married an Owenite, Jules Gay. Through Véret, Wheeler joined the circle around the Saint-Simonian women's journal *Tribune des femmes* and translated their articles for Owen's journal, *The Crisis*.[10] Writing to Fourier about Véret, Wheeler commented about their close friendship: "She is a great favourite of mine—for though I speak bad French, she comprehends the language of *my mind* better than many, whose language and my own are the same."[11] Wheeler became a well-known lecturer on socialism and women's rights, at a time when women were not often allowed to speak to mixed-sex groups.

Anna Wheeler was also associated with the Utilitarians. It was through her friendship with Jeremy Bentham (begun in Paris) that she met William Thompson, whose socialist economic theory so impressed Robert Owen. Thompson, also Anglo-Irish (a large landowner from Cork), formed a close relationship with Wheeler. Together they wrote *The Appeal of One Half the Human Race, Women, against the Pretensions of the Other Half, Men, to Restrain Them in Political and Thence in Civil and Domestic Slavery* (though it bears only Thompson's name, a long introductory letter gives credit to Wheeler). It was a reply to James Mill's essay on government in the *Encyclopedia Britannica* in which Mill, in less than a sentence, had dismissed women's rights as unnecessary because their interests were represented or "covered" by their husbands or fathers.

All the while Wheeler continued her networking for cooperative socialism. She was a major influence on the views of James Elishama Smith, the editor of *The Crisis*. When Flora Tristan visited London in 1839, Wheeler helped to show her around. The chapter in Tristan's *London Journal* on Bethlem Hospital relates an incident in which a French inmate, M. Chabrier, visited by Tristan, verbally attacks Anna Wheeler as an atheist who has killed God.[12]

When Thompson died in 1833, his will assigned an annual annuity of £100 to Wheeler; most of the rest of his estate he left to the Owenite cooperative movement for the building of an intentional community. His relatives contested the will, however, on the grounds that Thompson was insane; the process dragged on for a generation, so that she never received the money. Wheeler was invalided for her last years but lived to hear of the beginning of the 1848 Revolution in Paris.[13]

Wheeler's web-constructing efforts are not finally comprehensible apart from her thought and the particular feminist idiom in which it was expressed. One can get a sense of her little-known ideas and her position as an individualist feminist "mother" by briefly examining her key arguments.

Wheeler and Thompson's long, closely reasoned, and well-organized 1825 book, *The Appeal of One Half the Human Race,* takes up the proposition that a social system cannot provide for the greatest happiness for the greatest number if one-half that number is removed from consideration. It asks whether there is indeed an identity of interest between women and men, and various sections logically address various situations: single women without fathers, adult daughters living in fathers' houses, wives. As one might expect, the essay critiques marriage in the sharpest terms: "All women, and particularly women living with men in marriage . . . having been reduced . . . to a state of helplessness, slavery . . . and privations, . . . are *more in need* of political rights than any other portion of human beings."[14]

Finally, the book addresses the question, "Is there any way to secure happiness to a group but *by means of* equal civil and political rights?" Argued first is the issue of whether women can enjoy happiness without equal civil and criminal laws. This section shows the evil and degradation that women suffered under the unequal laws of the time. The second section inquires whether women can have any guarantee of equal *civil* and *criminal* law other than by possessing *political* rights. As it stands now, the authors point out, it could happen that "one fourth plus one" of the adults of the human race, would control "three fourths less one" (174). In other words, a simple majority of men could dictate to the rest of the men and all the women. (This of course takes no account of the fact that not even all men had the vote at that time.)

The essay as a whole is an unequivocal appeal for votes for women, the first to be cogently argued (Condorcet and Wollstonecraft had only hinted at it). The conclusion, a long "Address to Women," exhorts women to awaken to their degraded state and join with a system of cooperation in intentional community such as that espoused by Robert Owen's followers. In a long footnote Wheeler continues her quest to unify, across national borders, the disparate strands of socialism by discussing the similarities and differences between Fourier's system and Owen's. Both systems, she says, provide for equal education of all children, equal rights in marriage, and employment for both women and men. The main difference is that the Fourierist system of distribution is one of *inequality*, whereas Owen's goal is *equality* of distribution (204–5). Wheeler's thoroughgoing internationalism and knowledge of diverse situations and ideas made her contribution to Thompson's work essential. It was Wheeler who brought together the British Owenite and Utilitarian systems of thought with the French ideas of Fourier and the Saint-Simonians and applied them to the woman question. Through personal discussion and with long conversation and disputation, the argument in answer to James Mill must have been conceived and written by Thompson and Wheeler together. One can almost hear their daily discussion as they waited for Bentham (a personal friend of both) or someone else to answer James Mill in print. Thompson would have urged Wheeler to write a reply; she must have demurred but, in the heat of anger, dashed off the "Women of England" section. Finally, Thompson wrote up what he had taken down as notes from their ongoing conversation, and with her approval, published it.

A woman's perspective is obvious in the final section, the letter to the Women of England. The specific detail about the sexual degradation of women (187–88, 209), "tiger passions" (210), the sorrows over the loss of four children (205), the slave labor analogy (196), and the difficulties of losing a husband (198) seem to have been written by someone with personal knowledge of those experiences. At just about this time, Henrietta was ill in Paris, and Anna would have been involved in the protracted legal proceedings about the inheritance she never received after Francis Massey Wheeler's death.

Comparing the style and detail of her lecture at Finsbury Square Chapel with the *Appeal* seems to confirm that there was, at the least, a collaboration. The *Appeal*'s language in series ("demand *equal* civil and criminal laws, an *equal* system of morals, and, as indispensable to these, *equal* political laws, to afford you an *equal* chance of happiness with men,"

195) is reiterated in the lecture: "We then fearlessly ask for education; *equal* right to acquire and possess property; *equal* morals; women themselves responsible for their conduct as members of society; *equal* civil and political rights. Then what a diminution of crimes we shall have!"[15] The *Appeal* is a collaboration between two people, one of whom was a woman with strong international links—and it is a more powerful document because of that.

Anna Wheeler was a well-known lecturer on women's rights and the various forms of the cooperative movement. In a famous address in 1829 at Finsbury Square Chapel, titled "Rights of Women," she surveyed and then demolished the main arguments given by men to justify their claim of superiority over women. After a long apology in which she mentioned her "depressed health" and "a deep domestic sorrow" (probably Rosina's impending divorce), Wheeler said she would speak "in my capacity as slave and woman." As a good Utilitarian, she noted that when men refuse to treat women as anything other than as an object of animal passion, men too are degraded; for "in refusing to cultivate women's intellectual faculties, men are caught in their own snares; and the ignorance, that they would exclusively confine to women, soon becomes general. . . . *Prejudice* becomes *fixed principle*" and, like Pandora's box, spills evils throughout all society. It is good for the whole society to recognize women's capacities.[16]

At the end of her speech, she called on women to press for "a sound and liberal education" for their daughters, not being content to wait for others. Women must, she said, form groups of like-minded people, "the ultimate object of which will be to obtain, by all legal means, the removal of the disabilities of women, and the introduction of a national system of *equal education* for the Infants of both sexes."[17] This call for an *organization* of women, demanding equal education and equal property and political rights, marked Wheeler as one of the earliest and most radical of feminists. Invoking the name of Frances Wright, she showed her intellectual linkage to her freethinking contemporary, who was at the time organizing the working class in New York. Wright, said Wheeler, was a woman advocating general education for all who understood that only with the system of cooperation, as well as democratic education, could the wrongs to women be righted.

In other published pieces, under the pen name "Vlasta," she continued to promote equal education and equal civil and political rights for women, claiming that these were in *men's* self-interest. Because of her knowledge of various societies, Wheeler could look critically at women's position in each of them; she usually reserved her strongest criticism for English women. In a letter written in 1832, for example, she was very caustic about English women's inability to see their own oppression in the 1832 Reform Bill (which first put the word "male" into English law).[18] Earlier she had written Fourier that English women were socialized to their own oppression by being taught not to have their own opinions.[19]

Among the least recognized of Wheeler's legacies are the activities of her descendants. Her daughter Rosina (1802–82) was in her early life antagonistic to her mother's work. But after her disastrous marriage to novelist Edward Bulwer-Lytton, the ensuing Parliamentary scandal, and their separation, Rosina's own work (mostly novels) displayed many women's rights ideas, particularly with regard to married women's property rights and violence against women (at one point Bulwer-Lytton had her committed to an insane asylum).[20] And Rosina's granddaughter Lady Constance Lytton (1869–1923) was jailed and force-fed in the British suffrage fight at the turn of the century.

Clearly, in the tightly knit social world of early European socialism, Anna Doyle Wheeler was an important presence, a connector of people and ideas. Her language skills, as well as her personal contacts, enabled her to form an early node on the net as women, men, and ideas "radiated" to and from her. Though she never crossed the Atlantic herself, she influenced others—Fourierists, Owenites, and Saint-Simonians—who took the ideas to the New World and began cooperative societies there (see Chapter 6). Yet she is mentioned only as "Mrs. Wheeler and William Thomson" [sic] in the "Preceding Causes" chapter of History of Woman Suffrage,[21] and nearly erased from later history. Wheeler's presence as a "Mother of the Matrix" needs to be reclaimed.[22]

Elizabeth Cady Stanton, Transatlantic Mother

Elizabeth Cady Stanton's (1815–1902) international awakening should be dated to her wedding trip in 1840 when she and her new husband Henry Stanton traveled to England for the World's Anti-Slavery Convention. In London, in the midst of the controversy about the seating of American female delegates duly elected by such groups as the Female Anti-Slavery Society of Boston, she became acquainted with Lucretia Mott and others. She dated her awakened consciousness about the subjection of women to that experience: "As the convention adjourned, the remark

Elizabeth Cady Stanton and son, from *Eighty Years and More: Reminiscences 1815-1897* (New York: T. Fisher Unwin, 1898).

was heard on all sides, 'It is about time some demand was made for new liberties for women.' As Mrs. Mott and I walked home, arm in arm, commenting on the incidents of the day, we resolved to hold a convention as soon as we returned home, and form a society to advocate the rights of women." She analyzed the event in her autobiography, emphasizing its biblical aspects (since at the time she wrote, she was working hard on *The Woman's Bible*): "Deborah, Huldah, Vashti, and Esther might have questioned the propriety of calling it a World's Convention, when only half of humanity was represented there; but what were their opinions worth compared with those of the Rev. A. Harvey, the Rev. C. Stout, or the Rev. J. Burnet, who, Bible in hand, argued woman's subjection, divinely decreed when Eve was created."[23]

On that wedding trip in 1840–41 she spent ten months abroad, traveling to France, England, Scotland, and Ireland. After the convention she visited the homes of many of those she had met there, as well as other notables, including Lady Byron, Harriet Martineau, and the Irish patriot Daniel O'Connell. Stanton was frankly awed by them all: "Having read of all these people, it was difficult to realize, as I visited them in their own homes from day to day, that they were the same persons I had so long worshiped from afar!" (91).

Even though most of the rest of her trip was an unhurried Grand Tour, the basis for many more transatlantic links had been laid. The Seneca Falls Women's Rights Convention of July 1848 was a direct result of Stanton's 1840 crossing and her meeting with Mott. According to Bonnie Anderson, Stanton's opening speech (which remained unpublished for twenty years), linked it very specifically to the 1848 European revolutions of February, March, and June; thus Stanton was already conscious of the international significance of what the American women were doing.[24] That speech invoked progress and the lack of it for women, linking civilization to the position of women and a movement toward a kind of religious millennium, for "not even under what is thought to be the full blaze of the sun of civilization is [the sphere of woman] what God designed it to be."[25]

Seneca Falls and subsequent conventions (Rochester, N.Y., 1848; Salem, Ohio, 1850; Akron, Ohio, 1851; Worcester, Mass., 1850 and 1851; West Chester, Pa.,1852; Syracuse, N.Y., 1852; Philadelphia, 1854) placed Stanton and the American women's rights movement at the center of the international stage. Harriet Taylor Mill referred to the Worcester Convention in her first major article, "The Enfranchisement of Women"

Elizabeth Cady Stanton, daughter Harriot, and granddaughter Nora, from Elizabeth Cady Stanton, *Eighty Years and More: Reminiscences, 1815-1897* (New York: T. Fisher Unwin, 1898).

(1851);[26] Harriet Martineau wrote a long letter of support, setting forth her agreement with Taylor Mill.[27] And Pauline Roland and Jeanne Deroin wrote to American women at Worcester from St. Lazare Prison in Paris in 1851, calling on all women for support. The failure of the 1848 revolutions, they said, was caused by the failure of the revolutionaries to include women—"half of humanity"—and their right to liberty, equality, and fraternity."[28]

Stanton did not travel abroad again until her children were grown. In 1880, when she began her diary on her sixty-fifth birthday, her daughter Harriot was studying in France and her son Theodore was in Germany. Later, Harriot married an Englishman and resided in England; Theodore married French Protestant Marguerite Berry and lived in Paris. Thus, Stanton became literally as well as figuratively a transatlantic mother.

Mistakenly, Stanton says in her autobiography that she sailed for Bordeaux, France, with Harriot in May 1892; it was actually 1882. She spent three months in Toulouse, at La Sagesse convent, while Harriot learned French. With various members of the university faculty, Stanton was able to discuss social and political issues:

> That three heretics—I should say, six, for my daughter, son, and his wife often joined the circle—could thus sit in perfect security, and debate, in the most unorthodox fashion, in these holy precincts, all the reforms, social, political, and religious, which the United States and France need in order to be in harmony with the spirit of the age, was a striking proof of the progress the world has made in freedom of speech. The time was when such acts would have cost us our lives, even if we had been caught expressing our heresies in the seclusion of our own homes. But here, under the oaks of a Catholic convent, with the gray-robed sisters all around us, we could point out the fallacies of Romanism itself, without fear or trembling. Glorious Nineteenth Century, what conquests are thine! (342).

Thus she explored and debated religious, social, and political ideas, especially as they related to women, in an entirely international context.

Stanton's international talents extended also to editorial and translation work. She had come to France to rest after finishing the second volume of *The History of Woman Suffrage,* but it was not to be; instead, she functioned as a translator and editor for manuscripts sent to Theodore for his book, *The Woman Question in Europe:* "So, away off in the heart of France, high up in the Black Mountains, surrounded with French-speaking relatives [at the home of Theodore's mother-in-law] and patois-speaking peasants, I found myself once more putting bad English into the best I could command, just as I had so often done in America, when editor of *The Revolution,* or when arranging manuscript for 'The History of Woman Suffrage'" (344).

In November 1882 she traveled to London for the marriage of her daughter to William H. Blatch; the service took place at Portland Street Chapel and was conducted by an American, William Henry Channing. In London she made the rounds of movement women, visiting Frances Power Cobbe, Lydia Becker, Josephine Butler, Octavia Hill, and Emily

Faithful (just returned from a lecture tour in the United States). She also called on Elizabeth Pease Nichol and Jane and Eliza Wigham, whom she had first gotten to know at the World's Anti-Slavery Convention in 1840. Stanton was quite critical of English oratory but praised the women: "They have no speakers to compare with Wendell Phillips, George William Curtis, or Anna Dickinson, although John Bright is without peer among his countrymen, as is Mrs. [Annie] Besant among the women. The women, as a general rule, are more fluent than the men" (353).

In Scotland, she helped celebrate the passage of the municipal suffrage for women and gave a speech. Here she critiqued the making of resolutions, the organization of meetings, and Queen Victoria herself: "The Queen is referred to tenderly in most of the speeches, although she has never done anything to merit the approbation of the advocates of suffrage for women" (354).

She had a long meeting with Frances Power Cobbe, talking especially of the latter's anti-vivisection campaign. Daughter Harriot was able to turn the tables when Cobbe said she would refuse to shake hands with the renowned German scientist Virchow (a vivisectionist) but not with "statesmen, scientists, clergymen, lawyers, or physicians who treat women with constant indignities and insult." "Then," said Harriot, "you estimate the physical suffering of cats and dogs as of more consequence than the humiliation of human beings. The man who tortures a cat for a scientific purpose is not as low in the scale of beings, in my judgment, as one who sacrifices his own daughter to some cruel custom" (363).

Ernestine Rose, who had sat on the same platform so often with Stanton, was also living in London and "as deeply interested as ever in the struggles of the hour" (366). In Birmingham Stanton stayed with a relative of Joseph Sturge, who had been so stringently opposed to seating women at the 1840 convention, and in whose home she had visited forty years before (367). It is likely that this relative was his daughter Sophia Sturge, a Quaker peace activist and feminist who was then doing reform work for women in England and Ireland and thus making international connections as a part of the next generation.

Back in America on her seventieth birthday (November 12, 1885), she received cards, telegrams, and letters from England, France, Germany, and all over the United States. By that time the network was richly stranded, and Stanton's transatlantic mothering was very much a fact. In October 1886 she returned to England and then spent six months with Theodore in Paris. There she met key members of the women's movement in France—Maria Deraismes, Léon Richer, Isabelle Bogelot (who later attended the 1888 women's congress in the United States). She also encountered the Norwegian playwright Bjørnstjerne Bjørnson, who, along with Henrik Ibsen, was so important to the women's cause in Scandinavia.

She returned from this sojourn—nearly two years abroad—only in March 1888, just in time for the International Council of Women in Washington. She had decided not to attend, and only Susan B. Anthony's pleas and cablegrams persuaded her to change her mind. From England, she sailed to New York with the beautiful young Baroness Aleksandra Gripenberg of Finland, "a very charming woman, to whom I felt a strong attraction" (410). Thus, Stanton's transatlantic mothering came full circle, as the next generation began its work.

Mothers of the Matrix (II)

Fredrika Bremer, Frances Power Cobbe and "World"-Traveling

The power of the Idea, and the power of example, are the great movers of our time, and go from heart to heart, from land to land, with electric shock.
                                        —Fredrika Bremer to Dorothea Dix, 1850

The more I live and see of the world the more I feel that this indeed ['the elevation of woman to her true character and social position'] is the question on which depends the true liberation of mankind. I long to learn what you do for the great cause in America, and I will tell you by and by what I try to do and want to do for it in Scandinavia.
                                        —Fredrika Bremer to Dr. Harriot Hunt, 1855

Of all the movements, political, social and religious, of past ages there is ... not one so unmistakably tidelike in its extension and the uniformity of its impulse, as that which has taken place within living memory among the women of almost every race on the globe. ... [T]his movement has stirred an entire sex, even half the human race.
                                        —Frances Power Cobbe, Introduction to
                                        The Woman Question in Europe, 1884

Unlike Wheeler and Stanton, Fredrika Bremer and Frances Power Cobbe stressed women's difference from men; although not alike in religious belief, in age, or in language, they were similar in their attitude toward woman as daughter, sister, and mother. Both wrote prolifically; both remained unmarried. Like Wheeler, Stanton, and Mott, both created richly textured international networks of correspondents, visitors, and readers.

It was to them that hundreds of women turned for a referral or the latest argument on an issue of the day.

Because they were not only single women but outsiders in other ways as well, their situations were analogous to the ontological one described by María Lugones in 1987.

"World"-Traveling as Metaphor: A Hypothesis

In a classic article María Lugones examines the concepts of "worlds," "world-traveling," and "loving perception" relative to the existential status of "outsiders," those who inhabit boundaries and borders. For Lugones a "world" may be a physical place, but it is also a socially constructed space. It is possible, she says, to inhabit more than one "world" at the same time: "Most of us who are outside the mainstream of, for example, the U.S. dominant construction or organization of life, are 'world travelers' as a matter of necessity and of survival. . . . Inhabiting more than one 'world' at the same time and 'traveling' between 'worlds' is part and parcel of our experience and our situation."[1] Such "travel" between worlds has ontological dimensions: "The shift from being one person to being a different person is what I call 'travel'" (283). Travel to another "world" is a way of coming to understand its inhabitants "lovingly": "by traveling to their 'world' we can understand *what it is to be them and what it is to be ourselves in their eyes*" (289).

Lugones contrasts her view of "loving perception" to that of Johan Huizinga (in *Homo Ludens*), for whom Western civilization is agonistic play: "Agonistic travelers fail consistently in their attempt to travel because what they do is to try to conquer the other 'world.'" They "try to erase the other world," she asserts. "That is what assimilation is all about" (287). "Without knowing the other's 'world,' one does not know the other, and without knowing the other, one is really alone in the other's presence because the other is only dimly present to one," she concludes (289).

Although Lugones is intent on describing the situation of contemporary women of color, her suggestive metaphors and analysis can also be applied to nineteenth-century women who physically traveled great distances—across national borders, continents, and oceans—to become international networkers. My research indicates that the most-enduring connections were made, as might be expected, between women whose cultures were the most alike—that is, the cultures of nations in the industrializing Western world. Indeed, most of the international women whose accounts I have read were highly ethnocentric, able to do very little "loving" travel between extreme "worlds" of female experience. When they encountered radically novel cultural situations and practices, they were too often intolerant and judgmental.

The exceptions to this pattern were those women whose own "border" or "boundary" experience may have enabled them to identify with others. I thus hypothesize that women who were themselves *in border situations vis-à-vis the dominant culture* would have been uniquely capable of extending "loving perception" and of "traveling" ontologically between worlds. Thus single women, lesbians, and those whose mother tongue was not well known would have been better positioned to "know the other's world." Fredrika Bremer (single, Swedish) and Frances Power Cobbe (single, lesbian) were themselves in those boundary situations and thus in a better position than other Mothers of the Matrix to "travel" between worlds.[2]

The "outsider" status of the expatriate or the American living in Europe was often remarked in the nineteenth century, especially by such novelists as Henry James and Edith Wharton. In Wharton's *The Buccaneers,* for example, the character of the American governess, Miss Testvalley, identifies with Italian exiles in England and comments on the contradictory nature of her position. She has both the freedom of the outsider who does not know the rules and the stringent demands placed on a newcomer, particularly a woman: if she makes one false move, she is consigned to oblivion.

Singleness too bestowed marginality, even in the nineteenth century when England had an abundance of "redundant" or "superfluous" (single, unemployed) women. What to do with the excess of middle-class single women called forth many proposals and schemes: subsidized immigration to the colonies, such as Canada, South Africa, and Australia; employment as governesses; better education for women (see Appendix D). Both Bremer and Cobbe were single, as were many other women included in this work: Susan B. Anthony, Selma Borg, Adelaïde Ehrnrooth, Sarah Grimké, Aleksandra Gripenberg, Harriot Hunt, Anne Knight, Edmonia Lewis, Harriet Martineau, Florence Nightingale, Helena Schjerfbeck, Sophia Sturge, Flora Tristan, Malwida von Meysenbug, Maggie Walz, Frances Willard. In a society in which woman's place was determined by her relationship first to a father and then to a husband, the so-called "ever-single woman" was a kind of outcast. Both Bremer and Cobbe made a conscious choice for singleness, however, and both spoke often about its advantages in a society that made married women legal ciphers. When she was twenty-two years old, Bremer wrote in her diary, "18th March [1823].—Never marry, Fredrika! Be firm; thou wilt bitterly, bitterly repent it if thou allowest the weakness of thy heart to induce thee to such a step. Watch, pray, struggle, and hope!"[3]

Bremer (and other Nordic women with international links) were from out-of-the-way countries with small populations and languages that few in other nations spoke, thus ensuring that the educated citizens of Sweden and Finland, for example, perforce had extraordinary language facility. "Out-of-the-way" is another expression of marginal existence—at the edge, on the border. Thus one might have reason to expect that Nordic women long ago developed the skills and sensibilities required to be genuinely international citizens. Since they offer something of an ideal model of such internationality today, it is useful to speculate about its origin and causes. Citizens of peripheral countries must learn several languages from an early age, never assuming that others will speak their own. Thus, these women would be better able to view others with "loving perception" and understand the other's world. Significantly, Bremer's correspondence is in English, Swedish, French, and German, and her English markedly improved after her sojourn in the United States.

Romantic friendships, to use Lillian Faderman's term, became much more common in the nineteenth century as single women gained more independence. Female couples, or "Boston marriages," were well known in the Atlantic community; they were frequently urban and international (as in the expatriate community in Florence, Italy), but many couples lived happily in rural areas as well. In any case, all such couples by necessity inhabited at least two worlds, the women's world of romantic friendships, and the traditional heterosexual world. The American actress Charlotte Cushman (1816–76) was involved in a number of these relationships. In Florence she lived with Emma Stebbins, an American sculptor. Of Cushman, Faderman has written: "What she sought in a romantic friend seems to be what most woman-identified professional women of the next few decades thought to be their ideal too—a woman who understood the demands of their occupational life because she worked under such demands as well, and who could give support and sympathy when needed, who was self-sufficient to the extent that she had a whole life of her own, but who also had energy for another, more intimate life with an equal."[4]

Using the hypothesis that single women, lesbians, and those whose mother tongue was not well known would be the most likely candidates for "world"-traveling, one finds data that seemed insignificant taking on new meaning. Noting which women were single, widowed, or separated becomes more important. One thinks of the intimate "borderland" relationship between Anne-Charlotte Edgren-Leffler of Sweden—actress, playwright, and novelist—and Russian emigré and mathematician Sonya Kovalevsky, although neither was single (both had married for convenience).[5] Edgren-Leffler was early disposed to international relationships, since she traveled on the Continent from a young age. A "difference feminist," she spoke of "women's emancipation of the heart." She wrote her most famous play, *Sanna Kvinnor* (True women), in modern Swedish, the first to do so. Later, she traveled especially in England, meeting Annie Besant, Eleanor Marx, and other well-known women. In England she met Sonya Kovalevsky and persuaded her brother Gösta Leffler, a mathematics professor, to arrange for Kovalevsky to come to Sweden as the first woman mathematics professor. The special "romantic friendship" between Edgren-Leffler and Kovalevsky continued until the latter's death.

"World"-travelers from Finland were growing more numerous as upper-class families visited the Continent and added to their language facility. Frances Power Cobbe related meeting a group of Finnish women in Italy in 1864 at a *pension* in Naples: "Everybody is charmed with their grace and astonished by their accomplishments, but no one can guess their nation—they talk to each other in a tongue we cannot recognise. Somebody takes courage and asks their country, and they reply—that they come from a remote part of Finland! The English members of the party confess in private they believed the Finns to wear seal-skin clothes and drink train-oil!"[6] In such ways are stereotypes broken. In boundary situations themselves, these women were therefore empowered to "know the other's world" in gestures of "world traveling."

Although English, Cobbe was very much aware of her own unorthodox state, writing in the preface to her autobiography that the world of 1894 was "markedly" different for women and for "persons like myself holding heterodox opinions."[7] She chose the issues of redundant women and her own preferred state of singleness as her first causes in the women's movement. As an inhabitant of two worlds she continued to work with married women and with men in all her efforts, especially the anti-vivisection campaign. Likewise, Bremer was well aware of her status as a single person in a married people's world. Although most of her work was with women, both married and single, she corresponded with many men as well.

Fredrika Bremer, *Citoyenne du Monde*

As a young woman, Fredrika Bremer (1801–65) traveled throughout Europe for her health.[8] By 1837 she was making vital connections with women in other countries. In that year she wrote a long critique of Englishwoman Harriet Martineau's discussion of women's political rights in the latter's *Society in America* (1837), especially the chapter "The Political Non-Existence of Women."[9]

Her mature travel took place after she determined that her mother and an ailing sister could be cared for by her married sister and after her novels had been translated into English and other languages. The range of her European acquaintanceships was extraordinary: for example, she met Dora d'Istria, the Romanian-born feminist; American artists in Italy; Elizabeth Barrett Browning, the poet; and Mary Somerville, the British mathematician. This was because Bremer actually set out to become an international person, *une citoyenne du monde.*

Her first major journey was to the United States in 1849–51. There, Bremer visited many notable women, including Lucretia Mott, Harriet Beecher Stowe, Dorothea Dix, Lydia Maria Child, Lucy Stone, Elizabeth Peabody, and Fanny Kemble. Dr. Harriot Hunt of Boston was at first her physician and soon became her lifelong friend. Bremer also met slave and Indian women, abolitionists and slaveowners, working women and privileged women of leisure. She rewrote and published her letters home to sister Agathe (who died before Fredrika returned in 1851) as *The Homes of the New World.* That long account of her sojourn can be analyzed in terms of the narrator's ironic juxtaposition of her stance as a "separate spheres" woman (reflected in the "homes" of the title) and her position as a "masculine" explorer-traveler ("the new world").[10] She wrote to her friend Anne Howland in Charleston, South Carolina, that the letters were "conceived in the homes of my friends in America, and to these friends they will be dedicated." A few months later she wrote of the sisterly bond of her transatlantic friendship: "[To] me it is a precious memory that the friends I most prized, in the new world, became to me as sisters and brothers."[11]

An accomplished artist, Bremer sketched and painted many of those

Fredrika Bremer, from Märta von Alfthan's *Sju Årtionden med Unioni Naisasialiitto Suomessa* (Helsinki: Söderström, 1965).

she met, from Lucretia Mott and Maria White Lowell to Choctaw Indian women in Alabama. Her works also depict the flora and fauna she discovered in her travels: flowers and birds in Cuba; cypress swamps in St. Johns, Florida; tropical flowers in Charleston, South Carolina. Always interested in different cultures, she described new foods such as bananas, okra, and gumbo; the soft warm air, brilliant flowers, and birds of the tropical Carolina coast; the households of Indian and slave women.[12] In her long letter to Queen Carolina Amelia of Denmark (April 1851), she emphasized what she perceived to be the superior position of women in the United States, especially in regard to education:

> The American woman is being formed for a citizen of the world; she is teaching herself to embrace the whole of humanity. . . . It is with justice that we are accustomed to estimate the measure of a nation's cultivation by the estimation in which woman is held, and the place which she occupies in society, because it requires no small degree of spiritual culture to value a being whose highest power is of a spiritual character. The people of America have shown themselves to be possessed of this, and it will increase in the same proportion as the women of the country make themselves deserving of it.[13]

After her return to Sweden, Bremer corresponded at length with the people she had met, treating not only of family and friends, but of politics, women's rights, new ideas, books. She wrote letters of introduction, planned American friends' visits, and pleaded to have American newspapers sent to her. Of the seventy-five letters in English in the *Collected Letters* dated after her return, the majority are addressed to women. Her best friends—Americans Anne Howland and Rebecca Spring—she repeatedly called "sister" and "Scandinavian in mind."[14]

In replying to Dorothea Dix's query about whether Dix might accomplish reforms for the mentally ill in Sweden, Bremer answered that Sweden must do it herself although Dix's example would be the best catalyst: "But believe me, dear Miss Dix, what you have done, what you are doing in America, will, when properly disclosed—as it ought to be, and must be, to Sweden—work more for a bettering of the insane asylums there than a gift of ten millions could in their behalf. The power of the Idea, and the power of example, are the great movers of our time, and go from heart to heart, from land to land, with electric shock."[15] Thus, in language that reflected the premises of middle-class liberalism, Bremer emphasized the importance of inspiring examples of individual effort in building reform networks.

In 1854 Bremer and other Swedish women philanthropists proposed an international federation of women's groups, set up to communicate country by country to a central committee. "We propose," she wrote, "to consider ourselves as having the same native country, as belonging to the same family, and, whatever diversity of opinion there may be among us, yet to join hands [as] sisters." She called for women of all lands to join her: "Sisters . . . in whose existence we believe and hope, here and there among the ancient kingdoms of Asia, the steppes of Siberia, or in the Imperial cities of Russia; sisters of the western countries of Europe; . . . and you, sisters in that vast new land beyond the Atlantic Ocean; . . . and you, Christian women among the nations of Africa; Christian women in the isles of the South Sea; mild, loving sisters, all over the earth . . . give us your hands! May the earth thus become encircled by a chain of healing, loving energies."[16]

Bremer's plan was published in the *Times* (London) on August 28, 1854.[17] Although she couched her argument in terms of the *Christian* responsibility of women, her organizational strategy was still quite radical: she called all women sisters, reaching for commonality beyond diversity; she asked for an organization whose basic task would be communication of different work based on the variety of national contexts; she noted that even though her own group was from a small country, it was a place to begin. But the proposal did not become reality. Not only the *Times* editors but even Harriet Martineau ridiculed its "floating religiosity."[18] During World War I, however, when the International Council of Women met (1915) in The Hague, Netherlands, it was reprinted by the Swedish National Council of Women. The ICW sent women's delegations to the heads of state of belligerent nations in 1915 to propose "continuous mediation."[19] Bremer's forward-looking dream of an international women's alliance had, by that time, already come into existence, for the Hague congress was the genesis of the Women's International League for Peace and Freedom.

On her 1856–61 trip through Europe, Bremer first attended the International Congress on Philanthropy in Brussels; interestingly, she was the only woman delegate—yet within two decades most of the significant philanthropy in Europe was being carried on by women. She critiqued the absence of Christian ministers and priests at the conference but resurrected women's history by visiting institutions such as "le Grand Béguignage" in Ghent, a lay women's community founded in the Middle Ages.[20]

As she did everywhere, in Switzerland Bremer investigated the rights and position of unmarried women, an issue on which she had worked for many years in Sweden. Geneva, she said in *Life in the Old World*, was justly called *le paradis des vieilles filles,* the paradise of unmarried women: "It is so, in fact, because they can there so easily satisfy that hungering after the food of intelligence, which is being awakened more and more in the women of the present time, and which the unmarried have more time to satisfy than they who have husband, and children, and housekeeping duties, to occupy them. Besides which, women, in this Canton, attain to a legal majority at the age of twenty, and by this means, whether in or out of the paternal house, to a certain degree of independence" (I:310).

Bremer remained in Italy for some months, meeting and visiting with most of the prominent members of the expatriate communities in Rome and Florence. She met American artists, among them Harriet Hosmer, as well as the American astronomer Maria Mitchell. A visit to the room in which the young Swedish queen Christina died prompted an analysis of Christina's faults and virtues—and a lesson in women's history for the reader (2:294, 297–98). Like many others of her generation, Bremer had as a young girl been much influenced by Madame de Staël and toured the island of Ischia in the Bay of Naples to relive *Corinne* (2:340).

As a result of her five-year sojourn, she was able to make astute observations about national character and the position of women, especially unmarried women. She published four volumes on this trip—*Life in the Old World, or Two Years in Switzerland and Italy* (2 vol., 1860) and *Greece and the Greeks* (2 vol., 1863). In establishing international connections, Fredrika Bremer was a remarkable networker. She was able to use "loving perception" to identify with many she met on her journeys—from Catholics in Italy (where, although she was passionately Protestant, she did a month-long retreat to learn more about Catholicism, using an early form of "participant-observation") to women of the harems in Turkey—and thus to "world"-travel.[21]

One should note that despite her energetic connection-making and enthusiasm for sisterhood, Bremer remained an "equality-in-difference" feminist. Her position was squarely in the "separate spheres" camp, for she believed that women are given "something higher than law, something more important than legislation, that is the moral spirit." As she stated in her 1837 critique of Harriet Martineau, "Woman's participation in public life would, in the same way as Man would destroy her womanliness, take away the benefit of her influence on life and morals, and during the battle against men, the Male sex would soon be for her the same as Washington Irving's old Aunt called it: 'the opposite sex.'" She linked this analysis to her concept of God. God includes Nature, she asserted, and "Nature is the female (Womanly) principle in the Divinity. God is Man, Nature 'Manna.'"[22] ("Manna" is Bremer's neologism, merging a feminine ending on "Man," with the meaning of "manna" as spiritual food.)

Martineau, for her part, disagreed; she wrote in her *Autobiography* that "philosophical research with a view to truth is quite out of her [Bremer's] way. As she thinks every woman's influence springs from a hot-bed of sentiment, she naturally supposes that my influence must be destroyed by my having taken root on an opposite ground." Martineau nevertheless praised Bremer's international work: "It would be a worldwide benefit if this gifted woman could . . . discharge while she lives the special function by which she scatters a rare delight broadcast over whole nations."[23]

Bremer wrote articles for American periodicals about Jenny Lind;[24] referred to Louise Otto, Fanny Lewald, Malwida von Meysenbug, and other German feminists;[25] hosted Margaret Howitt (daughter of her translator Mary Howitt) in her home for a year;[26] and generally functioned as the first lady of Nordic feminism, both at home and abroad.

In the year of her death, Bremer was still responding to international ideas, especially through her voluminous correspondence. A friend sent her Frances Power Cobbe's *Essay on the Theory of Intuitive Morals* (1855). In her typically generous fashion she reacted first to the *person* and only secondarily to the ideas—with which she disagreed, since Cobbe was a Unitarian theist: "First of all, let me thank you, dear Louisa, for making me acquainted with this noble and strong minded woman, and for the true enjoyment that I have derived from many parts of her book, and most especially from the pure and highminded character which breathes in it throughout. I like, I love, I revere it. Not so well her doctrine."[27] She criticized especially the omission of Christian revelation.

Bremer, well known by the end of her life for her international un-

Harriet Martineau, from *Autobiography* (London: Smith, Elder, 1877).

dertakings on behalf of women, liked to call herself "the Wanderer." Biographer Ellen Kleman takes up that metaphor: "With her eye constantly fixed on the looming though unattainable goal, the perfect community, with men and women working together for its benefit, she, the *Wanderer*, . . . walked through the countries of the New and the Old World, looking for signs, promising a bright future, certain in her hope and her faith, but ever searching for the path that leads to the goal."[28] Wandering between worlds and bridging them with her linguistic facility and her empathetic understanding, Bremer truly came to know the other with loving perception.

Frances Power Cobbe, "World" Traveler

Growing up in County Dublin, Ireland, Frances Power Cobbe (1822–1904) was part of a privileged Anglo-Irish family distinguished by British military service and Anglican positions of power. Her great-great-grandfather, the Archbishop of Dublin, had entertained John Wesley and (on the premiere of *Messiah*) George-Friedrich Händel. Her father served in the Light Dragoons in India, and other family members held posts in Malta, South Africa, and elsewhere in India. Thus, stories of foreign travel and adventure abounded, and her home always contained Indian china and other items of foreign origin. One of her favorite governesses, a Mlle Montriou, taught her French history and literature, as well as a love for maps and geography.

She claims in her autobiography to have been aware of women's issues even as a child and adolescent.[29] From various home tutors and her own reading in her father's splendid library, she received a classical education, including Greek and mathematics, but she hated her two years at a girls' finishing school in Brighton, England (of course, her brothers were educated at Oxford and in Germany). International travel was acceptable for women, and she went to England with her family at least once a year, but as we have seen, women were not expected to travel alone.

The family was very religious, practicing evangelical, philanthropic Christianity, holding daily prayers, and attending weekly Anglican services. Her parents embraced an Arminian theology of the Clapham school which departed from strict Calvinism by not holding to absolute predestination (1:70). By age eleven, however, Frances had begun to question orthodox beliefs, first by doubting the feeding of the five thousand and other miracles and later by denying immortality, the divinity of Christ, the Trinity, and the divine inspiration and authority of the Bible. She kept the extent of her "heresies" to herself for years, until after her mother's death (Frances was twenty-four). When she told her father, he sent her away to the wilds of County Donegal to live with a brother for nearly a year. Finally, her father bade her return to be his housekeeper.

In the meantime, Cobbe had developed her own beliefs, moving from agnosticism through deism to theism. She ultimately advocated an *intuitive* belief in God, morality, and immortality. In this, she said, she was much influenced by the American theologian Theodore Parker's 1842 book, *A Discourse of Matters Pertaining to Religion* (1:78–95), and her correspondence with Parker led to other associations with Americans, particularly in Italy. After Parker's death Cobbe edited the fourteen-volume edition of his works. Significantly, Parker's theology critiqued the Judeo-Christian patriarchal concept of God as king and judge and substituted his own idea of God as "not a king but a Father and Mother, infinite in power, wisdom and love."[30] Cobbe in her preface to Parker's *Collected Works* emphasized this view of the masculine *and* feminine characteristics of God—"God is Himself and alone (as Parker often rightly addressed Him in his Prayers) 'The Father and Mother of the World'"—and went on to criticize traditional Christianity: "Too long has the Catholic Church separated off this *Mother Side* of Deity into another object of worship; and more fatal still has been the error of the Reformed Churches, who in rejecting the Madonna, have rejected all that she imaged forth of the Divine mansuetude and tenderness."[31] As Barbara Caine points out, Cobbe's rejection of her father's theology was also the beginning of her own feminism.[32]

She secretly wrote her first book, *Essay on Intuitive Morals* (1855 and 1857), while her father was still alive and she was in her thirties. Divided into "Theory of Morals," and "Practice of Morals," it presented a Kantian perspective on moral law, possessed intuitively: "The essential property of a right action is, *that it ought to be performed by a rational free agent,* and that there is no possibility of severing the idea of Right from that of Obligation."[33] Under "Religious Obligations" Cobbe wrote of God as "Father of the universe" and "Mother of the world," who "adds to our existence every unhurtful pleasure which the tenderest of woman's hearts could devise for the innocent happiness of her child."[34] Already in this early work Cobbe was attacking the double standard in morals for women and men. Noting, as a good scholar, that Greek philosopher

Frances Power Cobbe as a younger woman, courtesy of Mary Evans Picture Library, London.

Frances Power Cobbe as an older woman, from *Life of Frances Power Cobbe by Herself* (Boston: Houghton, Mifflin, 1894).

Antisthenes "insisted on the identity of nature between male and female virtue," she argued: "The absurd difference between the male and female Codes of Honour must be done away with. The lie which would disgrace the Man must not be treated as venial in the Woman. The unchastity which is the Woman's irretrievable dishonour must not be without shame for the partner of her sin. The cowardice which would bring ignominy to the Man must not be *taught* to the woman as the proper ornament of her sex."[35]

Reviews in religious journals attacked this quite unorthodox work as un-Christian and, worse, unfeminine (although it was published anonymously, her authorship became known). In her autobiography Cobbe delighted in quoting the *Christian Observer,* "Our dislike is increased when we are told it is a female (!) who has propounded so unfeminine and stoical a theory . . . and has contradicted openly the true sayings of the living God" (quoted in 1:101).[36]

As an only daughter, Cobbe could neither pursue her own career nor think of marrying while caring for her father; at his death in 1857 she received a small inheritance of £200 a year, with which she did her first traveling. As she notes ruefully, however, she was immediately thrust into poverty, since previously she had been given £130 annually just for spending money, and now she had to leave the family home at Newbridge (inherited by her eldest brother), rejecting a life there as "the maiden aunt."

On a year-long sojourn, Cobbe spent much time in the expatriate communities of Italy, especially Florence, meeting Elizabeth Barrett Browning, Mary Somerville, and Isabella Blagdon, as well as Theodore Parker and Harriet Beecher Stowe (with whom she argued about Theodore Parker's theology [2:347–48]). She also encountered the American sculptors Harriet Hosmer and Emma Stebbins and American actress Charlotte Cushman. Several of these women had established intimate relationships: Cushman had earlier lived with Matilda Hayes, the translator of George Sand, and then with Emma Stebbins. In Italy Cobbe also met French artists Rosa Bonheur and Natalie Mica, another "Boston marriage" pair. These independent women showed Cobbe a different way of living, one that she came to desire for herself. Indeed, it was Mary Somerville who introduced her to sculptor Mary Lloyd, later to become Cobbe's lifelong companion.[37] It is safe to say that Cobbe's years abroad broadened her horizons and helped her to become more aware of possibilities for how women might structure their lives.

Within a few years of her return to London, she was living with Mary Lloyd in an intimacy that lasted thirty-four years—until Lloyd's death in 1896. Although in her autobiography Cobbe refused to discuss the true nature of the relationship, there is much evidence in correspondence with close friends. A letter to Millicent Garrett Fawcett after Lloyd's death is clear about the emotional and spiritual commitment between the two women: "The end of such a friendship, 34 years of unbroken affection, is of course almost a mortal blow & I have yet to learn how I am to live without the one who has shared my thoughts and feelings so long. But I am very thankful that the pain and loneliness is mine, not hers as it would have been had I gone first & she been left alone. She died calmly and bravely resting on my arm and telling me we should not long be separated. . . . For such a friendship as I have enjoyed & its painless close, we can best thank God."[38]

Blanche Atkinson, editor of the posthumous edition of Cobbe's *Life*, wrote that Lloyd's and Cobbe's relationship was "perfect in love, sympathy, and mutual understanding." Atkinson told of Cobbe's grief after Lloyd's death: "I remember once being alone with her in her study when she had been showing me boxes filled with Miss Lloyd's letters. Suddenly she turned from me towards her bookshelves as though to look for something, and throwing up her arms cried, with a little sob, 'My God! how lonely I am!'"[39]

Both her personal life and her theological and moral ideas enabled Cobbe to travel between the two "worlds" of which she was a part, giving her generosity and insight to different groups in the campaigns for women. Her work on violence against women and their legal status derived from her growing beliefs about the value of the single state for women. Article and pamphlet titles reflect her journalistic fervor. For example, in "Criminals, Idiots, Women, and Minors: Is This Classification Sound?" she discussed marriage law as it would look to a visitor from another planet: "Why is the property of the woman who commits Murder, and the property of the woman who commits Matrimony, dealt with alike by your law?" she mischievously inquired.[40] In "What Shall We Do with Our Old Maids?" she vented her wrath on various schemes to send "redundant" women to the colonies and showed that single women have better lives than married ones. She also spoke in favor of women in the pulpit, in "The Fitness of Women for the Ministry of Religion."[41] "The Final Cause of Woman" enunciated her position that woman must not be defined in terms of others; only a theory of "woman as Noun," not "woman as Adjective," was acceptable to her.[42] Women are morally autonomous, but they are also daughters and potential mothers and therefore have qualities that set them apart from men. This insistence on sexual difference as well as equality is an essential ingredient of Cobbe's feminism.

Cobbe viewed the problem of violence against wives as part of the unequal status of married women: "I conceive then, that the common idea of the inferiority of women, and the special notion of the rights of husbands, form the undercurrent of feeling which induces a man, when for any reason he is infuriated, to wreak his violence on his wife." She proposed that Parliament pass a bill to protect wives from brutal assault, by means of a protection order, similar to a legal separation. The bill became law May 27, 1878, "An Act to Amend the Matrimonial Causes Acts." She looked back with great satisfaction on the success of her lobbying and organizing for this bill.[43]

She also connected violence against women to violence against animals, and her strongest arguments against vivisection castigated violent men who would beat their wives or torture animals. Many of the pamphlets of the National Anti-Vivisection Society (with which she was closely identified) carried illustrations captioned "How We Treat Dogs" (horrific pictures of live dogs on vivisecting tables, bound and tied, legs stretched out, muzzle up) and "How Dogs Treat Us" (pictures of St. Bernards rescuing people in the snow, or dogs jumping into water to save masters). The texts often included quotations by leading Continental vivisectionists, one of which exposes the apparently requisite love of violence of the successful scientist:

> He who shrinks from cutting into a living animal, he who approaches a vivisection as a disagreeable necessity, may very likely be able to repeat one or two vivisections, but will never become an artist in vivisection. He who cannot follow some fine nerve-thread, scarcely visible to the naked eye, into the depths, if possible sometimes tracing it to a new branching— with joyful alertness for hours at a time; he who feels no enjoyment when at last, parted from its surroundings and isolated, he can subject that nerve to electrical stimulation; or when, in some deep cavity, guided only by the sense of touch of his fingerends, he ligatures and divides an invisible vessel; to such a one there is wanting that which is most necessary for a successful vivisector.[44]

Cobbe corresponded with people from all over the world, especially in her anti-vivisection campaign. The number of letters she wrote
and received is vast, although they are not all extant. According to an
early biographer and her servants, she had the ability to read a book and
write a letter at the same time. She also possessed the astonishing ability
to write a letter with each hand simultaneously! (This must be why her
correspondence is nearly illegible.)[45]

She helped gain a commuted sentence for Louise Michel after the
ill-fated Paris Commune in 1871 (see her *Life*, 2:456–57), met Elizabeth
Cady Stanton and her daughter Harriot Stanton Blatch in 1882,[46] consulted with people in New South Wales on poor-law legislation,[47] and
entertained many American and Australian visitors—who, she said, often stayed too long (2:458). The New York women's club Sorosis made
her an honorary member (2:534). John Stuart Mill wrote Cobbe in 1869,
asking her to fulfill the request of Isabel Hooker, sister of Harriet Beecher
Stowe, that she write an article on the woman question for the American
magazine *Putnam's* (2:469). Cobbe often referred to American or Continental women or events in her columns and articles. In all these ways is a
network built.

On Frances Power Cobbe's eightieth birthday in 1902 a citation or
"Address" certificate was presented to her with the signatures of nearly
three hundred prominent women and men from England, France, Germany, Italy, and the United States. The fifty-nine American signatures
included those of Julia Ward Howe, Elizabeth Cary Agassiz, Elizabeth
Blackwell, Grover Cleveland, and Mark Twain. The address praised her
work for women's higher education, workhouse reform, and antivivisec-
tion, as well as noting her writings on religion and ethics.[48]

By the end of her life, then, Cobbe was internationally renowned in
many areas. According to Barbara Caine, her writings—especially those
against violence toward women and animals—were better known than
those of any other British woman in the last third of the century.[49] Partly
this was because most of her work was in pamphlet or journalistic form,
widely circulated in newspapers such as the daily *Echo* or journals such
as *Fraser's Magazine*. Although she did not travel abroad after 1870, the
contacts she had made earlier and the linkages resulting from her writings made her a genuine Mother of the Matrix, moving between the
"worlds" of single and married women yet always eager to point out
women's identity as daughters with similar moral duties. Cobbe liked to
end the lecture she called "Women's Duty to Women" with a revision of

Terence's famous Roman quotation: "I am a *woman*. Nothing concerning the interests of women is alien to me" (2:554).

"A Golden Cable of Sympathy"

Aleksandra Gripenberg, the Finland Connection, and the 1888 Council of Women

Hereafter there will be a golden cable of sympathy between you and us. Every victory you will win shall be ours; you work not only for the women of your country, but for the women of the whole world.
  —Alli Trygg-Helenius, 1888, at the International Council of Women

Often I wonder if you have an idea of how much you and Mrs. Stanton have influenced my life. You may know—you can see it—how much you have influenced the women of your own country; but I want that you should know how vividly we Finnish women feel our gratitude to you, how we follow what you speak and write. Is it not wonderful how great ideas unite different peoples? Thousands of women here in Finland cannot read English, but still they know you, have read your speeches and enjoyed your articles.
  —Aleksandra Gripenberg to Susan B. Anthony, 1903

This book has sought to unlock part of the "secret" of the emergence of a fully mature international women's consciousness and organizational articulation by the end of the nineteenth century. That there came into being a pre-organizational matrix (or network, or web) made up of complex lines of international contact, association, friendship, argument, and correspondence is, I hope, indisputable. Denser, stronger, and more productive than scholars have heretofore seen, this matrix becomes from now on an important explanatory factor in understanding the growth in our century of women's internationality and transatlantic connectedness. Made possible by the communications revolution, prepared for by

Catholic orders and Protestant evangelists, the matrix formed in complex patterns of crossing, overlapping, and repeating. What I have depicted is not a particularly coherent or always intentional phenomenon; indeed, much about the matrix is contradictory and haphazard. That linkages caused by literary celebrity should be discussed alongside utopianism, refugee migrations, temperance, and tourism will strike many readers as arbitrary and their interweaving as improbable. To such skeptics I must simply answer with what seems to be a preponderance of evidence.

I close by offering yet one more narrative account. Its significance is that it allows one to see in the triumphal event of 1888 the invocation of the very thing I have been at pains to reveal. Though not called a "matrix," its existence as a place of gestation was much on the minds of the protagonists. And in the activities of "granddaughter" figures from the margins such as Aleksandra Gripenberg, Maggie Walz, and Ida B. Wells-Barnett, one is enabled to see how potent were the structures originating at the center of an Atlantic community—forming a "place" to which women could now lay a firm claim.

International Council of Women, 1888

In November 1883, at the end of their separate trips abroad, Elizabeth Cady Stanton and Susan B. Anthony met in Liverpool with Millicent Garrett Fawcett, Elizabeth Blackwell, Harriet Hosmer, Olive Logan, Priscilla Bright McLaren, Margaret Bright Lucas, Margaret E. Parker, and Alice Scatcherd. This was the genesis of the first international women's congress, as Stanton noted in her autobiography: "Here the wisdom of forming an international association was first considered. The proposition met with such favor from those present that a committee was appointed to correspond with the friends in different nations. Miss Anthony and I were placed on the committee.... [T]he idea of the intellectual cooperation of women to secure equal rights and opportunities for their sex was the basis of the International Council of Women, which was held ... in Washington, D.C., in March, 1888."[1] The Call to Council in 1887 invited all associations of women, not just suffrage organizations, saying in part, "In an International Council women may hope to devise new and more effective methods for securing the equality and justice which they have so long and so earnestly sought. Such a Council will impress the important lesson that the position of women anywhere affects their

Susan B. Anthony, from Elizabeth Cady Stanton, *Eighty Years and More: Reminiscences, 1815-1897* (New York: T. Fisher Unwin, 1898).

position everywhere. Much is said of universal brotherhood, but . . . more subtle and more binding is universal sisterhood."[2] The council was therefore transatlantic and international from its inception.

This may be one reason for its relative success and long life, in contrast to an earlier attempt made in France. Paris was the location of the International Woman's Rights Congress in 1878, called and promoted by Léon Richer and Maria Deraismes and attended by representatives of six European countries and the United States. Its difference from the meeting in Washington ten years later was that the Paris meeting did not result in the founding of an international organization.[3]

Stanton was reluctant to return from England in 1888, but Susan B. Anthony's dire cables persuaded her. When she said she had no speech ready, Anthony, according to her own account, shut Stanton in her room at the Riggs House in Washington and told her to write.[4] The opening council speech that resulted was full of references to the current international political scene: the debates on international copyright law, the three-mile fishing limit, religious tests in national constitutions, political prisoners. Stanton averred that women everywhere were bound together by a universal "mother-tongue" of women, "by which with a sigh or a tear, a gesture, a glance of the eye, we know the experiences of each other in the varied forms of slavery." She called up a veritable international who's who of women as she praised those who had gone before: Mary Wollstonecraft, Madame de Staël, Madame Roland, George Sand, Fredrika Bremer, Elizabeth Barrett Browning, Frances Wright, George Eliot, and many Americans as well.

She went on to suggest that women's international organizing might even bring about a cessation of war: "Closer bonds of friendship between the women of different nations may . . . strengthen . . . international arbitration, . . . that thus the whole military system . . . may be completely overturned."[5] In this view, she was reiterating Bremer's 1854 Women's Peace Alliance proposal (see Chapter 6).

Stanton's closing address, however, came close to red-baiting, as she warned of dire consequences if "wild women" were not directed to useful reform: "Awake to their own wrongs, as they never have been before, and exasperated with a sense of the prolonged oppressions of their sex, it requires no prophet to foretell the revolutions ahead, when women strike hands with Nihilists, Socialists, Communists, and Anarchists, in defense of the most enlarged liberties of the people."[6]

The council was attended by representatives of some fifty different

Elizabeth Cady Stanton, as an older woman, from Elizabeth Cady Stanton, *Eighty Years and More: Reminiscences, 1815-1897* (New York: T. Fisher Unwin, 1898).

organizations from ten nations. The program was divided into sessions on Education, Philanthropy, Temperance, Industry, Professions, Organizations, Legal Conditions, Social Purity, Political Conditions, the Pioneers, and the Religious Symposium. Fifteen women were appointed to an international council, and a decision was reached to hold an international congress of women every five years. Thus a self-sustaining organization was set in place that continued well into the twentieth century.

The Finland Connection

One can learn much about the matrix by noting how it grew at both its central and peripheral areas. Recalling the material and metaphorical significance for women of the submarine Atlantic cable, a particular irony in the history of communication in Finland deserves noting. The Finn-

Women at the 1888 International Council of Women: first row, from left, Virginia Minor, Rev. Zerelda Wallace, Laura Ormiston Chant, Susan B. Anthony, Isabelle Bogelot, Elizabeth Cady Stanton, Matilda Joslyn Gage, Aleksandra Gripenberg and an unnamed delegate; second row, from left, Rev. Ada Bowles, Rev. Anna Howard Shaw, Frances Willard, Lillie Blake, Alice Scatcherd, Antoinette Blackwell, Elisabeth Saxon, May Wright Sewall, Margaret Moore, and an unnamed delegate; third row, from left, Rev. Elizabeth Harbert, Rachel Foster Avery, Bessie Starr Keefer, Sophie Groth, Hannah Whitall Smith, Victoria Richardson, Alli Trygg, Caroline Merrick. From Märta von Alfthan's *Sju Årtionden med Unioni Naisasialiitto Suomessa* (Helsinki: Söderström, 1965).

ish interest in international cables was fed not only by the excitement over the transatlantic undersea link in the 1850s and 1860s but by Western Union's agreement with Russia to lay a land line from St. Petersburg across Siberia and the Bering Strait through Alaska (still Russian territory) to the west coast of North America. Finland, then a grand duchy of Russia, would have been very much aware of these efforts as it sought to assert its own autonomy in the latter part of the century. After Cyrus Field and his colleagues won the Europe–North America communication contest, Russia ultimately contracted with the Danish Great Northern Telegraph Company to connect Scandinavia and Russia with China and Japan.[7] Finland, however, continued to look west, not east.

Alli Trygg-Helenius (1852–1926), whose "Golden Cable of Sympathy" speech brought down the house on the last day of the 1888 women's congress, was one of the two Finnish delegates. She had begun her professional life as a primary school teacher and, after traveling to Paris in 1878 to see the world's fair and Finland's exhibits, was one of the founding members of the Finnish Women's Association. She met Frances Willard and became an activist in the temperance movement in Finland, founding the White Ribbon group there and the YWCA (Young Women's Christian Association) as well, centering her activism in working-class neighborhoods in Helsinki.[8] Her speech emphasized the commonalities binding women even across language and culture borders. She was able, she told the gathering, to speak in English because her language skills had been so much improved by attending the congress; still, she apologized for her errors and asked that delegates "only think of the feeling of my heart." Using much biblical rhetoric and comparing herself to Jacob crossing the Jordan, Trygg-Helenius said the "great dream of [her] life" had been such an international gathering. The event itself had exceeded her expectations, "because I now have the sincere belief in women's love, women's power, women's ability, women's energy, which can never fail."[9]

When Aleksandra Gripenberg (1857–1913) came to the United States in 1888, she contributed to the international network of women already laboring for women's rights, temperance, and other reforms in industrializing countries. Gripenberg traveled widely throughout Europe and America and became one of the most knowledgeable proponents of women's rights. Her three-volume work, *Reformarbetet till förbättrande av kvinnans ställning* (1893–1903), surveyed the movement in various

Alli Trygg-Helenius, from Märta von Alfthan's *Sju Årtionden med Unioni Naisasialiitto Suomessa* (Helsinki: Söderström, 1965).

countries. President of the Finnish Women's Association at two different times, she worked ceaselessly for female suffrage in Finland, which was granted in 1906.[10] She was one of nineteen women elected to the first Finnish Diet (1907); they were the first elected women parliamentarians in the world, representing five different parties, both bourgeois and working class.[11]

By 1899 Gripenberg's personal library included at least four hundred volumes by renowned women writers in Europe and the United States, plus nearly fifty newspapers and magazines. She owned all of Harriet Beecher Stowe, most of George Eliot, Stanton's *History of Woman Suffrage* and *The Woman's Bible*, as well as Theodore Stanton's *The Woman Question in Europe* and Jules Michelet's *Woman (La Femme)*. Her collection included also a great number of reports on women's organizations and congresses—from London, Chicago, Paris, New Zealand.[12]

On her way to the United States in 1888 she traveled first to England, where she met many women, including foremothers Ernestine Rose and Marion Kirkland Reid (see Chapter 1). The Biggs sisters were her particular friends in England, and after her visit she corresponded regularly with them about women's rights. Writing in June 1888 from the United States to Caroline Ashurst Biggs, she asked bluntly, "Are you in love with Lucy Stone? I like her letters and speeches so much and her daughter whom I saw when in England, is delightful."[13]

In the United States Gripenberg wanted to meet all the women whose work she had followed for so long, as well as the great American authors of the day. In particular, she sought an introduction to Harriet Beecher Stowe and hoped to visit the grave of Helen Hunt Jackson, whose works (*Uncle Tom's Cabin* and *Ramona,* respectively) had brought the issues of the treatment of African Americans and Native Americans to the attention of people around the world.[14] Gripenberg toured the country for six months following the congress, seeing women activists from coast to coast, riding trains from Chicago to California. The older women with whom she traveled were quite taken with her, mothering her and—to Gripenberg's disgust—"matchmaking" (she never married). Her account of her travels, *A Half Year in the New World* (1889), is a fascinating travelogue from a foreigner's perspective on the situation of American women in different regions, especially the Southwest.

On Gripenberg's return from her year abroad, Finnish women gave her a gala reception, including a tribute (in Swedish) from feminist journalist and poet Adelaïde Ehrnrooth, better known as A—ï—a. The second stanza of the long poem "To Miss Aleksandra Gripenberg, Nov. 24, 1888" exalted Gripenberg's international work:

> Beyond the deep waves of the ocean in the West
> You brought the message of Finland
> To a Congress where the greatest questions of our times
> Were dealt with.
> Gathered together in the distant West
> You met guests from the whole world
> A workshop of freedom and light
> Whose aim is to loose chains,
> Smithed to the woman by a thousand years of oppression.[15]

In Finland she continued her international activity as an officer in the International Council of Women, helping to plan and attending many of the international meetings that followed the first. Her correspondence with other officers around the world is voluminous. She often traveled for the ICW, helping to set up national organizations as far away as Bulgaria and Greece. She helped Finnish women emigrants to the United States begin a women's group in 1897 in Calumet, Michigan, by responding to Maggie Walz's Finnish letters (see below), and sending books for a lending library. In Finland, however, she was often thought to be divisive and hard to work with; when the Finnish women's movement split in 1892, she chose not to be a part of the Unioni (*Unionen Kvinnosaksförbund i Finland,* or Union of Finnish Feminists), but stayed with the original, more conservative Finnish Women's Association.[16]

In a letter she wrote later to Susan B. Anthony, Gripenberg documented the importance of Stanton, Anthony, and other women's rights champions for the activities of women around the world. Its tone betrays the wide-eyed excitement of someone who has moved from margin to center, yet as a text demonstrating the strength of women's internationality it is matchless.[17] The speeches and articles of Anthony and Stanton that she referred to had been in great part translated and circulated in Finland and Sweden by Gripenberg herself. She also wrote a popular account of Elizabeth Cady Stanton and the history of the women's rights movement, which she gave as a lecture in Stockholm in 1896.[18]

In 1911, Theodore Stanton, son of Elizabeth Cady Stanton and long time scholar-activist in feminist circles on the Continent, visited Gripenberg in Finland, helping to complete the circle.

Aleksandra Gripenberg, courtesy of the Finnish Literature Society (SKS), Helsinki.

Other Granddaughters

Maggie Walz (1861–1927?) was another of the symbolic granddaughters of Lucretia Mott's generation who established a conscious network of transatlantic connections among women. Born Margareete Johanna Konttra Niranen, she came to the United States from Finland in 1881 as a domestic and settled in the copper country of the Keweenah Peninsula, Michigan. So many Finnish-speaking people dwelt there that most institutions and work details were language-segregated; thus it was possible to shop, work, worship, and read only Finnish. But Maggie Walz was determined to learn English and succeed as a businesswoman. She worked for English speakers and got a position at an English-speaking store. Selling sewing machines, pianos, and organs door to door—items that women would buy, though itinerant selling was usually a man's job—she gradually built up her stock and her reputation. In 1887 she returned to Finland to recruit young women for domestic positions, assisting them with the paperwork and money for passage; by helping fourteen young women get jobs, she started a successful employment agency. She also provided support for her new emigrés with night classes in English and in American homemaking skills and English services for the Finnish community—notary public, currency exchange, letter-writing, tickets to and from Finland.

In 1893 she traveled to Indiana, for a year's business and accounting course at Valparaiso University. At the same time she was heavily involved in the local Northern Star Temperance Society (she came from a conservative Laestadian Lutheran background in Finland) and cofounded the Calumet Finnish Women's Society in 1894. She wrote to Aleksandra Gripenberg—then president of the Finnish Women's Association in Helsinki and the best-known Finnish feminist—for ideas and books. On letterhead that read, "The Finnish Ladies Society of Calumet Michigan. An Organization for the Protection of Women's Rights," Walz asked that Gripenberg mention their society in her Finnish periodical, requested more books, sent subscriptions to the Finnish women's newspaper, and invited Gripenberg to come to the United States again.[19] Interestingly, Walz's letters are written in very poor Finnish; she had been away for a long time, and more important, she had had very little Finnish education to begin with. It is also fascinating that Walz chose to communicate with Finnish feminists, rather than contacting Americans for help in setting up her early women's group. Many of the women she

Maggie Walz, courtesy of the Finnish American Historical Archives, Suomi College, Hancock, Michigan.

organized would not have been able to read English, however, so she needed Finnish feminist printed sources.

Later Maggie Walz became business manager for a local newspaper, built and rented out a three-story business building, ran a women's clothing store and sold shares to other women. In 1903 she organized a community on Drummond Island in Lake Huron, where homesteaders were to run a sawmill, brickyard, and flour mill cooperatively, each family also homesteading their own 160 acres. But the community did not prosper; socialist factions took over in 1914, and Maggie Walz withdrew. In the meantime she continued her other enterprises and established links with American women's groups, especially suffrage and temperance organizations. She was a Michigan delegate to one of the national women's suffrage conventions and, in 1910, an American delegate to the International Women's Christian Temperance Union convention in Scotland. Continuing her financial schemes, she attempted to develop homes and training centers for domestic women workers in Marquette, Michigan; Houston, Texas; and Florida.[20]

After Finland granted suffrage to women in 1906, the U.S. suffrage movement regularly called on Finnish women immigrants such as Maggie Walz to participate in parades and rallies, noting Finland's position as the first nation in the Atlantic community to give women the vote. In 1911 Aleksandra Gripenberg received a request from Anna Howard Shaw, then president of the National American Woman Suffrage Organization, for some help in organizing Finnish immigrant women for the suffrage campaign. She responded, "It is rather difficult to reach the finnish women in America. Ignorant as they are and not knowing english, they are not able to develop mentally, and they are also usually cut off from all intellectual communication with their mother country [original capitalization]."[21] This remark belies the communication from the Calumet women's group but represents Gripenberg's own classism.

The Finnish connections have continued for a century. Finnish feminists have usually brought the largest per capita delegations to international women's conferences in Costa Rica (1993), New York (1990), Beijing (1996), and Australia (1996), from their country's tiny five million population. There is a national, government-sponsored women's studies office in Finland and women's studies programs and institutes in all Finnish universities, plus ten women's studies professorships around the country.

Ida B. Wells-Barnett (1862–1931) was a very different symbolic granddaughter of Lucretia Mott. In organizing the antilynching movement, she traveled to England in 1893 and again in 1894, utilizing Lucretia Mott's earlier abolitionist British network to bring pressure on the United States by means of the British press. Her first journalistic forays in New York (after she was burned out of her newspaper office in Memphis, she was hired by the African American *New York Age*) were not successful in gaining access to white newspapers, so she took her campaign to England and Scotland. There she had a triumphant lecture tour, speaking at many of the same places that Mott had in 1840–41, especially in the Quaker and old abolitionist circles of Newcastle, Birmingham, Manchester, Edinburgh, Glasgow, Aberdeen, London. Her speeches and press releases were carried by all the newspapers; she spoke to various denominational groups—Quaker, Unitarian, Baptist, Methodist, Presbyterian, Congregational—and at temperance, community, working-class, and YMCA gatherings. In all cases, many of her contacts were with women. By the end of her 1894 campaign the British Anti-Lynching Committee had been formed, headed by the Duke of Argyle; the first contributions came from a group of African students, including two women. Discussion of her tour and the British response was carried in detail by the American press, both secular and denominational, so that when she returned home, she had an entrée to white groups and publications.[22]

In 1893, when she and Frederick Douglass (former U.S. ambassador to Haiti, 1889–91) wrote *The Reason Why the Colored American Is Not in the World's Columbian Exposition* and distributed 10,000 copies of the pamphlet at the Haitian building at the Chicago World's Fair, she spread the word around the world about her antilynching campaign, as well as the many contributions African Americans had made to American civilization.[23] In the process she participated in what may have been the first sit-in: as she and Douglass integrated the Boston Oyster House, a whites-only lunch counter near the Chicago fairgrounds.[24]

Wells-Barnett was the first to show that lynching usually had economic rather than sexual causes, using accounts in white newspapers to gather statistics on age, sex, race, and charges against the victims.[25] She also confirmed lynchings of women, children, and white men to counteract stereotyped beliefs about black men. For our purposes, what is important about Ida B. Wells-Barnett's work is that she utilized transatlantic contacts, many with women, which had been set up two generations earlier.

By the time of the first International Council of Women, then, and certainly within the next decade, women on both sides of the Atlantic were using these slowly built-up friendships, groups, meetings, and contacts—this web of networks—for their campaigns *against* lynching, alcohol, and white slavery and *for* woman suffrage, international peace, and women's economic rights. The "golden cables of sympathy" were stretched below and above the Atlantic as women gained strength and energy from the strategies of their sisters in very different cultures.

There is much more to this story; peripheral webs can be drawn for the artistic community, for governesses, for women entrepreneurs, for translators, for phrenologists and spiritualists, for scientists and intellectuals (see the Appendixes). But perhaps enough has been told to encourage scholars to break free of national boundaries and concentrate on the crossing, breaking, and transcending of them.

"Golden cables of sympathy" linking women across the Atlantic in the nineteenth century were put together with countless individual connections. Most of the women who formed them were unaware of the significance of their work for women's future; some believed that most women should not engage in such public behavior as they themselves did. But a good number of those examined here knew how important it was that women see themselves as part of a transnational group—women. From the "unprotected women" traveling to exotic locations, through the religious zeal of Pentecostal and Catholic women, the literary celebrity of Harriet Beecher Stowe and the infamous George Sand, the developing female consciousness of revolutionary and expatriate women and of various reformers and utopian communalists, and finally to the Mothers of the Matrix—Lucretia Mott, Anna Doyle Wheeler, Elizabeth Cady Stanton, Fredrika Bremer, and Frances Power Cobbe, those women fully aware of their position in building a movement for the future—the Atlantic community in the nineteenth century was crisscrossed by webs of linkages between women, as the matrix gestated the next generation of the women's movement.

Susan B. Anthony's photograph collection includes Lucretia Mott, Ernestine Rose, Elizabeth Cady Stanton, and a group portrait from the International Council of Women. The latter image is reproduced elsewhere in this volume. Courtesy of the Library of Congress, LCJ 601-81497.

Appendix A

Some Atlantic Community Women with International Links

Appendix A. Some Atlantic Community Women with International Links

Years of Greatest Activity	UNITED STATES	BRITISH ISLES	CONTINENT
1820–1850	Sarah Grimké 1792-1873	Elizabeth Fry 1780-1845	Suzanne Voilquin 1801-1877
	LUCRETIA MOTT *1793-1880*	**ANNA DOYLE WHEELER** *1785-1848*	Flora Tristan 1803-1844
	Frances Wright 1795-1852	Anne Knight 1786-1862	**GEORGE SAND** *1804-1876*
	Lydia Maria Child 1802-1880	Elizabeth Jesser Reid 1794-1866	Pauline Roland 1805-1852
	Maria Weston Chapman 1806-1885	Anna Jameson 1794-1860	Jeanne Deroin 1810-1894
	Cornelia Connelly 1809-1879	Harriet Martineau 1802-1879	Mathilda Franziske Anneke 1817-1884
	Margaret Fuller 1810-1850	Marion Kirkland Reid *(dates unknown)*	Natalie Herzen 1817-1852
	Caroline Healey Dall 1822-1888		Louise Otto-Peters 1819-1895
	Ednah Dow Cheney 1824-1904		
1850–1870	Harriot Hunt 1805-1875	Mary Somerville 1780-1872	**FREDRIKA BREMER** *1801-1865*
	Phoebe Palmer 1807-1874	Mary Howitt 1799-1888	Christina Belgiojoso 1808-1871
	Ernestine Rose 1810-1892	Mary Seacole 1805-1881	Aurora Karamzin 1808-1902
	Harriet Beecher Stowe 1811-1896	Florence Nightingale 1820-1910	Jenny P. d' Héricourt 1809-1875
	ELIZABETH CADY STANTON *1815-1902*	**BARBARA BODICHON** *1827-1891*	Johanna Kinkel 1810-1858
	Susan B. Anthony 1820-1906	Josephine Butler 1828-1906	Malwida von Meysenbug 1816-1903
	Sarah Remond 1826-1894	Maria Rye 1829-1903	Dora D' Istria 1829-1888
	Amanda Berry Smith 1837-1915	Catherine Booth 1829-1890	Marie Riegrová-Palacká 1833-1891
		Jessie White Mario 1832-1906	
1870–1900	**ELIZABETH CADY STANTON** *1815-1902*	**FRANCES POWER COBBE** *1822-1904*	Marie Goegg 1826-1899
	Matilda Joslyn Gage 1826-1898	Emily Faithful 1835-1895	Hedvig von Haartman 1826-1902
	Hannah Whitall Smith 1832-1911	Millicent Garrett Fawcett 1847-1929	Maria Deraismes 1828-1894
	Frances Willard 1839-1898	Sophia Sturge 1849-1936	Selma Borg 1838-1922
	May Wright Sewall 1844-1920	Harriet Stanton Blatch 1856-1940	Bertha von Suttner 1843-1914
	Edmonia Lewis 1845-1909	Ishbel Aberdeen	Sonya Kovalevsky 1850-1891
	Jane Addams 1860-1935	Caroline Ashurst Biggs	Alli Trygg-Helenius 1852-1926
	Maggie Walz 1861-1927		**ALEXANDRA GRIPENBERG** *1859-1913*
			Helena Schjerfbeck 1862-1946

Boldface = Most Important Networkers

Appendix B

The Relevance and Irrelevance to This Study of Social Network Analysis

Sociological theory has provided the historian with many sophisticated tools, among them ideal type analysis, alienation theory, and the concept of "civil ecology."[1] Network analysis as a method of social research began in anthropology in the mid-1950s and spread to sociology and political science.[2] Sociology is the discipline in which it has seen its most significant flowering. Network analysis serves the larger purpose of placing *structures* rather than individuals and psyches in the foreground. By focusing on the concrete relations that pervade and give coherence to organizations, interest groups, nation-states, and informal units (neighborhoods, crowds), network theorists seek to "confront directly the structural basis of social life," in the words of Barry Wellman; network analysis "forms part of a worldwide scientific shift ... toward structural analytic interpretation of phenomena in the light of their linkages with other members of systems."[3]

Besides Wellman, other leading figures in developing the method include Ronald Breiger, Samuel Leinhardt, Edward Laumann, S.D. Berkowitz, Nancy Howell, and Harrison White. By the late 1970s a rapidly expanding group had elaborated a set of core concepts and produced major research. Many of the concepts are drawn from the metaphoric sources discussed in my introduction: matrix, net, and web. Thus, network analysts speak of nodes, links, matrices, ties, bridges, chains, lattices, clusters, and connections; however, their vocabulary is supplemented by terms drawn from systems theory, economics, mathematics, information theory, chemistry, group dynamics, and a bewildering array of other domains. "Cliques," "matrix of interlocks," "degree of centrality," "embeddedness in local subsystem," "blockmodeling," "isolates," "transfer phenomena," "system openness," "liaisons," "multistranded ties," "dyads," "structural equivalence," "balancing"—such terms and formulations are standard fare in the literature.

Furthermore, network analysis is heavily quantitative in orientation. In Laumann's words, "Close examination reveals that network analysis is, at least in part, some rather old ideas that have been refurbished and made more attractive by being combined with sophisticated mathematical and quantitative tools."[4] The "sociometric" tendency of network analysis is not universal but very pervasive. Lacking any mathematical notation, a sentence like the following from Breiger is far from the most technical that one can encounter: "Whereas the analysis of the previous section was predicated on knowledge of the translation matrix A, this section indicates that information about 'reachability' in either the person-to-person or the group-to-group matrix may be derived from knowledge of its dual matrix."[5] Moreover, in the hands of network analysts, such familiar terms as "link" or "tie" have been operationally defined so as to render them suitable for quantitative manipulation. Thus, a "liaison" is "an individual who links two or more cliques in a system, but who is not a member of any clique."[6]

In 1979 John Barnes, a Cambridge University sociologist, wrote "Network Analysis: Orienting Notion, Rigorous Technique, or Substantive Field of Study?" He concluded that network theorists bring to their efforts such a diversity of interests and objectives that "there is at best what Wittgenstein calls a family resemblance among the various manifestations of network analysis."[7] More recent commentators agree.[8] This state of affairs is, I believe, an advantageous one for historians who wish to draw upon some of the insights, terminology, diagramming strategies, and intellectual energy of network analysis—without, however, being required to use it as an authoritative framework of interpretation. Certainly in the historical materials worked on by network analysts, no "standard approach" has been developed.

One is thus free to regard network analysis as "an orienting notion" only—and that is the approach adopted in this book. This means that although I do not wish to describe woman-to-woman international relations in equation form, I must recognize and acknowledge that a quantitative dimension exists and could be explored. To assert, as I do, that the nineteenth-century network binding women became increasingly dense and complex is to suggest a historical change in the sheer magnitude of contacts. In addition to its attempts to picture networklike relations in diagrams and figures, what I have found most useful in network analysis is some of the terminology: "broker," "node," "liaison." Yet I resist the idea that network analysis holds a monopoly on the definitions of words associated with the metaphors of matrix, net, and web. One need not feel bound to use only a network analysis lexicography in doing this kind of work.

Appendix C

Adventurers and Invalids

Chapter 2 examined the communications revolution and the rise of a new and controversial species of traveler: "the unprotected female." To provide a sense of just how wide and inviting the new horizons of geographical mobility were, I briefly discussed the emergence of such female adventurers as Isabella Bird and Ida Pfeiffer. That they were usually loners who found the Atlantic community too restrictive disqualified them as subjects for this book, yet I argued that their writings might well have encouraged the sort of journeying that *did* contribute to the matrix: the less rigorous travels of a Bremer, a Stowe, or a Cobbe. To remind readers that women were up to a great deal more, however, I include here materials on Harriet and Alexine Tinne and Amelia Edwards.

Another category inviting further attention by historians of women's internationality is the invalid. There is evidence to suggest that the ancient practice of making pilgrimage to places of healing might well have worked to the advantage of female-to-female contacts in the nineteenth century. It seems clear that particular climatic environments became important sites for the formation of women's international connections, especially in Italy.[1] There, Elizabeth Barrett Browning, Mary Somerville, the novelist Ouida, and a host of others formed large expatriate communities. Lucie Duff Gordon and Hester Stanhope elected to remain for their "cures" in the Arab cultures of Egypt and Lebanon.

Invalids traveled originally for their health but became expatriates when they stayed abroad for years. The physical climate became only one reason they stayed; the psychological climate of greater freedom and independence became important to them; additionally, they could live abroad more cheaply. Many became *salonnières* as international travelers journeyed to see them. The experience of Mary Somerville briefly illustrates this line of further historical inquiry.

The Tinnes

Harriet Tinne and her daughter Alexine were wealthy aristocrats and traveled in that style, with both Dutch and Egyptian servants and all the stores, provisions, and luxuries needed: live chickens and sheep for food, pet dogs, horses and donkeys, gifts for rulers they might encounter, even a piano for Alexine. They were traveling at the time when Western Europe was trying to abolish the Arab slave trade in Africa, as well as explore, establish colonies, and exploit the resources of the region. Reading about them now, one is shocked at the expense and flamboyance of their entourage. In some ways, they survived simply because they were so naive as to believe that they could indeed do anything they set out to do *because* they were ladies. Above Khartoum, however, disease struck; Alexine supervised the carrying out of the bodies of her mother, her aunt, and her trusted servants so that they could be shipped home for burial. She herself never returned to the Netherlands but continued her adventures in North Africa. Her last expedition was an attempt to cross the Sahara and live among the Tuareg—for whom she brought elaborate gifts, including a sewing machine, ice makers, alarm clocks, invisible ink, magnifying glasses, and a microscope.[2] In 1869, when she was thirty-three, the party was ambushed in an intertribal feud; she was killed, along with most of her guides, and her expedition completely looted. Although there was an investigation by Libyan authorities, no one was ever charged with the murder.

Some of the Tinnes' actions seem appalling from a twentieth-century perspective. At various points in their journeys up the Nile they came across slave traders, and they often stopped at *zeribas*, or holding stations for captured slaves. Several times they were asked to accept children from slave mothers; at one point Alexine decided to purchase a family of six Dinka slaves from the White Nile area in order to save them (the family disappeared a few weeks later; perhaps they were retaken or escaped). A more heinous act involved their buying a twelve-year-old girl and presenting her, along with a yellow silk dress and scarf of Alexine's, as a wife to the governor of Barbar in the Sudan, because they "could think of no [other] suitable gift" (90). Later, the Tinnes were accused of engaging in the slave trade. When Alexine was living in Tripoli, she tried to make amends by setting up a home for liberated slaves, in order to relieve the hunger and suffering of a few (200).

Alexine Tinne remains an enigmatic figure, never content to live as "female Other" in polite society but becoming instead an outsider or pariah, determined to control her own space and time. As an unprotected female she paid with her life, said her critics—but some European *male* explorers were also killed by native peoples.

Amelia Edwards

Beginning as a tourist, Amelia B. Edwards (1831–92) quickly became an adventurer; she was also a novelist, journalist, and archaeologist. Her parents died when she was not yet thirty; this freedom, along with income from her novels, gave her independence to travel. Her first travel book, *Untrodden Peaks and Unfrequented Valleys* (1873), is about two "unprotected females" in the Dolomites and is inscribed, "To my American friends in Rome," reflecting her transatlantic bent. She was very specific in her advice to women travelers. They should always carry certain provisions, including "a small store of tea, arrowroot, and Liebig's extract, a bottle or two of wine and brandy," and a sidesaddle.[3] Her most famous work, *A Thousand Miles up the Nile,* recounts her 1877 journey with a female friend, still "unprotected." On her return she helped to establish the Egypt Exploration Fund in 1882, a group that organized and funded archaeological research in Egypt. In 1888–89 she lectured in the United States—in New England and on west to Milwaukee—and received three honorary degrees. The awards cited her explorations and her academic importance as a woman.

Mary Somerville

Like many women who went abroad for their health, Mary Somerville (1780–1872) stayed on to become an expatriate and a meeting point on the network. After her husband's death she went to Italy on doctor's orders in 1852, traveling "unprotected," taking her daughters with her. Remaining in Italy for the last twenty years of her life, she first settled in Florence, then in Spezia, and finally in Naples. She is known for her mathematical and scientific writings, especially for *The Connection of the Physical Sciences* (1858), an explanation of Laplace's theories; in Paris she visited with his widow Madame de Laplace, through whom she was introduced to society.

Following a pattern of women of her generation, Somerville was influenced by Madame de Staël, though she never met her. She describes de Staël's dislike of the company of women: "[she] was exceedingly impatient of women's society, would not deign to enter into conversation with any of the ladies."[4] (De Staël was evidently an unwitting builder of the women's network.) The Somerville biography includes letters from various notable persons—English, French, German, Italian—both men and women; a letter in Italian from the Countess Bon-Brenzoni of May 28, 1853, flatters Somerville's learning and her position as a woman in science (297–99). She also met and corresponded with Frances Power Cobbe and others in the expatriate community; Cobbe even mounted an unsuccessful campaign to have her buried in Westminster Abbey.

Somerville participated, from abroad, in the movement to grant university degrees to women in England; she compared the English situation negatively to that in Paris, where women were already (in the 1860s) earning university degrees in the sciences and mathematics. She signed the petition for woman suffrage presented to Parliament by J.S. Mill. She was in Florence for the Italian revolution of 1859; sympathetic with the liberals, she rejoiced at the successive steps to unite Italy. Even after her health improved, she never returned to England, preferring to remain in the sunny climate of Italy. No longer a traveler but a settler, an expatriate, she lived to the age of ninety-one, keeping her intellectual acumen, seeing foreign visitors, and continuing her mathematical calculations to the end of her life.[5]

Appendix D

International Governesses

That the international ties I have been exploring were the work mostly of middle- and upper-class women is a fact that leads interestingly to the question of how much their working- and service-class helpers participated in web-making. Here again is a lead to be followed up by other researchers. That such an effort might prove very fruitful is shown by the example of governesses—a group of women who, as in the case of Anna Leonowens, made abundant and possibly significant connections.

Educated, single, and working in new and unusual surroundings, these women were uniquely positioned to leave a written record of their impressions. Their responsibilities often involved extensive travel, and governesses often wrote letters, journals, and diaries. Additionally, they were uniquely situated to associate with other women, both the young women who were their charges and the mothers who were their employers. Many returned to their original home country after several years abroad, sometimes publishing accounts of their experiences on their return. Others stayed in their adopted country to teach or to marry there. Some of these women we know a great deal about, especially if they published in later life or participated in the public sphere. Others we know only by a letter or two or from statistics of the Female Middle-Class Emigration Society.

What sorts of connections did they make to other women, and how conscious were they of the importance of these transatlantic, transpacific, and other international linkages? For the most part, the governesses seemed not cognizant of the wider implications of what they were doing, their descriptions remaining at the specific level. Some few, however, most notably Rosalie Roos, became involved in various campaigns and work for women on their return, drawing especially on their experiences abroad and the differences they had seen in independence, opportunities, and public roles for women in other cultures. This was true especially of those who went to Australia and the United States.

The Female Middle-Class Emigration Society was founded in 1861 by Maria Rye (1829–1903), a strong member of the Society for Promoting Employment of Women, which had been organized by members of the Langham Place Group (such as Barbara Bodichon) in response to the numbers of "redundant" (unemployed) women in England. This surplus of women existed because of male population losses due to emigration, war, and disease. For middle-class women, the surplus was substantial enough to cause considerable government and press discussion, as the numbers of educated women without employment or possibilities continued to rise. Maria Rye had begun her law-copying firm, employing only women; Emily Faithful opened a publishing house (Victoria Press); and Isa Craig started a firm employing women as telegraph operators. But for every opening there were nearly one hundred applicants, and women wrote pitiful letters begging for jobs.

With Jane Lewin, Maria Rye undertook an emigration plan for educated women which advanced interest-free funds for passage, gave them letters of introduction, organized places for them to stay on disembarkation, and provided respectable organizations as sponsors. In an 1861 address to the Social Science Congress in Dublin, Rye outlined her plan and its early successes, asking for donations for the loan fund.[1] In its twenty-five years of existence, the organization sponsored only 302 women, most of whom went to Australia; other destinations were New Zealand, South Africa, New York, Canada, India, and Russia. Because Maria Rye kept the organization before the public with her letters to the *Times* and her public presentations, it had an enormous effect on public opinion. Additionally, the organization kept good records and retained all the letters written by its sponsored governesses as they were repaying their loans. These letters, collected and saved in letterbooks, give an unparalleled firsthand picture of life abroad.[2] Rye was so involved with her project that she made several visits to Australia, New Zealand, and Canada between 1860 and 1868 in order to understand emigration from the standpoint of the settlers. Orphans and destitute children were also of concern, and much of her later life was taken up with a campaign to find jobs and homes for them, whether in England or in Canada.[3]

The one woman who went to Russia, Josephine Stoney, understood the importance of the international associations she was making. Governesses were needed, she wrote, to teach English, German, French, and music, and the most sought-after teachers were those who had all those accomplishments. A few letters are extant from North American governesses; a Mrs. M. Carruthers wrote in 1872–73 about her situation as matron in an orphanage in New Jersey; her three daughters, significantly, were also employed—as a nanny, a governess, and a student in a teacher-training course. "We do not regret coming," she writes, "although our pleasure is hoping to return to purchase a more advanced school."[4]

Rosalie Roos (1823–98) came to the United States from Sweden in 1851 to teach at Limestone Female High School in Charleston and stayed on there as governess with a wealthy family. In all, she was in the United States for over four years. Her story is an intriguing one because she reflected on her situation as a woman, as well as on women's position in the United States and on her determination to work toward a less stifling role for (unmarried) women in middle-class society in Sweden. Along the way she revealed her ambivalence about the complexities of the great social issue of the time—slavery—and took her countrywoman Fredrika Bremer to task for not being sufficiently cognizant of those complexities in her earlier travels in America.[5]

On her journey back to Europe, she sailed first to England, on shipboard making many new acquaintances, including Julia Griffiths, an Englishwoman returning after a six-year stay in the United States as secretary of the Ladies' Anti-Slavery Society in Rochester and editorial assistant on Frederick Douglass's journal the *North Star.* These connections, which led to others during stops in London, Paris, Hamburg, and Cologne, were invaluable as Roos began making her way in the world of women's reform and philanthropy in Sweden. Two years after her 1855 return she married a widower from Uppsala, a Professor Olivecrona, and embarked on her new career as wife and mother. After her sojourn in America, however, this was not going to be enough. In 1859 she and dear friend Sophie Leijonhufvud became coeditors of *Tidskrift för Hemmet,* the periodical of the fledgling Swedish women's movement (later renamed *Hertha* in honor of Bremer's pioneering novel).[6] Together she and Sophie traveled on the Continent and in England, visiting women's organizations.

Julia Gertrude Stewart was the younger daughter of James Stewart of Stewart Castle, Trelawney, Jamaica; her father was a planter from Galloway, Scotland, and a member of the Jamaican House of Assembly. In Paris in 1836 she married John Oliphant Murray, the British attaché. The marriage was unhappy, and Stewart decided to become a governess, assuming again her maiden name. Her child, Ellen Jane Marion Murray Stewart, was cared for at the boarding school of the Misses Martin in Paris. During the 1848 French revolution the Martins fled to England, and Jane was taken to the British Embassy in Paris until she could obtain safe passage to London. Julia Stewart, then a governess in Ireland, had to give up her position as a result of the Irish potato famine and resulting economic depression. In 1850, therefore, she and daughter Jane arrived in Melbourne on the ship *Amity Hall*, "without connection in the Colony," and she proceeded to gain a position as governess in Australia.[7] Little can be determined about conscious female connections from her letters, but Stewart's descendants are very interested in genealogy and the fact that Lady Byron was a relation.

Compared with the norm, Emmeline Lott's governess position was truly exotic. For two years she was governess to the Grand Pasha Ibrahim of Egypt. In her two-volume work, *The English Governess in Egypt: Harem Life in Egypt and Constantinople* (1866), she wrote about her experiences, making conscious comparison with Lady Mary Wortley Montague's earlier *Persian Letters*. Details of the horrors of life in seclusion (dirty bed linens, inedible food) are interspersed with discussions of the problems that lack of education brings—at all levels of government, as well as in marriage and between sex partners. Lott was undoubtedly making connections to women internationally; whether these were at all useful to either party is doubtful.

Appendix E

Women Transatlantic Entrepreneurs
in the Nineteenth Century

The experiences of women entrepreneurs in the nineteenth century is as interesting as it is difficult to research. It is clear that a number of women entrepreneurs founded successful international businesses, moving especially between Europe and North America. These women varied from small-business entrepreneurs—dealing in cheeses or pickles—to executives of larger enterprises managing women's emigration or gold mining in Siberia; others were entertainers, translators, or journalists. Whether these women originated in the working class or the bourgeoisie, their common purpose was financial independence and success. Often, the connections were made between colony and mother country or between European nation and emigrant's destination.

Business Entrepreneurs, Rural and Urban

Women who worked hard in food production in the nineteenth-century countryside quickly saw that they could advance their livelihood by selling. Although most simply took their dairy or vegetable products to the local weekly market, some discovered an international market as well. Hanne Nielsen (1829–1903), a cheesemaker of Denmark, traveled across the Continent, tasting and comparing and selling. She developed and marketed Havarti cheese, named after her dairy.[1] Other rural women sold baskets, candles, buttons, lace, and all kinds of textiles. Unfortunately, as the Industrial Revolution advanced, fewer and fewer subsistence farms survived. Both the enclosure movement of common lands (especially in England) and the move toward single-cash-crop economies (such as sugar beets or wheat in Eastern Europe) forced peasants and sharecroppers to give up livestock and kitchen gardens to the detriment of women especially.

One Mrs. B. Beaumont of Woodville, Mississippi, daughter of British reformer Joseph Bentley, visited England following the Civil War in order to buy stock for her dry goods store. In *A Business Woman's Journal* (1888), her comparisons of the economic situation in the U.S. South and in England, and how business transactions were handled (banking, insurance, billing, etc.) make fascinating reading.[2]

One of the most successful small-business entrepreneurs was Mary Seacole, a Jamaican Creole who sailed to London as an adolescent and there sold pickles and preserves for two years before returning to Jamaica. Her next venture took her to other Caribbean islands to collect rare shells for sale at home. Between travels she learned herbal medicine from her mother and was thus able to make a living as a "doctress." After the death of her mother and her husband, she resolved to support herself and not remarry: "It was from a confidence in my own powers, and not at all from necessity, that I remained an unprotected female."[3] Traveling to Cruces, Panama, she helped manage her brother's hotel and restaurant for California gold rush prospectors. Here she not only helped female travelers, but endured the taunts and jibes of Southern racists both male and female.

When the Crimean War started in the spring of 1854, Seacole was determined to participate. Traveling first to London, she offered her services to Florence Nightingale and the nursing corps. Continually rebuffed, probably because of her race, she worked instead with a male partner to set up her own convalescent facility, hotel, restaurant, and boarding house—the "British Hotel"—outside of Sebastopol. Her establishment was known all over the front, not only because she managed to stock luxury items from home but also because she was so skillful at "doctoring." Her many colorful adventures there are recounted in her autobiography. She also made a good profit on the war and was somewhat disappointed when it was over. Called "Mother Seacole" by her "sons" in the army, she knew that she would not be able to continue the same relationship back in England. Evidently, the autobiography was undertaken on her return as a financial venture, for it asked for subscriptions from some of the prominent men to whom she had ministered. She worked for the cause of war widows and orphans and was decorated by the French, Turkish, and English governments. Later, she became a masseuse for the Princess of Wales and died in relative prosperity in 1881.[4]

Although Mary Seacole's best connections were not to women but to men in the British military, they were certainly international; she was able to capitalize on her entrepreneurial skills on three continents.

Significant too is the example of Minna Canth (1844–97) of Finland. She supported her family as a haberdasher after her husband's early death and wrote controversial plays realistically portraying women's role. Her dramas, written in Finnish, were also produced in the Finnish-American immigrant community in upper Michigan. She became a spokeswoman in the fledgling Finnish women's rights movement and corresponded with emigrants to the United States and Canada.[5]

Maggie Walz (see Chapter 9), who began as a door-to-door salesperson provides an example of a transatlantic entrepreneur who branched out in many directions. As she advanced from a small business venture to larger enterprises, she deliberately constructed a network between women transatlantically.

The best example I have found of a woman running a large enterprise internationally in the nineteenth century is Aurora Karamzin (see Chapter 5).

Entertainers

One of the most fertile areas in which to find international entrepreneurial connections among women is in entertainment. Most of the famous female musicians, opera stars, actresses, and circus performers in the nineteenth century worked for larger groups or managers and therefore could be described as employees rather than independent entrepreneurs. For example, Jenny Lind, "the Swedish nightingale," was to vocal music what Stowe or Sand were to the novel: she created a system of "publics" throughout the Atlantic community, but, managed and handled by P.T. Barnum, she was hardly independent. Adelaide Kemble was a successful international actress and opera star, well known in England, Italy, France, and the United States, but she too was evidently part of a larger production company.[6] Some did work for themselves, however, organizing their own shows, doing publicity and subscriptions, hiring halls, writing press releases, and figuring out alternative ways to make a living as well.

Selma Borg (1838–1922?) is one of these international entrepreneurial entertainers. She grew up on the west coast of Finland, and her greatest desire was to travel to the West; Boston and Baltimore were favorite pretend destinations in play with her brothers. Educated in Stockholm and Lausanne in music, art, history, and languages, she was finally able to travel to the United States in 1864, along with other members of the "Swedish Ladies' Quartet." She soon decided to stay, supporting herself as translator of Swedish and German novels by women, as musician, and as lecturer. She worked with an American writer, Marie Brown, who edited and polished her translations. One of those whom Borg translated was Marie Sophie Schwartz, author of *Gerda* and *Gold and Name*. A letter exists in which Borg offers reasons for the poor sales of the translation and asks Schwartz to send her a book from Sweden on the rights of women, one she especially wants to read.[7] Among other works Borg translated was the autobiography of Maria Zakrzewska of Boston, one of the first woman doctors in the United States.

Her family having lost its fortune during the financial crisis resulting from the Franco-Prussian War (1870–71), she was even more dependent on her own resources and determined to succeed on the lecture circuit. In 1875 she returned to Finland on a lecture tour; her topics included the position of women in American society and publicity about the upcoming 1876 World Exhibition in Philadelphia. She was commissioned by the Finnish Senate to organize the country's entries for the exhibition and enthusiastically lectured in Vasa, Oulu, Kuopio, and Viborg as well as Helsinki and Stockholm, putting particular emphasis on women.[8] (Ironically, since Finland was then a grand duchy under Russia and not an independent nation, the entries were not allowed at the exhibition.) During her stay abroad she also sent back travel columns to American newspapers.

Back in the United States, she continued her speaking and music work, combining lectures on Finnish folklore with renditions by the Swedish Ladies' Vocal Quartet. She also published the music for many Finnish and Swedish songs, translating the texts herself. After the quartet disbanded, she directed orchestras in Philadelphia, New York, Providence, and Boston, playing the music of Finnish composers Filip von Schantz and Sibelius, as well as folk melodies and marches. Most reviews commented on the uniqueness of seeing a woman conductor but complimented her forcefulness and grace with the baton.[9] The *Providence Press* of February 12, 1879, had the most to say about this unusual woman, commenting that she was not "one of those furious reformers with which this country has been blessed, or cursed, of late"; instead, she was "natural, truthful, and ingenuous, [taking] her large audience by

Selma Borg, courtesy of Sibelius Museum, Åbo Akademi University, Turku, Finland.

storm."[10] She was proud of being the first to translate the initial runes of the Finnish national epic, the *Kalevala,* into English blank verse;[11] she often read parts of her translation during her lectures. Evidently the poet Henry Wadsworth Longfellow attended at least one of her lectures in Cambridge, Massachusetts.

To her friend Elisabeth Blomqvist, headmistress of the most important girls' school in Helsinki, Borg wrote from Philadelphia, telling of her singing and translation work, asking for news from home, and indicating that she would like guests from Finland. Later she wrote to Finland about two young Finnish women, Eva and Anna Ingman, who had visited her in America, and inquired whether another female friend was then in Dresden.[12] In this correspondence she was providing a node on a Finnish international female network.

Borg continued to publicize Finnish life and culture throughout her life. In her later years she lived in Camden, New Jersey, with Sarah Hill, a member of the Swedish Church of the New Jerusalem in Philadelphia; she died in Atlantic City in the early 1920s. In 1986 her personal effects—including a beautiful director's baton of ebony with her name engraved in silver, plus sheet music, programs, photographs, newspaper clippings, and press releases—were given to the Sibelius Museum at Åbo Akademi in Turku, Finland, by Sarah Hill's granddaughter, Elsie Vosseller.

Borg was a model of the true international entrepreneur, working to make transatlantic connections as a part of gaining a livelihood. I have so far been unable to find many personal letters to tell us more about what kind of person she was. The photographs show a determined and independent woman. How many of her transatlantic connections were with women is also a question, but we do know that she often spoke in her lectures of the importance of women in Finland and provided hospitality to Finnish female guests in the United States.

Translators and Journalists

Nineteenth-century translators were often women who knew languages; they could do the work at home and would accept the very low pay for such labors. Translating work was like piecework, but at least those who did it were working for themselves. Women translators, some of whom were immigrants, furthered the network of ideas and works. According to Marie Zebrikoff's essay on nineteenth-century Russian women in Theodore Stanton's *The Woman Question in Europe,* many Russian women supported themselves at this time by translating, "but, as Russians are generally proficient in foreign languages, the market is overstocked and the pay is 15 rubles or less for sixteen printed pages."[13] As noted above, Selma Borg partly supported herself in the United States by translating, as did Fredrika Runeberg in Finland and Anna Doyle Wheeler in England. Catherine Winkworth translated many hymns from German, and George Eliot (Mary Ann Evans) translated David Strauss's *Life of Jesus*.

Mary Howitt (1799–1888) was a British translator and writer who made a real career of her work in Victorian England, collaborating with her husband, William Howitt. Together they translated most of the German and Scandinavian authors for English-speaking audiences. She became so well known that many international guests visited her—authors whose work she had translated and others in literary circles as well. She brought Fredrika Bremer to English-speaking readers, for example, and they became good friends. By the end of her life (which she spent in Italy, where she converted to Catholicism—she had begun as a Quaker), she and her husband had written or translated more than 180 volumes.[14]

Journalists were not usually true entrepreneurs, since they often worked as employees for newspapers. But sometimes, especially as international writers, they did freelance work and could therefore be considered here; Margaret Fuller (1810–50) and Mathilde Franziska Anneke (1817–84) are discussed in Chapter 5.

What characteristics or ideas are there in common among these international entrepreneurs? First, they were often connected with some immigrant group, in order to make the contacts—Maggie Walz with Finnish immigrants to the United States; Selma Borg, who used her Swedish language and Finnish culture as the means and substance of the career she carved out for herself in entertainment; Mathilde Franziske Anneke, who worked with German immigrants in the United States, then returned to German-speaking Switzerland as a correspondent during the Civil War. Other women who made entrepreneurial connections were often from a higher class or educated in several languages (international journalists such as Margaret Fuller; wealthy widows such as Aurora Karamzin).

Second, many of these women were widows who took over the business dealings of their husbands or decided that by necessity they must make a living on their own. Widow Mary Seacole of Jamaica decided not to remarry; Annie Nelles, a book agent in Indiana, left a bigamous relationship; Minna Canth in Finland continued her husband's haberdashery business and wrote her plays on the side; Aurora Karamzin became an owner and manager of great wealth after her husband died. In common with widows, single women faced the necessity of earning a living. Neither Maggie Walz nor Selma Borg ever married. Margaret Fuller was single when she went to Italy as a correspondent. Mathilde Franziska Anneke was separated from her husband when she returned from Switzerland.

For the most part, the businesses chosen were acceptable for women, related to private domestic life—hotels or restaurants, cooking or sewing, entertainment, translation. In sales, too (though there was not as much international selling as one might expect), women dealt mostly in items appropriate to their "sphere": pickles, pianos, sewing machines, cheeses, clothes, and dry goods.

In sum, nineteenth-century women in small business and larger enterprises—entertainment, translation, and journalism—were managing to make a living, learning skills that enabled them to negotiate between cultures and languages. Their lives and stories seem worthy of much more attention, for they too made vital connections between cultures and between women. I speculate that in indirect ways they added to the matrix—just how and to what degree remain inviting questions.

Appendix F

Women Artists Abroad

Except for Stowe and Sand, the arts as a domain productive of international woman-to-woman contacts has remained largely undiscussed—another example of an area to which important future work might be directed. Many artists continued their international peripatetic existence after the French Revolution. A well-known example is Marie Louise Elisabeth Vigée-Lebrun, 1756-1842, portrait painter, who was born and educated in Paris before the Revolution. Escaping the Terror, she lived in Italy, then in England, and traveled all over Europe, spending much time in Russia painting portraits of royalty at the Czar's court. Her memoirs focus on the revolutionary and Napoleonic periods and her many connections to upper-class women. Vigée-Lebrun was persuaded to publish her *Memoirs* by her close friend Princess Dolgoruki of Russia in 1835. That significant material is not lacking may be demonstrated by reference to the experience of Nordic women painters.

Like their American counterparts, a great number of Nordic women artists went abroad to study art in the nineteenth century. In the 1860s they went to Germany; in the 1880s Paris was the place to be. The most important place for art after the Franco-Prussian war, Paris drew people from the United States and the whole of Europe. At least one hundred Nordic women artists studied and worked in Paris during that decade. Here is a partial listing. From Sweden: Julia Beck, 1853–1935; Eva Bonnier, 1857–1909; Wilhilmina (Mina) Carlson-Bredberg, 1857–1943; Karin Larsson, 1859–1928; Emma Löwstädt-Chadwick, 1855–1932; Jenny Nyström, 1854–1946; Hanna Pauli, 1864–1940; Hildegard Thorell 1850–1930. From Norway: Harriet Backer, 1845–1932; Kitty Kielland, 1843–1914; Asta Nørregaard, 1853–1933; Signe Scheel, 1860–1942; Sofie Thomesen-Werenskiold, 1849–1926. From Denmark: Anna Ancher, 1859–1935; Edma Frölich-Stage, 1859–1958; Sofie Holten, 1858–1930;

Agnes Lunn, 1850–1941; Emilie Mundt, 1842–1922; Emmy Thornam, 1852–1935; Ludovica Thornam, 1853–1896; Bertha Wegmann, 1847–1926. From Finland: Elin Danielson-Gambogi, 1861–1919; Amélie Lundahl; Helene Schjerfbeck, 1862–1946; Helena Westermarck, 1857–1938; Maria Wiik, 1853–1928.

At home, these women had won prizes, had been admitted to art schools and awarded travel grants. But on the Continent they had to contend with the prejudice against women artists, prohibitions on using nude models, and conservative views about women's education and autonomy. In Paris, for example, only two schools accepted female students, Académie Colarossi and Académie Julian. The international women artists' community established in these schools served these young women for the rest of their lives, as they continued their associations with people they met from Italy, England, France, Germany, Switzerland, and the United States. (The American women sculptors in Rome—Harriet Hosmer, Edmonia Lewis, and others—were thought by the Nordic women to be very masculine.) Most of these American artists were very much a part of the American-English expatriate communities of Rome and Florence.[1] Unfortunately, this chapter of feminist art history is not well known in the United States.[2]

Fanny Churberg (1845–1892) was of the earlier generation who studied in Germany. Of the Düsseldorf school, she worked in a very unusual naturalistic style, painting somber winter-light landscapes. In 1880 she became involved in the Finnish nationalist movement, founding the Friends of Finnish Handicrafts. As her way of working for women, art, and nationalism, she organized a textile exhibit for Copenhagen in 1888 and for the Paris World Art and Industry Exhibition in 1889. This involvement terminated her career as a painter.[3] Other Finnish women who studied in Germany were Victoria Åberg (1824–92), who remained on the Continent as a successful artist in Paris, London, Rome, and Berlin; and Ida Silfverberg (1834–99). According to Synnöve Malmström, many of these women, as part of the movement to dress more simply, refused to wear crinolines in the 1850s.[4]

Helene Schjerfbeck (1862–1946) is the best known of a group of "Painting Sisters" that included Helena Westermarck, Maria Wiik, Amélie Lundahl, and Elin Danielson, all of whom studied in Paris in the 1880s. Schjerfbeck went to Paris in 1880 and spent her summers first in Brittany and then in St. Ives, England, with a good friend, the Austrian Marianne Preindelsberger. In 1888 her painting *The Little Convalescent* won a place at the Paris Salon. Later she traveled to Italy, Austria, and Russia, copying pictures at the great museums to support herself, as did many of her colleagues. Although keeping herself apart from the Helsinki art community on her return to Finland to care for her mother and teach, she continued to paint and maintained her contacts with international friends she had made in Paris.[5] Her remarkable series of self-portraits, the last one painted just before her death, displays a gradual winnowing away of all that was unessential.

A quotation from her diary shows her awareness of her artistic foremothers: "That which lies innermost—passion—that I would like to reveal, but then one is ashamed of oneself and can't conjure it up—because one is a woman. Women have seldom become such conjurers. Fanny Churberg did."[6] Criticized at home for being "foreign," Schjerfbeck was able to maintain her integrity partly because she isolated herself from the traditional, competitive Finnish art scene and "world-traveled" in Lugones's sense (see Chapter 8), opening up to new possibilities—Japanese block-printing, cubism, expressionism—gained from books and art journals. In this way she came to know others' worlds and, even in her solitariness, related to them with loving perception. The evidence for this attitude is in her late paintings, her unique abstract expressionistic style.[7]

Maria Wiik (1853–1928), a close friend of Schjerfbeck, received many portrait commissions and won awards from the Paris Salon. At Académie Julian in Paris she became friends with Marie Bashkirtseff, a young Russian artist whose autobiography—published after her death at age twenty-three—became a cause célèbre of the "new woman." Bashkirtseff wrote about her work at the academy and about several of the Nordic women artists, especially Louise Breslau, her great rival. Anna Nordlander, Anna Nordgren, and Maria Wiik are all mentioned, as are Americans and other Europeans. Although a wealthy aristocrat, Bashkirtseff became part of the international community at Julian's art school; in 1877 she wrote in her journal about the social equality at the school: "In the studio all distinctions disappear. One has neither name nor family; one is no longer the daughter of one's mother, one is one's self—an individual—and one has before one art, and nothing else. One feels so happy, so free, so proud!"[8]

Elin Danielson-Gambogi (1861–1919) did not return to Finland for some time but stayed abroad, marrying an Italian artist whom she met while making copies of pictures in Florence. Her *At the Tea Table*

(1890) nicely illustrates the "new women" these young women felt themselves to be: leaning on the table in a pensive mood, smoking, seeming independent by choice. Ellen Thesleff (1869–1925) studied in Paris a bit later and spent much time in Italy as well. Of the Symbolist school, she minimized color, calling her method "black colorism."[9]

Women artists in Finland received more awards than did men (though they enjoyed only one-third the income), especially up to about 1870. Thereafter, the country's attitude toward women artists shifted to the more conservative separate-spheres philosophy of the rest of Europe. Ironically, life became more difficult for women artists in Finland at the *end* of the nineteenth century than earlier.

Notes

Introduction

1. Bright, *Submarine Telegraphs*, 91.
2. Thompson, *Wiring a Continent*, 427–39.
3. Field, *The Story of the Atlantic Telegraph*, 393.
4. Ibid., 210. The ceremonies were held in 1858; several days later that first cable failed.
5. Ibid., 393.
6. See, e.g., Tyrrell, *Woman's World, Woman's Empire*; Rupp, "Constructing Internationalism" and her *Worlds of Women*; Hurwitz, "The International Sisterhood"; Sherrick, "Toward Universal Sisterhood"; Polasky, "Internationalism in the Age of Nationalism"; Kuehl, "Concepts of Internationalism in History"; Wikander, "International Women's Congresses, 1878–1914."
7. The contested term "feminism" is the subject of much current debate. One must recognize different strands of feminism, but all of them, at the very least, perceive the historical inequity of women's position and encourage its eradication. See the longer discussion in Chapter 7, Offen's "Defining Feminism" in *Signs*, and the subsequent discussion in later issues.
8. See, e.g., Fox-Genovese and Genovese, *Fruits of Merchant Capital*; Kolchin, *American Slavery, 1619-1877*; Foner and Genovese, *Slavery in the New World*. Additionally, Vincent Carretta's edited collection, *Unchained Voices*, gives evidence from black writers of the eighteenth-century Atlantic world.
9. Gilroy, *The Black Atlantic*, 15.
10. "Connections" is less suggestively rich than the other three metaphors. "Connectedness" is a word that has recently come into vogue as a concept in feminist jurisprudence. Robin West in *Caring for Justice* asserts a concept of "connectedness" in opposition to the Rule of Law view of the physically "boundaried" autonomous self (see Slavin, "Authenticity and Fiction in Law"). "Connectedness" in this book means all those ways and means of people's being bound to one another (usually across physical distance), including kin connections but not including institutional hierarchical connections.
11. Kramarae and Treichler, *A Feminist Dictionary*, 299.
12. *Webster's II New College Dictionary* (Boston: Houghton Mifflin, 1995).
13. Witt, Reed, and Peakall, *A Spider's Web*, 5.
14. As an aside, we might be reminded of the wonderful "Spider-Web Chart" of women and women's organizations and connections to "the Socialist-Pacifist

Movement" used in the Red-baiting era in 1924 to discredit feminism. It is reprinted in Cott, *The Grounding of Modern Feminism*, 242.

15. The phrase "communicative action" is suggested by Habermas in *Theorie des Kommunikativen Handelns*, trans. as *The Theory of Communicative Action*.

16. See Boissevain, "Network Analysis: A Reappraisal."

17. See, e.g., Burt, "Models of Network Structure." *Social Networks* has been published since 1975.

18. See Rupp and Taylor, "Women's Culture and the Continuity of the Women's Movement"; Rupp, "Conflict in the International Women's Movement, 1888–1950"; Holton, "To Educate Women into Rebellion."

19. Boissevain, "Networks."

20. Appendix B explains in some detail the way sociological network analysis can usefully function as an "orienting notion"—as opposed to a rigorous frame of reference.

Chapter 1. Weaving the Delicate Web

1. Boissevain, *Friends of Friends*, 41.

2. Mott, *Slavery and "The Woman Question."* Page references to this work are noted parenthetically in the text. Also see Sklar, "Women Who Speak for an Entire Nation."

3. Helsinger, Sheets, and Veeder, *The Woman Question*, 1:5.

4. Ibid., 128 n. 17.

5. Boissevain, *Friends of Friends*, esp. 41.

6. Knight's marked copy of *A Plea for Woman* by Mrs. Hugo Reid, 146. Bonnie Anderson, "The Lid Comes Off," uses Anne Knight's firsthand experience and analysis of women's demands in the 1848 Revolution as evidence of international feminist connections in that revolutionary decade. See also Malmgreen, "Anne Knight and the Radical Subculture."

7. Biggs to Aleksandra Gripenberg, 1889.

8. "A Colored Lady Lecturer."

9. The reference to "first order" comes from Boissevain, *Friends of Friends*, 26.

10. Ibid., 41.

11. In Boissevain's words, "Brokers are thus highly expert network specialists. . . . [A] social broker places people in touch with each other either directly or indirectly. . . . He bridges gaps in communication between persons, groups, structures and even cultures" (ibid., 147).

12. See Daly and Caputi, *Websters' First New Intergalactic Wickedary of the English Language*, and Daly, *Outercourse*, for many examples of her brilliant use of feminist metaphors of spinning, spinsters, webs, websters, etc.

13. Bodichon, *An American Diary*, 63.

14. Herstein, *A Mid-Victorian Feminist*, 57, 62.

15. Gleadle, *The Early Feminists*, 177–83.

16. Herstein, *A Mid-Victorian Feminist*, 70–79.

17. Bodichon, *An American Diary,* 140, 141.

18. Ibid., 156–58.

19. See McFadden, "Boston Teenagers Debate the Woman Question."

20. Bodichon, *An American Diary,* 142.

21. Hirsch, "Barbara Leigh Smith Bodichon."

22. See Bodichon, "Slavery in America"; "An American School"; "Slave Preaching"; "Algiers: First Impressions"; "Middle Class Schools for Girls"; and "Cleopatra's Daughter, St. Marciana, Mama Marabout and Other Algerian Women."

23. Rye, "Emigration of Educated Women."

24. Others who could be studied in this context are Marie Pouchoulin Goegg (1826–99) and Jenny P. d'Héricourt (1809–75). Goegg, born in Geneva, founded and organized the Association Internationale des Femmes in 1868 and worked tirelessly for women's rights, writing letters and articles in French, German and English. A useful collection of reprinted documents on her life and work is Rahm, *Marie Goegg.* Goegg also wrote the article on Switzerland for Theodore Stanton's *The Woman Question in Europe.* On Jenny P. d'Héricourt, see Offen, "A Nineteenth-Century French Feminist Rediscovered."

25. See Schappes, "Ernestine L. Rose"; and Basch, "The Rose of America."

26. Gripenberg, Matkapaïväkirjoja (Travel diaries), Oct. 6, 1888.

27. Sturge to Aleksandra Gripenberg, July 30, [1890?].

28. Hughes, *Sophia Sturge,* 44.

29. Sturge to Gripenberg, July 30 [1890?].

30. Bremer, *Appeal to the Women of the World.*

31. Hughes, *Sophia Sturge,* 81–110.

32. Sklar, "Women Who Speak for an Entire Nation," 314.

Chapter 2. Paving the Way

1. Klancher, "Reading the Social Text," 184–85.

2. Zboray, *A Fictive People,* 84.

3. C. Beecher, *Harriet Beecher Stowe in Europe,* 320. Further page citations to this work are noted parenthetically in the text.

4. Fuller, *The American Mail,* 110, 125.

5. Zboray, *A Fictive People,* 13.

6. Fuller, *The American Mail,* 70.

7. Hargest, *History of Letter Post Communication,* 18.

8. Fuller, *The American Mail,* 213.

9. Robinson, *The British Post Office,* 233, 230.

10. Ibid., 308.

11. Gourvish, "Railways 1830–1870," 57, 77; Robinson, *The British Post Office,* 242.

12. Tute, *Atlantic Conquest,* 6; *Encyclopedia Britannica,* 15th ed., s.v. "Samuel Cunard."

13. Robinson, *The British Post Office,* 308.

14. Wyman, *Round-Trip to America*, 6.

15. Usherwood, "Travel Agents Extraordinary," 650–51.

16. Marx, "Communist Manifesto," 17.

17. Pemble, *The Mediterranean Passion*, 78. For a detailed look at the connection between industrial capitalism and the realm of leisure as embodied in the tourism industry, see Böröcz, "Travel-Capitalism."

18. Wright, *Society and Manners*.

19. See Trollope, "An Unprotected Female at the Pyramids," and "The Unprotected Female Tourist." Henry James's caricatured female characters, such as the excited school teacher in "Four Meetings," were less often "unprotected." See also Pemble, *The Mediterranean Passion*, 77–78.

20. Trollope, "The Unprotected Female Tourist," 39, 40, 42.

21. See, e.g., [Lowe], *Unprotected Females in Norway;* [Lowe], *Unprotected Females in Sicily;* Tristan, *Nécessité de faire un bon accueil aux femmes étrangères.* Also see Jones, *European Travel for Women;* and Mansfield, *The American Woman Abroad.*

22. [Lowe], *Unprotected Females in Norway,* 3. The book was published anonymously, as was the second in the series (*Unprotected Females in Sicily*). Since the narrator of the second book refers often to the first journey (to Norway), we can assume they were written by the same person; another piece of evidence is the fact that Cobbe refers to "the handsome young 'Unprotected Female' from Norway and Sicily" in her *Italics,* 422.

Duke University's copy of the first gives "Emily Lowe" as the author; the copy of the second in the Library of Congress cites "Helen Lowe" as author. See also Ryall, "Reisebeskrivelser," which examines the problems involved in using travel writing as factual source. It focuses particularly on a new annotated Norwegian translation of Lowe's text whose editor, Åse Enerstvedt, has discovered that indeed "Mrs. and Miss Lowe from England" stayed at Sontums Hotel in Bergen, August 29, 1856—but the problem of the given name is not solved.

23. Kirkland, *Holidays Abroad,* quoted in Dulles, *Americans Abroad,* 75.

24. Lowe has some amusing things to say about Sicilian attitudes to the fact that she and her mother were traveling "unaccompanied": "Till fairly inside the carriage, no one believed we would start, as to see ladies travel alone in Sicily is as uncommon as in Norway; the countenance of a native alone could express the dismay at women who 'Girare senza esser accompagnate!!' ('Travel unaccompanied!!!') that is the sum of horror, an escort being as indispensable as money to an Italian lady unhappy enough to be obliged to travel twenty miles; and a hint at the ascent of Ætna, put them into a fury of 'Impossibile!' which encouraging expression accompanied us to the foot of the mountain" (*Unprotected Females in Sicily,* 41).

25. John Murray, *Handbook for Travellers in Southern Italy,* xlvii. Murray published a series of such handbooks for different countries, the first ones appearing in the 1830s; each was regularly updated.

26. Gordon, *Letters from Egypt,* 155.

27. Cobbe, *Life,* 1:201. Further page references to this work are included parenthetically in the text.

28. Cobbe, *Italics*, 428.
29. Bremer, *The Homes of the New World*.
30. See A. Smith, *Eastern Pilgrims;* and Price, *The Ladies of Castlebrae*.
31. Gladstone, *Travels of Alexine*, 12, 75, 78.
32. Stark, *The Freya Stark Story*, "Author's Note," vi.
33. Levine, Introduction to *Untrodden Peaks and Unfrequented Valleys*, xx.
34. There are, by now, many studies of this complex relationship. For a variety of perspectives, see Brantlinger, *Rule of Darkness;* Spivack, *In Other Worlds;* Burton, "The White Woman's Burden"; Rupp, "Challenging Imperialism in International Women's Organizations"; Mohanty, Russo, and Torres, *Third World Women*.
35. Hatem, "Through Each Other's Eyes."
36. See Lott, *Harem Life in Egypt and Constantinople;* Leonowens, *The English Governess at the Siamese Court,* and *The Romance of the Harem;* and Roos, *Travels in America*.
37. Seacole, *Wonderful Adventures of Mrs. Seacole in Many Lands*.
38. Cunningham, *Cummy's Diary*, esp. 47–49, 54–55, 93.

Chapter 3. The Ironies of Pentecost

1. Thistlethwaite, *The Anglo-American Connection*, 86, 87.
2. For an earlier version of this chapter, see McFadden, "The Ironies of Pentecost: Phoebe Palmer, World Evangelism, and Female Networks."
3. E. Thomas, *Women Religious History Sources*, 169–80.
4. Ewens, "The Leadership of Nuns in Immigrant Catholicism," 101.
5. Code, "Mother Cornelia Connelly."
6. Connelly, *A Religious of the Society*. See also Flaxman, *A Woman Styled Bold*.
7. See Guérin, *Journals and Letters*.
8. See Code, "Mother Philippine Duchesne"; Mooney, *Philippine Duchesne;* and pamphlets from Old St. Ferdinand's Shrine, Florissant, Mo.
9. Ewens, "The Leadership of Nuns in Immigrant Catholicism," 107.
10. Quoted from *Berättelse och Redovisning af Fruntimmers Bibel-Sällskapets i Stockholm Comité* (1828, 18), in Åberg, "Revivalism, Philanthropy and Emancipation," 404.
11. Carwardine, *Transatlantic Revivalism*, 107, 106. See also Hardesty, *Women Called to Witness*.
12. Gillespie, "The Clear Leadings of Providence," 214–16.
13. Cott, "Feminist Theory and Feminist Movements," 50.
14. O. Anderson, "Women Preachers in Mid-Victorian Britain."
15. Ibid., 480.
16. Significantly, however, in the Associated Press obituary for Catherine Bramwell-Booth (dead in 1987 at 104), granddaughter of William and Catherine Booth and daughter of Bramwell Booth, no mention is made of Catherine Booth as cofounder of the Salvation Army, or of Evangeline Booth (her aunt) as its first woman general. The article says only that Catherine Bramwell-Booth was appointed commissioner, "the highest rank below the movement's only general,"

in 1927 ("Obituary: Salvation Army Leader in England"). This is how women's history is erased and lost.

17. E.C. Stanton, Anthony, and Gage, *History of Woman Suffrage*, 1:424.

18. J. Wesley, Letter to Mary Bosanquet, June 13, 1771. See also E.K. Brown, "Women of the Word."

19. [Palmer], *Promise of the Father*, vi.

20. Gillespie, "The Clear Leadings of Providence," 211.

21. Amanda Smith, *An Autobiography*, 278–79.

22. Mildred Duff, *Hedvig von Haartman*, 25.

23. Gulin, *En Herrgårdsfröken i uniform.*

24. Noted in Hardesty, "Minister as Prophet? Or as Mother?" 88, citing S. Olin Garrison, ed., *Forty Witnesses* (New York: Phillips & Hunt, 1888; rpt., Freeport, Pa: Fountain Press, 1955), 73. See also Bordin, *Frances Willard*, 156. Bordin asks for caution in interpreting Willard's diaries from the time of her Holiness experience. The fact remains, however, that Palmer was influential in Willard's life and her later international perspective. Tyrrell analyzes astutely the connections between millennialism, Holiness, and international temperance work in *Woman's World/Woman's Empire*, esp. 23–26.

25. Another example of an early international female preacher is Australian Catherine Helen Spence, who left the Anglican faith for the Unitarian so that she would be able to preach. Her published work includes some sixty extant sermons; she preached in England and the United States as well as in Australia. Her papers are in the Mortlock Library, State Library of South Australia, Adelaide.

26. Quoted in Raser, *Phoebe Palmer*, 249. Cott, among others, has noted (in *The Bonds of Womanhood*, 90) the frequent correlation between women's conversion experiences and the deaths of their children.

27. H.A.R. Rogers, *Experience and Spiritual Letters*. It is worthwhile noting that the "spiritual letters" are often addressed "My Dear Sister"; the concept of sisterhood which was first used by secular feminists in the early nineteenth century must surely be traced to the idea of "sisterhood in Christ," as well as to the French Revolution's ideal of *Fraternité*.

28. Carwardine, *Transatlantic Revivalism*, 182–83.

29. [Palmer], *Four Years in the Old World*, e.g., 382–86, 403, 411–12.

30. Carwardine, *Transatlantic Revivalism*, 183–84.

31. Hovet, "Phoebe Palmer's 'Altar Phraseology.'"

32. Ibid., 278–79; Palmer, *Promise of the Father*, 311–21; Charles Taylor, *Hegel*, 563.

33. Palmer, *Promise of the Father*, 98–99.

34. Amanda Smith, *An Autobiography*, 498.

35. Flexner, *An American Saga*, 160–61.

36. D. Campbell, "Hannah Whitall Smith," 88.

37. Quoted in B. Strachey, *Remarkable Relations*, 102. The similarity to Virginia Woolf's famous sentences in *Three Guineas* (1938) is almost too striking: "As a woman, I have no country. As a woman I want no country. As a woman my

country is the whole world" (109). Granddaughter Ray married Oliver Strachey, and granddaughter Karin married Adrian Stephen, Virginia Woolf's brother.

38. D. Campbell, "Hannah Whitall Smith," 81.

39. Quoted in ibid., 95.

40. *Report of the International Council of Women*, 114–16.

41. Quoted in R. Strachey, *A Quaker Grandmother*, 131.

42. Cott, "Feminist Theory and Feminist Movements," 50–52.

Chapter 4. Unwitting Allies

1. I analyze Stowe before Sand, even though Sand's notoriety preceded Stowe's by some twenty years, because of internal structural considerations: Stowe's reading of Sand's novels provides the link between them; additionally, ending the chapter with Sand's connections to the early Russian revolutionaries leads the way to the political women in the next chapter.

2. C.E. Stowe, *Life of Harriet Beecher Stowe*, 160. Further references to this work are cited parenthetically in the text as *Life*.

3. "Uncle Tomitudes," 99.

4. Many were shown in the "Sunny Memories" exhibit, 1993–94.

5. C. Beecher, *Harriet Beecher Stowe in Europe*, 34. Subsequent page references to this work are cited parenthetically in the text as Beecher.

6. Rodgers and Hammerstein, *The King and I*, 135–63.

7. Landon, *Anna and the King of Siam*, 376. See also Leonowens, *The English Governess at the Siamese Court*, and *The Romance of the Harem*.

8. Landon, *Anna and the King of Siam*, 385. Donaldson discusses "The Small House of Uncle Thomas" in *Decolonizing Feminisms*, 32–51; her argument emphasizes the imperialist penchant for reducing the Other to the Same.

9. Charles Beecher's journal was not published until 1986. H.B. Stowe, *Sunny Memories of Foreign Lands*, has never been republished since 1854 and is not included in the sixteen-volume *Writings of Harriet Beecher Stowe* (1896).

10. See Shepperson, "Harriet Beecher Stowe and Scotland."

11. Cited in ibid., 41.

12. Cobbe, *Italics*, 416.

13. "Introductory" to H.B. Stowe, *Sunny Memories*, 1:xxxviii.

14. Ibid., xx.

15. Ibid., xxiv.

16. The closely woven mesh of international women's connectedness is nicely illustrated here. In 1867 Louise Belloc became the mother-in-law of Bessie Rayner Parkes, English feminist and close friend of Barbara Bodichon (see Chapter 1). Bessie Belloc's second child was Hilaire Belloc (1870–1953), the English writer, politician, and Roman Catholic intellectual. See Wilson, *Hilaire Belloc*, 5, 6, 21.

17. H.B. Stowe, *Sunny Memories*, 2:389.

18. Bremer, *The Homes of the New World*, 2:653–54.

19. Thurs. Sept. 1, 1853: "Hatty read Miss Bremer's *Homes in the West* and I read the end of *Bleak House*."

20. Thomson, "George Sand and English Reviewers."

21. E.C. Stanton, Anthony, and Gage, *History of Woman Suffrage*, 3:896a.

22. Stites, *The Women's Liberation Movement in Russia*, 23–24.

23. Ibid., 22.

24. Naginski, *George Sand*, 168.

25. McKenna, "George Sand's Reception in Russia."

26. Stites, *The Women's Liberation Movement in Russia*, 378–80.

27. Codman, *Brook Farm*, 106. Shaw was a neighbor of those at Brook Farm, a close friend of Lydia Maria Child and other abolitionist and reformer women, and the father of Col. Robert G. Shaw, commander of the first "colored" regiment, who was killed at Fort Wagner, S.C., in 1863.

28. Daniels, *Jessie White Mario*, 38–39. Gleadler, *The Early Feminists*, says that Ashurst worked with Matilda Hays and Edmund Larken on the project (60–62).

29. Cited from Fuller's *Memoirs* in Chevigny, *The Woman and the Myth*, 362.

30. Lesser, *Clarkey*, 105.

31. Lerner, *The Feminist Thought of Sarah Grimké*, 38.

32. Lydia Maria Child to Lucy Osgood, June 12, 1857, quoted in Clifford, *Crusader for Freedom*, 88.

33. T. Stanton, *The Woman Question in Europe*, 390.

34. Stenwall, *Den frivilligt ödmjuka kvinnan*, 23–24.

35. Hirsch, "Barbara Leigh Smith Bodichon," 179.

36. Mermin, *Godiva's Ride*, 20–21. See also P. Brown, "The Reception of George Sand in Spain."

37. Barry, *George Sand, In Her Own Words*, xxxviii.

38. Sand, "To Members of the Central Committee of the Left."

39. See O'Brien, "George Sand and Feminism."

40. Letter to Lucy Osgood, June 12, 1858, in Child, *Selected Letters*, 316.

41. Sand, *Histoire de ma vie*, 2:117–18; trans. and quoted in Naginski, *George Sand*, 20.

42. Malmström, "Kvinnliga pionjärer inom finländsk bildkonst från 1840- till 1880–talet," 40.

43. Dekker and van de Pol, *The Tradition of Female Transvestism*, 2.

44. Garber, *Vested Interests*, 17. See also Wheelwright, *Amazons and Military Maids*.

45. Quoted from Sand's correspondence in Naginski, *George Sand*, 21. Naginski's whole chapter is relevant here.

46. Yellin, *Women and Sisters*, 10–19.

Chapter 5. A Developing Consciousness

1. Lattek, "Women in Exile."

2. Ashton, *Little Germany*, 219.

3. Lattek, "An International Network of Women," typescript.

4. Ashton, *Little Germany*, 210.

5. Kinkel, Letter to Auguste Heinrich, June 20, 1852, quoted in Adelheid von

Asten-Kinkel, "Johanna Kinkel in England," *Deutsche Revue* 26 (Jan.-Mar. 1901):75.

6. See portions translated in Meysenbug, *Rebel in Bombazine.*

7. See Secci, "German Women Writers and the Revolution of 1848," 169.

8. See Joeres, "The Triumph of the Woman."

9. See Ashton, *Little Germany,* 201–2.

10. Lattek, "An International Network of Women," 15–16.

11. Ashton, *Little Germany,* 211.

12. Ibid., 212–17.

13. Zucker, "German Women and the Revolution of 1848," esp. 250–51.

14. Leitenberger, "Austria," 186–87.

15. See Anneke, *Mathilde Franziska Anneke in Selbstzeugnissen und Dokumenten,* and Wittke, "Mathilde Franziska Anneke."

16. Wagner, "A German Writer and Feminist," 161.

17. Different stories are told about her costume. Secci ("German Women Writers," 157) quotes Anneke's defense against the gossip about her masculine attire and weapons: "I was at my husband's side, unarmed, and in my usual woman's clothing, with only the addition of linen trousers for riding."

18. Wittke, "Mathilde Franziska Anneke."

19. "National Honor Sought for Madame Anneke."

20. Wagner, "A German Writer and Feminist," 171–72.

21. Deroin and Roland, "Letter to the Convention of the Women of America," June 15, 1851.

22. Moses, *French Feminism in the Nineteenth Century,* 149.

23. See Riot-Sarcey, "La conscience feministe des femmes de 1848"; and Moses, *French Feminism.* See also Riot-Sarcey, *La democratie à l'epreuve des femmes;* and Scott, *Only Paradoxes to Offer.*

24. Quoted in "Anne Knight, a Woman's Pioneer."

25. E. Willard, "Letter to DuPont de l'Eure on the Political Position of Women." I thank Karen Offen, Stanford University's Center for Research on Women and Gender, for providing a copy of this document.

26. For background on Kossuth and the Hungarian Revolution, see Headley, *The Life of Louis Kossuth*; and Spencer, *Louis Kossuth and Young America.*

27. Pulszky and Pulszky, *White, Red, Black,* 2:111–12, 301, 306–15.

28. Ibid., 1:156–57.

29. Ibid., 2:6–8.

30. For this story and many other interesting ones, particularly in the area of women's philanthropy in Czechoslovakia, see Volet-Jeanneret, "La femme bourgeoise à Prague," 173,110.

31. Ibid., 109–10. See also Krásnohorská, "Bohemia."

32. Reinfeld, "Charlotte Garrigue Masaryk."

33. B. Smith, *Changing Lives,* 222.

34. Brombert, *Cristina,* 61–62. For more on Belgiojoso, see Veauvy, *Parole oubliées.*

35. Brombert, *Cristina,* 73.

36. See Belgiojoso, *Asie Mineure et Syrie;* and Brombert, *Cristina,* chap. 7, "The Last Odyssey," 196–209.

37. Brombert, *Cristina*, 212.

38. Daniels, *Jessie White Mario*, 38–39.

39. Ibid., chap. 4, "Prison and Marriage," 60–73.

40. Ibid., 79–81.

41. Ibid., chap. 6, "The Marios and the Redshirts," 87–99.

42. Ibid., 140, quoting letters from George Eliot.

43. On Margaret Fuller, see Chevigny, *The Woman and the Myth*.

44. M. Fuller, "These Sad but Glorious Days," 4. Subsequent page citations of this work are noted parenthetically in the text.

45. Quoted in Chevigny, *The Woman and the Myth*, 362, from Fuller's *Memoirs*.

46. Engel, *Mothers and Daughters*, 38; see also Zimmerman, "Natalie Herzen and the Early Intelligentsia."

47. Quoted in Carr, *The Romantic Exiles*, 64–65.

48. Karp, "George Sand and the Russians," 157.

49. Bremer, *Greece and the Greeks*, 1:271, 306, 271–72.

50. Much of Aurora Karamzin's correspondence is located in the National Archives in Helsinki and awaits analysis.

51. See Kennedy, *Little Sparrow;* and Leffler, *En Självbiografi.*

52. On Mikhailov, see Stites, *The Women's Liberation Movement in Russia*, 38–48.

53. On d'Héricourt, see Offen, "A Nineteenth-Century French Feminist Rediscovered."

54. Bonner, "Rendezvous in Zurich."

55. Engel and Rosenthal, Introduction to *Five Sisters*, xxiii.

Chapter 6. Higher Consciousness

1. See the suggestive sociometry on the various reform connections between the early women's rights women in Rossi, "Social Roots of the Woman's Movement," 276.

2. See Allen, "The Genealogy of German Feminism."

3. See, e.g., Rossi, "Social Roots of the Woman's Movement"; DuBois, *Feminism and Suffrage;* Rendall, *The Origins of Modern Feminism;* Hersh, *The Slavery of Sex;* B. Taylor, *Eve and the New Jerusalem;* Moses, "Saint-Simonian Men/Saint-Simonian Women"; Tyrrell, *Woman's World, Woman's Empire;* Bordin, *Woman and Temperance;* Liddington, *The Road to Greenham Common.*

4. The international women's organizations discussed in all the following sources are those of the later period at the end of the nineteenth and beginning of the twentieth centuries: Hurwitz, "The International Sisterhood"; Sherrick, "Toward Universal Sisterhood"; Rupp, "Constructing Internationalism," and *Worlds of Women;* Holton, "To Educate Women into Rebellion," and "From Anti-Slavery to Suffrage Militancy"; Tyrrell, *Woman's World, Woman's Empire.*

5. Bacon, *Mothers of Feminism*, 77.

6. Schappes, "Ernestine L. Rose," 346.

7. Thistlethwaite, *The Anglo-American Connection*, 123, quoting a letter from Child to E. Carpenter, Sept. 6, 1838.

8. Yellin, *Women and Sisters*, 10.

9. Mott, *Slavery and "The Woman Question,"* 23.

10. Thistlethwaite, *The Anglo-American Connection*, 123.

11. Published in 1843, it responded to the popular *Woman's Mission*, published in 1839 by Sarah Lewis. On Marion Kirkland Reid and Sarah Lewis, see Helsinger, Sheets, and Veeder, *The Woman Question*, esp. 3–20.

12. See Clifford, *Crusader for Freedom*, for Child's biographical details; for a good selection of her voluminous correspondence, see *Lydia Maria Child: Selected Letters*.

13. Child to Ellis Gray Loring, August 11, 1841.

14. Mott, *Slavery and "The Woman Question,"* 56.

15. Lerner, *The Grimké Sisters from South Carolina*; see also Bartlett, *Sarah Grimké's Letters on the Equality of the Sexes*.

16. Sklar, "Women Who Speak for an Entire Nation," 317n. 36.

17. See letters 47, 51, 54, e.g., in Taylor's *British and American Abolitionists*.

18. See letters in Lerner, *The Feminist Thought of Sarah Grimké*, 119–22, 149–51.

19. "A Colored Lady Lecturer."

20. D.P. Wesley, "Sarah Parker Remond"; also see Porter, "Sarah Parker Remond"; and Bogin, "Sarah Parker Remond."

21. McFeely, *Frederick Douglass*, 328–29.

22. See "Abolition Movement," in *Black Women in America: An Historical Encyclopedia* (Brooklyn, New York: Carlson, 1993), 1:8. See also Giddings, *When and Where I Enter*; Yee, *Black Women Abolitionists*; and Richardson, *Maria W. Stewart*.

23. See Buhle and Buhle, *The Concise History of Woman Suffrage*, 139–40, 150.

24. Mott, *Slavery and the "Woman Question"*; see, e.g., 32, 34.

25. Tyrrell, *Woman's World, Woman's Empire*, 13, quoting Willard Diary, Feb. 24, 1869, bk. 3, p. 3, roll 3, WCTU Series, 1982, Supp., Mich. Historical Collections, William R. Clements Library, University of Michigan; also printed in F. Willard, *Woman and Temperance*, 23.

26. Tyrrell, *Woman's World, Woman's Empire*, 12, 24.

27. Ibid., 20, quoting from Eliza Stewart, *The Crusader in Great Britain* (Springfield, Ohio: New Era, 1893), 83.

28. Ibid., 86–87; Ackermann, *Australia from a Woman's Point of View*.

29. Tyrrell, *Woman's World, Woman's Empire*, 28–29. For additional details, see Offen, "Contextualizing the Theory and Practice of Feminism."

30. Mott, *Slavery and "The Woman Question,"* 75.

31. Smith-Rosenberg, "Beauty, the Beast, and the Militant Woman"; Stansell, "Women, Children, and the Uses of the Streets"; and Walkowitz, *Prostitution and Victorian Society*. See also Berg, *The Remembered Gate*.

32. On Butler's life and work, see Forster, *Significant Sisters*, 167–202; Boyd, *Three Victorian Women*, 23–89; and Fisher, "Josephine Butler."

33. Käppeli, "Between High and Low."

34. See, for a good analysis of the connections, Tyrrell, *Woman's World,*

Woman's Empire, chap. 9, "A Fatal Mistake? The Contest for Social Purity," 191–220.

35. Barash, *Introduction to Peace Studies,* 61–62. See also Nuttall, *Christian Pacifism in History;* Alonso, *Peace as a Women's Issue;* and Cooper, *Patriotic Pacifism.*

36. Clayhills, "Fredsrörelsen [Peace Movement]," 140.

37. Quoted in Bremer, *Fredrika Bremers Brev,* 3:567.

38. Bremer, *Appeal to the Women of the World,* 5–6.

39. Rahm, *Marie Goegg,* esp. 81–85.

40. See Hamann, *Bertha von Suttner.*

41. Quoted in Brock-Utne, *Educating for Peace,* 41.

42. Lengyel, *And All Her Paths Were Peace,* 81.

43. Brock-Utne, *Educating for Peace,* 44.

44. Ritchie, "Visions of a United Europe."

45. Lengyel, *And All Her Paths Were Peace,* 116.

46. Costin, "Feminism, Pacifism, Internationalism"; and Braker, "Bertha von Suttner's Spiritual Daughters."

47. Cooper, "The Work of Women in Nineteenth Century Continental European Peace Movements," and her *Patriotic Pacifism.* Clayhills, "Fredsrörelsen [Peace Movement]," has summarized the situation of women in the history of the international peace movement, particularly from the Swedish perspective.

48. Also see Margaret McFadden, "Peace Movement and Women," *Women's Issues: Ready Reference* (Englewood Cliffs, N.J.: Salem Press, 1997), 2:656–57.

49. For the Shakers, see E.D. Andrews, *The People Called Shakers* and *The Hancock Shakers.* For an old but still useful comparative study, see Webber, *Escape to Utopia.* See also Foster, *Women, Family, and Utopia;* Chmielewski, Kern, and Klee-Hartzell, *Women in Spiritual and Communitarian Societies;* Kolmerten, *Women in Utopia;* Richter, *Utopias.*

50. Quoted in Shepperson, "The Comparative Study of Millenarian Movements," 52, from Richard T. Hooker, ed., *The Carolina Backcountry on the Eve of the Revolution* (Chapel Hill: Univ. of North Carolina Press, 1935), 78.

51. See Ruether and Keller, *Women and Religion in America,* vol. 1, *The Nineteenth Century.*

52. See Moses, *French Feminism in the Nineteenth Century;* and Grogan, *French Socialism and Sexual Difference.*

53. Quoted in Moses, "Saint-Simonian Men/Saint-Simonian Women," 264.

54. See Voilquin, *Souvenirs d'une fille du peuple.*

55. Voilquin, *Mémoires d'une Saint-Simonienne en Russie.* These letters were published only posthumously.

56. Voilquin may have practiced medicine in New Orleans, but little is known; see Albistur and Armogathe, "Introduction: Une Vie," 24.

57. Polasky, "Utopia and Domesticity."

58. Moon, "Feminism and Socialism," 23.

59. Tristan, *London Journal,* 208–12.

60. Moon, "Feminism and Socialism," 38–40.

61. B. Taylor, *Eve and the New Jerusalem,* 20.

62. Mott, *Slavery and "The Woman Question,"* 57. Owen had explained his system to her; she called it "altogether visionary" (51).

63. For a selection of Frances Wright's work, see Rossi, *The Feminist Papers.* Of several biographies, the best one is Eckhardt, *Fanny Wright.*

Chapter 7. Mothers of the Matrix (I)

1. The phrase was used by Elizabeth Pease in a letter to Maria Weston Chapman in 1853, and quoted in Sklar, "Women Who Speak for an Entire Nation," 320.

2. Offen, "Defining Feminism," and the subsequent discussion in later issues of *Signs.*

3. Offen, "Challenging Male Hegemony," 22. See also Snitow, "A Gender Diary"; and McFadden, "Feminism."

4. Doyle, *A Hundred Years of Conflict.*

5. Galgano, "Anna Doyle Wheeler."

6. Devey, *Life of Rosina,* "Autobiographical," 1-12. This volume includes Rosina's manuscript autobiography.

7. Earlier sources disagree as to the date of Francis Massey Wheeler's death. Galgano (ibid.) and Pankhurst, "Anna Wheeler," follow Devey, *Life of Rosina,* and use 1820, but Sadleir, *Bulwer and His Wife,* says 1823. I have been unable to locate a death certificate or grave marker in any available records in Clonbeg Parish or at the Diocesan Library in Cashel; records for Clonbeg and Galbally Parishes were among those destroyed in the fire at the Public Records Office in Dublin in 1922.

8. For an earlier version of this material, see McFadden, "Anna Doyle Wheeler." The available biographical materials on Wheeler are all dependent on two early sources, written in the wake of the scandal surrounding the separation between Wheeler's daughter Rosina and the British novelist Bulwer-Lytton in 1836.

Devey's *Life of Rosina* takes Rosina's side; Sadleir's *Bulwer and His Wife* puts all the blame on Rosina and reflects the Lytton attitude toward Rosina and her family: "[Sir John] chose resignation and quick departure, because by this means at least he would be rid of women who had only sought him out for what they could get. . . . Apprised of his immediate retirement to London, Mrs. Wheeler gave way to one final burst of rage and, late in 1816 or early in 1817, sailed for France. In a few months she had become 'Goddess of Reason' to a small group of embittered cranks in Caen. Her unhappy children played acolyte on either side of her altar" (Sadleir, 76). The most sympathetic view of Rosina was that she was the "product" of a terrible upbringing, her mother having abdicated her maternal responsibilities. Even in the sources sympathetic to Rosina, therefore, Anna is seen as money-grubbing and, worse, as a radical intellectual. This view is part of the reason that Anna has been erased from history. Like Mary Wollstonecraft and Frances Wright before her, her political views and personal life were anathema to respectable women, and so her life and works simply were omitted from later accounts of early feminism and socialism.

As might be expected, the sources available are not entirely dependable; they contain several errors and contradict each other. For example, although Ballywire is located in County Tipperary, in Devey's account Rosina says not only that it is in County Limerick (it *is* on the border of the two counties) but that it is on the western *coast* of Ireland. She describes in great detail the house at Ballywire, and in most respects she is correct (stone turret, marble fireplaces, carved ceilings), but the memory-imagination of the eight-year-old Rosina added to the surroundings a high cliff over crashing waves and a view of the sea to the west (10–11). This is pure fantasy; the view is the relatively tame Glen of Aherlow in the southwestern part of County Tipperary. Further, Anna Wheeler's father is said to be an archbishop in Sadleir and later sources (Devey says archdeacon); he was in fact an archdeacon and a prebendary, entirely different offices (Leslie, "Biographical Index of the Clergy of the Church of Ireland," 1:326). There was a *Catholic* archbishop Doyle (James Warren Doyle, bishop of Kildare and Leighlin) at this time in Ireland, so one can see how this error has crept in.

9. Gans, "Les relations entre socialistes de France et d'Angleterre."

10. E.g., Wheeler, trans., "Appel aux femmes," by Jeanne-Victoire [pseud.].

11. Wheeler, letter to Charles Fourier, 28 May 1833. I am indebted to Karen Offen, Center for Research on Women and Gender, Stanford University, for her notes on this letter and for calling it to my attention.

12. Tristan, *The London Journal,* 208–14.

13. Register of Deaths, Saint Pancras, 7 May 1848, 51 High Street, Entry of Death # 395 for "Ann Doyle Wheeler," General Register Office, London.

14. W. Thompson, *Appeal of One Half the Human Race,* 107. Further page references to this edition are noted parenthetically in the text.

15. Wheeler, "Rights of Women," 35.

16. Ibid., 13-14.

17. Ibid., 36.

18. Stephen Burke, "Letter from a Pioneer Feminist," 22.

19. Wheeler, letter to Charles Fourier, 30 July 1830. Again I am indebted to Karen Offen for her notes on this letter and for calling it to my attention.

20. See Blain, "Rosina Bulwer Lytton"; and McFadden, "Rosina Wheeler Bulwer-Lytton."

21. E.C. Stanton, Anthony, and Gage, *History of Woman Suffrage,* 1:42. This chapter, written by Matilda Joslyn Gage, ends with three paragraphs on European precursors.

22. A recent book on Thompson and Wheeler—Dooley, *Equality in Community*—unfortunately misrepresents my thesis and takes no account of the primary research and new material I use in McFadden, "Anna Doyle Wheeler."

23. E.C. Stanton, *Eighty Years and More,* 80–81, 82–83. Further references to this work are noted parenthetically in the text. One should remember that Stanton's autobiography was begun only very late in her life, and her memory of earlier events is colored by the later struggles and triumphs. Thus, her analysis of the 1840 convention fight to seat women is predicated on the work on theology and the Bible which culminated in her publication of *The Woman's Bible* (1895–98), completed in the same year as *Eighty Years and More.* As Ann D. Gordon points out in her afterword to *Eighty Years and More* (477), only after 1880,

the year that Stanton began keeping a diary, do events in the autobiography follow a close chronology rather than a structure based on Stanton's understanding and analysis of the *meaning* of the events of her life.

24. B. Anderson, "The Lid Comes Off." We should note, however, that Stanton did not mention the repression of the campaigns for women's rights that had taken place in Europe by July 1848.

25. E.C. Stanton, reprinted in K.K. Campbell, *Man Cannot Speak for Her,* 2:43.

26. Mill, "The Enfranchisement of Women."

27. Stanton, Anthony, and Gage, *History of Woman Suffrage,* 1:229–31.

28. Ibid., 1:234–37.

Chapter 8. Mothers of the Matrix (II)

1. Lugones, "Playfulness, 'World'-Traveling, and Loving Perception," 282. Further page references to this article are noted parenthetically in the text.

2. The term "lesbian" was not used in the nineteenth century for women whose romantic and/or sexual involvement was with other women. I use it here as a kind of shorthand, since the terms "romantic friendship" and "Boston marriage" refer to the relationship, not the individual.

3. C. Bremer. *Life, Letters & Posthumous Works of Fredrika Bremer,* 60.

4. Faderman, *Surpassing the Love of Men,* 225.

5. Anne-Charlotte Leffler, *En Självbiografi;* Kennedy, *Little Sparrow.*

6. Cobbe, *Italics,* 420.

7. Cobbe, *Life,* 1:v.

8. C. Bremer, *Life, Letters, & Posthumous Works of Fredrika Bremer,* 43.

9. The secondary literature on Fredrika Bremer in English is surprisingly sparse. The basic work is Rooth, *Seeress of the Northland,* which reprints much from the diaries and letters; there is also a biography, Stendahl, *The Education of a Self-made Woman.* The standard biography in Swedish is Qvist, *Fredrika Bremer och kvinnans emancipation.* See also Kleman, *Fredrika Bremer and America.*

10. Ryall, "Domesticating Geographical Exploration."

11. Bremer, letters to Anne Howland, Jan. 28, 1852, and April 15, 1852.

12. Rooth, *Seeress of the Northland,* 97.

13. Bremer, *The Homes of the New World,* 2:426–27.

14. Bremer, letters to Anne Howland, April 15, 1852, and April 2, 1853.

15. Bremer to Dorothea Dix, Nov. 2, 1850, in *Fredrika Bremers Brev,* 3:letter 761.

16. Bremer, *Appeal to the Women of the World,* 7–8.

17. Bremer, *Fredrika Bremers Brev,* 3:567.

18. Martineau, *Autobiography,* 428.

19. See Costin, "Feminism, Pacifism, Internationalism."

20. Bremer, *Life in the Old World,* 1:229. Further page references to this work are included parenthetically in the text.

21. Lugones, "Playfulness, 'World'-Traveling, and Loving Perception."

22. Bremer, *Fredrika Bremers Brev,* 1:478–79 (transl. by Ann-Catrin Östman).

23. Martineau, *Autobiography*, 428.

24. Bremer, "Jenny Lind."

25. Montén, *Fredrika Bremer in Deutschland*, 194.

26. Margaret Howitt published a book about her stay, *Twelve Months with Fredrika Bremer in Sweden*, 2 vols. (London: Jackson, Walford & Hodder, 1866).

27. Bremer, letter to Louisa Norderling, August 31, 1865, in *Fredrika Bremers Brev*, 4: letter 1298.

28. Kleman, *Fredrika Bremer and America*, 16.

29. Cobbe, *Life*, 1:13–14. Further page references to this work are included parenthetically in the text.

30. Parker, *Collected Works*, 1:306.

31. Ibid., xviii.

32. Caine, *Victorian Feminists*, 117–18.

33. Cobbe, *Essay on Intuitive Morals*, 9.

34. Cobbe, *Essay on Intuitive Morals, Part II*, 87.

35. Cobbe, *Essay on Intuitive Morals*, 173.

36. See Mermin, *Godiva's Ride*, 123–25.

37. For more details about this expatriate community of "emancipated women," see Caine, *Victorian Feminists*, 120–21. For details from Cobbe, see her *Italics*, 412–16.

38. Cobbe letter to Mrs. Henry Fawcett, Nov. 11, 1896.

39. Atkinson, introduction to *Life of Frances Power Cobbe*.

40. Cobbe, *Criminals, Idiots, Women, and Minors*, 5.

41. In Cobbe, *The Peak in Darien*, 197–262.

42. Cobbe, "The Final Cause of Woman," 21.

43. Cobbe, "Wife-Torture in England," quoted from *Contemporary Review* (1878) in Bauer and Ritt, "A Husband Is a Beating Animal."

44. Quoted in Cobbe, *Light in Dark Places*, 15–17.

45. Caskie, "Frances Power Cobbe," 50.

46. E.C. Stanton, *Eighty Years and More*, 362–3.

47. Carpenter, *In Memoriam: Frances Power Cobbe*, 12.

48. "Addresses to Miss Cobbe," Dec. 4, 1902.

49. Caine, *Victorian Feminists*, 104–5.

Chapter 9. "A Golden Cable of Sympathy"

1. E.C. Stanton, *Eighty Years and More*, 375.

2. *Report of the International Council of Women*, 10.

3. Although an international committee was formed, with representatives from twelve nations, to advance "the reforms called for by the congress and to issue the call" for the next international meeting, no second meeting was ever held; see E.C. Stanton, Anthony, and Gage, *History of Woman Suffrage*, 3:899.

4. Harper, *Life and Work of Susan B. Anthony*, 2:636.

5. *Report of the International Council of Women*, 33, 37.

6. Ibid., 436.

7. Bright, *Submarine Telegraphs*, 112–16.

8. *Kansallinen Elämäkerrasto* [Finnish National Biography] (Porvoo: Osa v. WSOY, 1934).

9. *Report of the International Council of Women*, 425, 437.

10. I should perhaps remind non-Nordic readers that Finland was the first European nation to give women the right to vote.

11. Markkola and Ramsay, *Yksi kamari—kaksi sukupuolta*.

12. Gripenberg, catalogue of personal library (a bound book, arranged by Gripenberg herself).

13. Gripenberg, letter to Caroline Ashurst Biggs, June 6, 1888.

14. Gripenberg, *A Half Year in the New World*, 73–80, 117, 189. Translated first into Swedish and then into Finnish in 1856, *Uncle Tom's Cabin* sold well in Finland (in German and English, as well as in Swedish and Finnish), according to Kero, "The United States during its First Century of Independence as It Appeared in Finnish Print," 40–41.

15. A—ï—a [Ehrnrooth], "To Miss Aleksandra Gripenberg," stanza 2.

16. See von Alfthan, *Sju Årtionden med Unioni Naisasialiito Suomessa*.

17. Gripenberg, letter to Susan B. Anthony, 1903.

18. Gripenberg, *Elizabeth Cady Stanton och Kvinnosaksarbetet*.

19. Maggie Walz, letters to Aleksandra Gripenberg, 1897–98.

20. Information on Walz is from K.M.W. Brown, "Three 'Founding Mothers' of Finnish America."

21. Gripenberg, letter to the Reverend Anne [*sic*] Shaw, Oct. 19, 1911.

22. Wells-Barnett, *Crusade for Justice*, esp. 87–224.

23. In her autobiography (ibid., 117) Wells records that she received communications about the work from Germany, France, Russia, and India.

24. Ibid., 120.

25. Wells-Barnett, *A Red Record*.

Appendix B.

1. Bellah, *Habits of the Heart*. I thank Leslie E. Gerber, my colleague in Interdisciplinary Studies, for much of what appears in this appendix.

2. A useful historical treatment is Wellman, "Structural Analysis."

3. Wellman and Berkowitz, *Social Structures*, i.

4. Laumann, "Network Analysis in Large Social Systems," 391.

5. Breiger, "The Duality of Groups and Persons," 91.

6. E.M. Rogers, "Network Analysis of the Diffusion of Innovations," 146.

7. Barnes, "Network Analysis," 420.

8. See, e.g., Berkowitz, "Afterword: Towards a Formal Structure for Structural Sociology," esp. 493.

Appendix C.

1. See, e.g., Pemble, *The Mediterranean Passion*.

2. Gladstone, *Travels of Alexine,* 208–9. Subsequent page references to this work are included parenthetically in the text.

3. Edwards, *Untrodden Peaks and Unfrequented Valleys,* xxxii.

4. Somerville, *Personal Recollections,* 160. Subsequent page references to this work are included parenthetically in the text.

5. See Patterson, *Mary Somerville and the Cultivation of Science.*

Appendix D.

1. Rye, "Emigration of Educated Women."

2. See Clarke, *The Governesses.*

3. Uglow, "Maria (Susan) Rye."

4. Clarke, *The Governesses,* 210–11.

5. R. Roos, *Travels in America.*

6. Ibid., 150–151.

7. Details from Stewart, Letterbook.

Appendix E.

1. B. Smith, *Changing Lives,* 141. See also Hansen, "Rural Women in Late Nineteenth-Century Denmark."

2. Beaumont, *A Business Woman's Journal.*

3. Seacole, *Wonderful Adventures of Mrs. Seacole in Many Lands,* 8.

4. W. Andrews, Introduction to Seacole, *Wonderful Adventures of Mrs. Seacole,* xxxiii.

5. Nevala, "Women in the Finnish Literary Establishment," 97.

6. Jameson, "Adelaide Kemble."

7. Borg, letter to Marie Sophie Schwartz [1874].

8. See stories in the *Morganbladet* (Helsinki) in 1875: e.g., Aug. 14, 1875, nr 186, p. 2; and Sept. 16, 1875, nr 214, p. 3.

9. E.g., Frederick Underwood, "The Inborn Power and Grace of Selma Borg's Baton at her Finnish Concert," *New York World*, Feb. 15, 1879; clipping from scrapbook in Selma Borg Collection, Sibelius Museum, Åbo Akademi University, Turku, Finland.

10. Providence Press, clipping from scrapbook in Selma Borg Collection, Sibelius Museum, Åbo Akademi University, Finland.

11. See *The Kalevala* (Cambridge: J. Wilson, 1882).

12. Borg, letter to Elisabet Blomqvist, Aug. 24, 1877; Borg, letter, Jan. 21, 1879, Finnish Literature Society (SKS), Helsinki.

13. T. Stanton, *The Woman Question in Europe,* 418.

14. Woodring, *Victorian Samplers,* 225.

Appendix F.

1. Malmström, "Kvinnliga pionjärer inom finlandsk bildkonst," 48; see J.M. Roos, "Another Look at Henry James."

2. For information on all of these Nordic women artists, see *De drogo till Paris,* esp. Werkmäster, "Frigjord eller bunder?" On the Finnish women artists, see Konttinen, *Suomalaisia naistaitelijoita 1880–luvulta* and Konttinen, *Totuus enemmän kuin kauneus.* See also Greer, *The Obstacle Race,* esp. 310–27.

3. Nikula, "Women in the History of Finnish Art," 84.

4. Malmström, "Kvinnliga pionjärer inom finländsk bildkonst," 40.

5. Konttinen, "Finska konstnärinnors 1880-tal." On Schjerfbeck there is a wealth of material, including her correspondence with Helena Westermarck (in the Åbo Akademi University Library Manuscript Collection) and the exhaustive catalogue of the 1992 International Retrospective Exhibition, *Helene Schjerfbeck,* which includes the complete list of works, a chronology, and seven scholarly interpretive articles. There are also earlier studies, including several pieces by Westermarck. Walter Sparrow's groundbreaking *Women Painters of the World* included material on Schjerfbeck in an article on Finnish women artists by Westermarck (see Leena Ahtola-Moorhouse and Lena Holger, "Helene Schjerfbeck memorandum" in *Helene Schjerfbeck,* 312).

6. *Ateneum Guide,* 105.

7. Holger, "Nothing Ventured, Nothing Gained."

8. Bashkirtseff, *Marie Bashkirtseff,* 162.

9. *Ateneum Guide,* 115–18. On the American women in Paris, see Jo Ann Wein, "The Parisian Training of American Women Artists," 43.

Works Cited

Åberg, Ingrid. "Revivalism, Philanthropy, and Emancipation: Women's Liberation and Organization in the Early Nineteenth Century." *Scandinavian Journal of History* 13 (1988): 399–420.

"Abolition Movement." In *Black Women in America: An Historical Encyclopedia.* Vol. 1, no. 8. Brooklyn, N.Y.: Carlson, 1993.

Ackermann, Jessie. *Australia from a Woman's Point of View.* London: Cassell, 1913.

"Addresses to Miss Cobbe," Dec. 4, 1902. Reprint, Fawcett Library, London.

Ahtola-Moorhouse, Leena, and Lena Holger. "Helene Schjerfbeck Memorandum." In *Helene Schjerfbeck,* 303-28. Helsinki: Finnish National Gallery Ateneum, 1992.

A—ï—a [Ehrnrooth, Adelaïde]. "To Miss Aleksandra Gripenberg, Nov. 24, 1888." Trans. Ann-Catrin Östman. Aleksandra Gripenberg Papers, Finnish Literature Society, Helsinki.

Albistur, Maïté, and Daniel Armogathe. "Introduction: Une Vie." In *Mémoires d'une saint-simonienne en russie (1839–1846).* Paris: Des Femmes, 1977.

Allen, Ann Taylor. "The Genealogy of German Feminism." *History of European Ideas* 8, nos. 4-5 (1987):615–19.

Alonso, Harriet Hyman. *Peace as a Women's Issue: A History of the U.S. Movement for World Peace and Women's Rights.* Syracuse, N.Y.: Syracuse Univ. Press, 1993.

Anderson, Bonnie. "The Lid Comes Off: International Radical Feminism and the Revolutions of 1848." *NWSA Journal* 10, no. 2(1998):1-12.

Anderson, Olive. "Women Preachers in Mid-Victorian Britain: Some Reflections on Feminism, Popular Religion, and Social Change." *Historical Journal* 12 (1969): 479–80.

Andreasen, Tayo, et al. *Moving On: New Perspectives on the Women's Movement.* Aarhus, Denmark: Aarhus Univ. Press, 1991.

Andrews, Edward Deming. *The Hancock Shakers.* Hancock, Mass.: Shaker Community, 1961.

———. *The People Called Shakers.* New York: Oxford Univ. Press, 1963.

Andrews, William. Introduction to Mary Seacole, *Wonderful Adventures of Mrs. Seacole in Many Lands.* New York: Oxford Univ. Press, 1988.

Anneke, Mathilde Franziska. *Mathilde Franziska Anneke in Selbstzeugnissen und Dokumenten.* Ed. Maria Wagner. Frankfurt/Main: Fischer-Tauschenbuch, 1980.

"Anne Knight, a Woman's Pioneer." *English Woman's Review,* Jan. 15, 1884, 11.

Anthony, Katharine. *Feminism in Germany and Scandinavia.* New York: Henry Holt, 1915.

Ashton, Rosemary. *Little Germany: Exile and Asylum in Victorian England.* Oxford: Oxford Univ. Press, 1986.

Ateneum Guide, from Isak Wacklin to Wäinö Aaltonen. Helsinki: Otava, 1987.

Atkinson, Blanche. Introduction to *Life of Frances Power Cobbe,* posthumous ed. London: Swan Sonnenschein, 1904.

Bacon, Margaret Hope. *Mothers of Feminism: The Story of Quaker Women in America.* San Francisco: Harper & Row, 1989.

Barash, David. *Introduction to Peace Studies.* Belmont, Calif.: Wadsworth, 1991.

Barnes, John. "Network Analysis: Orienting Notion, Rigorous Technique, or Substantive Field of Study?" In *Perspectives on Social Network Research,* ed. Paul W. Holland and Samuel Leinhardt. New York: Academic Press, 1979.

Barry, Joseph, ed. and trans. *George Sand, In Her Own Words.* New York: Anchor Books, 1979.

Bartlett, Elizabeth Ann, ed. *Sarah Grimké's Letters on the Equality of the Sexes and Other Essays.* New Haven, Conn.: Yale Univ. Press, 1988.

Basch, Françoise. "The Rose of America: Ernestine Louise Potowsky Rose (1810–1892), an International Feminist?" Paper presented to the National Women's Studies Association, Minneapolis, Minn., 1988.

Bashkirtseff, Marie. *Marie Bashkirtseff: The Journal of a Young Artist, 1860–1884.* Trans. Mary J. Serrano. New York: E.P. Dutton, 1919.

Bauer, Carol, and Lawrence Ritt. "'A Husband Is a Beating Animal'—Frances Power Cobbe Confronts the Wife-Abuse Problem in Victorian England." *International Journal of Women's Studies* 6 (March-April 1983): 109–110.

Beaumont, Mrs. B. *A Business Woman's Journal.* Philadelphia: T.B. Peterson, 1888.

Beecher, Charles. *Harriet Beecher Stowe in Europe: The Journal of Charles Beecher.* 1853. Ed. Joseph S. Van Why and Earl French. Hartford: Stowe-Day, 1986.

Belgiojoso, Cristina. *Asie Mineure et Syrie: Souvenirs de voyages.* Paris: M. Levy, 1858.

Bell, Susan Groag, and Karen Offen. *Women, the Family, and Freedom: The Debate in Documents.* 2 vols. Stanford, Calif.: Stanford Univ. Press, 1983.

Bellah, Robert N., et al. *Habits of the Heart: Individualism and Commitment in American Life.* Berkeley: Univ. of California Press, 1985.

Berg, Barbara. *The Remembered Gate: Origins of American Feminism—the Women and the City, 1800–1860.* New York: Oxford Univ. Press, 1975.

Berkowitz, S.D. "Afterword: Towards a Formal Structure for Structural Sociology." In *Social Structures: A Network Approach,* ed. Barry Wellman and S.D. Berkowitz, 477–95. New York: Cambridge Univ. Press, 1988.

Biggs, Caroline Ashurst, to Aleksandra Gripenberg, 1889. Gripenberg Papers, 312.83.8, Finnish Literature Society (SKS), Helsinki.

Blain, Virginia. "Rosina Bulwer Lytton and the Rage of the Unheard." *Huntington Library Quarterly* 53, no. 3 (1990): 211–36.

Bodichon, Barbara Leigh Smith. "Algiers: First Impressions." *English Woman's Journal* 6 (Sept. 1860): 21–32.

———. *An American Diary, 1857–58.* Ed. Joseph W. Reed Jr. London: Routledge & Kegan Paul, 1972.

———. "An American School." *English Woman's Journal* 2 (Nov. 1858): 198–200.

———. "Cleopatra's Daughter, St. Marciana, Mama Marabout, and Other Algerian Women." *English Woman's Journal* 10 (Feb. 1863): 404–16.

———. "Middle Class Schools for Girls." *English Woman's Journal* 6 (Nov. 1860): 168–77.

———. "Slavery in America." *English Woman's Journal* 2 (Oct. 1858): 94–100.

———. "Slave Preaching." *English Woman's Journal* 5 (Mar. 1860): 87–94.

Bogin, Ruth. "Sarah Parker Remond: Black Abolitionist from Salem." *Essex Institute Historical Collections* 110 (1974): 120–50.

Boissevain, Jeremy. *Friends of Friends: Networks, Manipulators, and Coalitions.* Oxford: Basil Blackwell, 1974.

———. "Network Analysis: A Reappraisal." *Current Anthropology* 20, no. 2 (1979): 393.

———. "Networks." In *The Social Science Encyclopedia,* ed. Adam Kuper and Jessica Kuper, 557. London: Routledge & Kegan Paul, 1985.

Bonner, Thomas Neville. "Rendezvous in Zurich: Seven Who Made a Revolution in Women's Medical Education, 1864–1874." *Journal of the History of Medicine and Allied Sciences* 44 (Jan. 1989): 7–27.

Bordin, Ruth. *Frances Willard: A Biography.* Chapel Hill: Univ. of North Carolina Press, 1986.

———. *Woman and Temperance: The Quest for Power and Liberty, 1873–1900.* Philadelphia: Temple Univ. Press, 1981.

Borg, Selma. Letter to Elisabet Blomqvist, August 24, 1877. Manuscript Collection, Blomqvistiana E.B. Helsinki University Library.

———. Letter to Marie Sophie Schwartz [1874]. Royal Library Manuscript Collection, Stockholm.

———. Letter, January 21, 1879. Finnish Literature Society (SKS), Helsinki, Finland.

———. Scrapbook. Selma Borg Collection. Sibelius Museum, Åbo Akademi University, Turku, Finland.

Böröcz, József. "Travel-Capitalism: The Structure of Europe and the Advent of the Tourist." *Comparative Studies in Society and History* 34, no. 4 (1992): 708–41.

Boyd, Nancy. *Three Victorian Women Who Changed Their World.* New York: Oxford Univ. Press, 1982.

Braker, Regina. "Bertha von Suttner's Spiritual Daughters: The Feminist Pacifism of Anita Augspurg, Lida Gustava Heymann, and Helene Stöcker at the International Congress of Women at The Hague, 1915." *Women's Studies International Forum* 18, no. 2 (1995): 103–11.

Brantlinger, Patrick. *Rule of Darkness: British Literature and Imperialism, 1830–1914.* Ithaca, N.Y.: Cornell Univ. Press, 1988.

Breiger, Ronald. "The Duality of Groups and Persons." In *Social Structures: A Network Approach,* ed. Barry Wellman and S.D. Berkowitz. New York: Cambridge Univ. Press, 1988.

Bremer, Charlotte, ed. *Life, Letters, & Posthumous Works of Fredrika Bremer.* Trans. Fredr. Milow. London: Sampson Low, 1868.

Bremer, Fredrika. *Appeal to the Women of the World to Form a Peace Alliance.* 1854. Reprint, Swedish National Council of Women. Stockholm: Aftonbladets Tryckeri, 1915.

———. *Fredrika Bremers Brev* (Fredrika Bremer's Letters). Samlade och Utgivna av Klara Johanson och Ellen Klemen. 4 vols. Stockholm: Norsted, 1915–20.

———. *Greece and the Greeks: The Narrative of a Winter Residence and Summer Travel in Greece and Its Islands.* Trans. Mary Howitt. 2 vols. London: Hurst and Blackett, 1863.

———. *The Homes of the New World: Impressions of America.* Trans. Mary Howitt. 1853. 2 vols. New York: Negro Universities Press, 1968.

———. "Jenny Lind." *Sartain's Magazine,* June 1850, 409–10.

———. Letters to Anne Howland, Jan. 28, 1852, April 15, 1852; April 2, 1853. Fredrika Bremer Collection, L2:31:II, Royal Library, Stockholm.

———. *Life in the Old World, or Two Years in Switzerland and Italy.* Trans. Mary Howitt. 2 vols. Philadelphia: T. B. Peterson, 1860.

Bridenthal, Renate, and Claudia Koonz, eds. *Becoming Visible: Women in European History.* Boston: Houghton Mifflin, 1977.

Bright, Charles. *Submarine Telegraphs: Their History, Construction, and Working.* 1898. New York: Arno Press, 1974.

Brock-Utne, Birgit. *Educating for Peace: A Feminist Perspective.* New York: Pergamon Press, 1985.

Brombert, Beth Archer. *Cristina: Portraits of a Princess.* Chicago: University of Chicago Press, 1983.

Brown, Earl Kent. "Women of the Word: Selected Leadership Roles of Women in Mr. Wesley's Methodism." in *Women in New Worlds,* ed. Hilah F. Thomas and Rosemary Skinner Keller, 69-87. Nashville, Tenn.: Abingdon, 1981.

Brown, K. Marianne Wargelin. "Three 'Founding Mothers' of Finnish America: Maggie Walz, Entrepeneur and Temperance Crusader." In *Women Who Dared: The History of Finnish American Women,* 151–57. St. Paul: Univ. of Minnesota, Immigration History Research Center, 1986.

Brown, Penny. "The Reception of George Sand in Spain." *Comparative Literature Studies* 25, no. 3 (1988): 203–24.

Buhle, Mari Jo, and Paul Buhle, eds. *The Concise History of Woman Suffrage.* Urbana: Univ. of Illinois Press, 1978.

Burke, Stephen. "Letter from a Pioneer Feminist—Anna Wheeler." *Studies in Labour History* 1 (1976): 19–23.

Burt, Ronald S. "Models of Network Structure." *Annual Review of Sociology* 6 (1980): 79–141.

Burton, Antoinette M. "The White Woman's Burden: British Feminists and 'The Indian Woman,' 1865–1915." *Women's Studies International Forum* 13, no. 4 (1990): 295–308.

Caine, Barbara. *Victorian Feminists.* Oxford: Oxford Univ. Press, 1992.

Campbell, Debra. "Hannah Whitall Smith (1832–1911): Theology of the Mother-Hearted God." *Signs* 15, no. 1 (1989): 79–101.

Campbell, Karlyn Kohrs. *Man Cannot Speak for Her.* 2 vols. New York: Praeger, 1989.

Carpenter, J. Estlin. *In Memoriam: Frances Power Cobbe.* London, 1904.

Carr, Edward Hallett. *The Romantic Exiles: A Nineteenth-Century Portrait Gallery.* 1933. Boston: Beacon Press, 1961.

Carretta, Vincent, ed. *Unchained Voices: An Anthology of Black Authors in the English-Speaking World of the Eighteenth Century.* Lexington: Univ. Press of Kentucky, 1996.

Carwardine, Richard. *Transatlantic Revivalism: Popular Evangelicalism in Britain and America, 1790–1865.* Westport, Conn.: Greenwood Press, 1978.

Caskie, Helen C. "Frances Power Cobbe: Victorian Feminist." 1981. Typescript. Fawcett Library, London.

Chevigny, Bell Gale. *The Woman and the Myth: Margaret Fuller's Life and Writings.* Old Westbury, N.Y.: Feminist Press, 1976.

Child, Lydia M., Letter to Ellis Gray Loring, August 11, 1841. Lydia Maria Child Collection, Letters, 1838–78. New York Public Library.

———. *Lydia Maria Child: Selected Letters, 1817–1880.* Ed. Milton Meltzer and Patricia G. Holland. Amherst: Univ. of Massachusetts Press, 1982.

Chmielewski, Wendy E., Louis J. Kern, and Marlyn Klee-Hartzell, eds., *Women in Spiritual and Communitarian Societies in the United States.* Syracuse, N.Y.: Syracuse Univ. Press, 1993.

Clarke, Patricia. *The Governesses: Letters from the Colonies, 1862–1882.* Sydney: Allen & Unwin, 1985.

Clayhills, Harriet. "Fredsrörelsen [Peace movement]." In *Kvinnohistorisk Uppslagsbok*, 139–43. Stockholm: Rabén & Sjögren, 1991.

Clifford, Deborah Pickman. *Crusader for Freedom: A Life of Lydia Maria Child.* Boston: Beacon Press, 1992.

Cobbe, Frances Power. *Criminals, Idiots, Women, and Minors: Is This Classification Sound?* Pamphlet. Reprinted from *Fraser's Magazine* 3 (Dec. 1868).

———. *Essay on Intuitive Morals.* London: Longman, Brown, Green & Longmans, 1855.

———. *Essay on Intuitive Morals, Part II: Practice of Morals.* London: John Chapman, 1857.

———. "The Final Cause of Woman." In *Woman's Work and Woman's Culture,* ed. Josephine Butler. London: Macmillan, 1869.

———. *Italics: Brief Notes on Politics, People, and Places in Italy in 1864.* London: Trübner, 1864.

———. Letter to Mrs. Henry Fawcett on the death of Miss Lloyd, Nov. 11, 1896. Autograph Letter Collection, vol. 8, pt. 6, Fawcett Library, London.

———. *Life of Frances Power Cobbe, by Herself.* 2 vols. Boston: Houghton Mifflin, 1894.

———. *Light in Dark Places.* London: Victoria Street Society for the Protection of Animals from Vivisection, 1897.

———. *The Peak in Darien: An Octave of Essays.* Boston: Ellis, 1882.

———. "Social Science Congresses and Women's Part in Them." In *Pursuits of Women,* reprinted from *Macmillan's Magazine.* Dec. 1861, 25.

———. "What Shall We Do with Our Old Maids?" In *Fraser's Magazine* 65 (1862): 594-606.

Code, Joseph B. "Mother Cornelia Connelly." In *Great American Foundresses,* 406–36. New York: Books for Libraries, 1968.

Codman, John Thomas. *Brook Farm: Historic and Personal Memoirs.* Boston: Arena, 1894.

"A Colored Lady Lecturer." *English Woman's Journal* 7 (July 1861):274–75.

Connelly, Cornelia. *A Religious of the Society: The Life of Cornelia Connelly, 1809–1879.* London: Longmans, 1924.

Cooper, Sandi E. *Patriotic Pacifism: Waging War on War in Europe, 1815–1914.* New York: Oxford Univ. Press, 1991.

———. "The Work of Women in Nineteenth Century Continental European Peace Movements." *Peace and Change* 9 (1984): 11–28.

Costin, Lela B. "Feminism, Pacifism, Internationalism, and the 1915 International Congress of Women." *Women's Studies International Forum* 5 (1982): 301–15.

Cott, Nancy. *The Bonds of Womanhood: "Woman's Sphere" in New England, 1780–1835.* New Haven, Conn.: Yale Univ. Press, 1977.

———. "Feminist Theory and Feminist Movements: The Past before Us." In *What Is Feminism?* ed. Juliet Mitchell and Ann Oakley. New York: Pantheon, 1986.

———. *The Grounding of Modern Feminism.* New Haven, Conn.: Yale Univ. Press, 1987.

Cunningham, Alyson. *Cummy's Diary.* 1863. Ed. Robert T. Skinner. London: Chatto & Windus, 1926.

Daly, Mary. *Outercourse: The Be-Dazzling Voyage.* San Francisco: Harper, 1992.

Daly, Mary, with Jane Caputi. *Websters' First New Intergalactic Wickedary of the English Language.* Boston: Beacon Press, 1987.

Daniels, Elizabeth Adams. *Jessie White Mario: Risorgimento Revolutionary.* Athens: Ohio University Press, 1972.

De drogo till Paris: Nordiska konstnärinnor på 1880–talet. Stockholm: Föreningen Norden, 1989.

Dekker, Rudolf M., and Lotte C. van de Pol. *The Tradition of Female Transvestism in Early Modern Europe.* New York: St. Martin's, 1989.

Deroin, Jeanne, and Pauline Roland. "Letter to the Convention of the Women of America," June 15, 1851. In *Women, the Family, and Freedom,* ed. Susan Groag Bell and Karen Offen, 1:287–90. Stanford, Calif.: Stanford Univ. Press, 1983.

Devey, Louisa. *Life of Rosina, Lady Lytton.* London: Swan, Sonnenschein, Lowren, 1837.

D'Istria, Dora. *Des femmes, par une femme.* 2 vols. Paris: Lacroix, Verboeckhoven, 1865.

Donaldson, Laura E. *Decolonizing Feminisms: Race, Gender, and Europe.* Chapel Hill: Univ. of North Carolina Press, 1992.

Dooley, Dolores. *Equality in Community: Sexual Equality in the Writings of William Thompson and Anna Doyle Wheeler.* Cork, Ireland: Cork Univ. Press, 1996.

Doyle, Arthur. *A Hundred Years of Conflict: Being Some Records of the Service of Six Generals of the Doyle Family, 1756–1856.* London: Longmans, Green, 1911.

DuBois, Ellen Carol. *Feminism and Suffrage: The Emergence of an Independent Women's Movement in America, 1848–1869.* Ithaca, N.Y., Cornell Univ. Press, 1978.

Duff, Mildred. *Hedvig von Haartman.* Helsinki: Utgifven af Frälsningsarmén, 1904.

Dulles, Foster Rhea. *Americans Abroad: Two Centuries of European Travel.* Ann Arbor: Univ. of Mich. Press, 1964.

Eckhardt, Celia Morris. *Fanny Wright: Rebel in America.* Cambridge, Mass.: Harvard Univ. Press, 1984.

Eduards, Maud, et al., eds. *Rethinking Change: Current Swedish Feminist Research.* Uppsala: Humanistisk-samhällsvetenskapliga forskningsradet, 1992.

Edwards, Amelia B. *Untrodden Peaks and Unfrequented Valleys: A Midsummer Ramble in the Dolomites.* 1873. Boston: Beacon Press, 1987.

Engel, Barbara Alpern. *Mothers and Daughters: Women of the Intelligentsia in Nineteenth-Century Russia.* Cambridge: Cambridge Univ. Press, 1983.

Engel, Barbara Alpern, and Clifford N. Rosenthal. Introduction to *Five Sisters: Women against the Tsar*. New York: Schocken, 1977.

Ewens, Mary. "The Leadership of Nuns in Immigrant Catholicism." In *Women and Religion in America*, vol. 1, *The Nineteenth Century*, ed. Rosemary Radford Ruether and Rosemary Skinner Keller, 101–13. San Francisco: Harper & Row, 1981.

Faderman, Lillian. *Surpassing the Love of Men: Romantic Friendship and Love between Women from the Renaissance to the Present*. London: Women's Press, 1985.

Field, Henry M. *The Story of the Atlantic Telegraph*. 1893. New York: Arno Press, 1972.

Fisher, Trevor. "Josephine Butler: Feminism's Neglected Pioneer." *History Today*, June 1996, 32–38.

Flaxman, Radegunde. *A Woman Styled Bold: The Life of Cornelia Connelly 1809–1879*. London: Darton, Longman & Todd, 1991.

Flexner, James Thomas. *An American Saga: The Story of Helen Thomas and Simon Flexner*. Boston: Little, Brown, 1984.

Foner, Laura, and Eugene Genovese, eds. *Slavery in the New World: A Reader in Comparative History*. Englewood Cliffs, N.J.: Prentice-Hall, 1969.

Forster, Margaret. *Significant Sisters: The Grassroots of Active Feminism, 1839–1939*. New York: Oxford Univ. Press, 1984.

Foster, Lawrence. *Women, Family, and Utopia: Communal Experiments of the Shakers, the Oneida Community, and the Mormons*. Syracuse, N.Y.: Syracuse Univ. Press, 1991.

Fout, John C., ed. *German Women in the Nineteenth Century: A Social History*. New York: Holmes & Meier, 1984.

Fox-Genovese, Elizabeth, and Eugene D. Genovese. *Fruits of Merchant Capital: Slavery and Bourgeois Property in the Rise and Expansion of Capitalism*. New York: Oxford Univ. Press, 1983.

Fuller, Margaret. *"These Sad but Glorious Days": Dispatches from Europe, 1846–1850*. Ed. Larry J. Reynolds and Susan Belasco Smith. New Haven, Conn.: Yale Univ. Press, 1991.

Fuller, Wayne. *The American Mail: Enlarger of the Common Life*. Chicago: Univ. of Chicago Press, 1972.

Furuhjelm, Annie. *Gryningen: Efterlämnade minnen ur kvinnorörlsens historia* (Dawn: Memories from the history of the women's movement). Helsinki: Söderström, 1939.

Galgano, Michael. "Anna Doyle Wheeler." In *Biographical Dictionary of Modern British Radicals*, ed. Joseph O. Baylen and Norbert J. Gossman, 1:519–24. Sussex, Eng.: Harvester Press, 1979.

Gans, J. "Les relations entre socialistes de France et d'Angeleterre au debut du XIXe siècle." *Le Mouvement Social* 46 (1964): 105–18.

Garber, Marjorie. *Vested Interests: Cross-Dressing and Cultural Anxiety.* New York: Routledge, 1989.

Garrison, S. Olin, ed. *Forty Witnesses.* 1888. Freeport, Pa.: Fountain Press, 1955.

Giddings, Paula. *When and Where I Enter: The Impact of Black Women on Race and Sex in America.* New York: Morrow, 1984.

Gillespie, Joanna Bowen. "'The Clear Leadings of Providence': Pious Memoirs and the Problems of Self Realization for Women in the Early Nineteenth Century." *Journal of the Early Republic* 5 (Summer 1985): 197–221.

Gilroy, Paul. *The Black Atlantic: Modernity and Double Consciousness.* Cambridge, Mass.: Harvard Univ. Press, 1993.

Gladstone, Penelope. *Travels of Alexine: Alexine Tinne, 1835–1869.* London: John Murray, 1970.

Gleadle, Kathryn. *The Early Feminists: Radical Unitarians and the Emergence of the Women's Rights Movement, 1831-51.* New York: St. Martin's Press, 1998.

Goegg, Marie. "Switzerland." In *The Woman Question in Europe,* ed. Theodore Stanton, 374–89. New York: Putnams, 1884.

Gordon, Lucie Duff. *Letters from Egypt, 1863–65.* London: Macmillan, 1865.

Gourvish, T.R. "Railways, 1830–1870: The Formative Years." In *Transport in Victorian Britain,* ed. Michael J. Freeman and Derek H. Aldcraft. New York: Manchester Univ. Press, 1988.

Greer, Germaine. *The Obstacle Race: The Fortunes of Women Painters and Their Work,* esp. "The Nineteenth Century," 310-27. New York: Farrar Straus Giroux, 1979.

Gripenberg, Aleksandra. Catalogue of Personal Library. Aleksandra Gripenberg Collection, Finnish Literature Society (SKS), Helsinki, Finland.

———. *Elizabeth Cady Stanton och Kvinnosaksarbetet.* Stockholm: Samson & Wallin, 1896.

———. *A Half Year in the New World: Miscellaneous Sketches of Travel in the United States.* 1888. Trans. and ed. Ernest J. Moyne. Newark: Univ. of Delaware Press, 1954.

———. Letter to Caroline Ashurst Biggs, June 6, 1888. Aleksandra Gripenberg Collection, 312.83.4, Finnish Literature Society (SKS), Helsinki.

———. Letter to the Reverend Anne [*sic*] Shaw. Oct. 19, 1911. Aleksandra Gripenberg Collection, 318.82.1, Finnish Literature Society (SKS), Helsinki.

———. Matkapaïväkirjoja (Travel diaries), 1881–88, vol. 4. Trans. from Swedish by Ann-Catrin Östman. Aleksandra Gripenberg Collection, Finnish Literature Society (SKS), Helsinki.

Grogan, Susan K. *French Socialism and Sexual Difference: Women and the New Society, 1803–44.* New York: St. Martin's, 1992.

Guérin, Mother Theodore. "Journals and Letters of Mother Theodore Guérin." Docs. 2 and 4 of "The Leadership of Nuns in Immigrant Catholicism," in *Women and Religion in America,* vol. 1, *The Nineteenth Century,* ed. Rosemary Radford Ruether and Rosemary Skinner Keller, 114–22, 128–30. San Francisco: Harper & Row, 1981.

Gulin, Helmi. *En Herrgårdsfröken i uniform: Drag ur Hedvig von Haartmans Liv.* Helsinki: Söderström, 1951.

Habermas, Jürgen. *Theorie des Kommunikativen Handelns.* Trans. as *The Theory of Communicative Action,* 2 vols. Cambridge: Polity Press, 1989.

Hamann, Brigitte. *Bertha von Suttner: A Life for Peace.* Trans. Ann Dubsky. Syracuse, N.Y.: Syracuse Univ. Press, 1996.

Hansen, Bodil K. "Rural Women in Late Nineteenth-Century Denmark." *Journal of Peasant Studies* 9, no. 4(1982): 231.

Hardesty, Nancy A. "Minister as Prophet? Or as Mother?" In *Women in New Worlds,* ed. Hilah Thomas and Rosemary Skinner Keller, 88–101. Nashville, Tenn.: Abingdon, 1981.

———. *Women Called to Witness: Evangelical Feminism in the Nineteenth Century.* Nashville, Tenn.: Abingdon, 1984.

Hargest, George E. *History of Letter Post Communication between the United States and Europe, 1845–1875.* Washington, D.C.: Smithsonian Institution Press, 1971.

Harper, Ida Husted. *Life and Work of Susan B. Anthony.* 3 vols. 1908. New York: Arno Press, 1969.

Hatem, Mervat. "Through Each Other's Eyes: Egyptian, Levantine-Egyptian, and European Women's Images of Themselves and of Each Other (1862–1920)." *Women's Studies International Forum* 12, no. 2 (1989): 183–98.

Headley, P.C. *The Life of Louis Kossuth, Governor of Hungary.* 1852. Freeport, N.Y.: Books for Libraries, 1971.

Helene Schjerfbeck. Catalogue. Helsinki: Finnish National Gallery Ateneum, 1992.

Helsinger, Elizabeth K., Robin Lauterbach Sheets, and William Veeder. *The Woman Question: Society and Literature in Britain and America, 1837–1883,* vol. 1, *Defining Voices.* Chicago: Univ. of Chicago Press, 1983.

Hersh, Blanche Glassman. *The Slavery of Sex: Feminist-Abolitionists in America.* Urbana: Univ. of Illinois Press, 1978.

Herstein, Sheila R. *A Mid-Victorian Feminist: Barbara Leigh Smith Bodichon.* New Haven, Conn.: Yale Univ. Press, 1985.

Hirsch, Pam. "Barbara Leigh Smith Bodichon, Artist and Activist." In *Women in the Victorian Art World,* ed. Clarissa Campbell Orr, 167–186. New York: Manchester Univ. Press, 1995.

Holger, Lena. "Nothing Ventured, Nothing Gained: Helene Schjerfbeck's Struggle for Her Painting from 1892–1917." In *Helene Schjerfbeck,* 55–63. Helsinki: Finnish National Gallery Ateneum, 1992.

Holland, Paul W., and Samuel Leinhardt, eds. *Perspectives on Social Network Research.* New York: Cambridge Univ. Press, 1979.

Holton, Sandra Stanley. "From Anti-Slavery to Suffrage Militancy: The Bright

Circle, Elizabeth Cady Stanton and the British Women's Movement." In *Suffrage and Beyond: International Feminist Perspectives,* ed. Melanie Nolan and Caroline Daley. N.Y.: New York Univ. Press, 1994.

———. "'To Educate Women into Rebellion': Elizabeth Cady Stanton and the Creation of a Transatlantic Network of Radical Suffragists." *American Historical Review* 99, no. 4 (1994): 1112–36.

Hovet, Theodore. "Phoebe Palmer's 'Altar Phraseology' and the Spiritual Dimension of Woman's Sphere." *Journal of Religion* 63, no. 3 (1983): 264–80.

Hughes, William R. *Sophia Sturge: A Memoir.* London: George Allen & Unwin, 1940.

Hurwitz, Edith. "The International Sisterhood." In *Becoming Visible: Women in European History,* ed. Renate Bridenthal and Claudia Koonz, 325–45. Boston: Houghton Mifflin, 1977.

Jameson, Anna, ed. "Adelaide Kemble and the Lyrical Drama in 1841." In *Memoirs and Essays,* 65–112. London: Richard Bentley [1843].

Joeres, Ruth-Ellen. "The Triumph of the Woman: Johanna Kinkel's *Hans Ibeles in London* (1860)." *Euphorion: Zeitschrift für Literaturgeschichte* 70, no. 2 (1976): 187–97.

Jones, Mary Cadwalader (Rawle). *European Travel for Women.* New York: Macmillan, 1900.

Käppeli, Anne-Marie. "Between High and Low: Prostitution in Geneva." In *Forgotten Women of Geneva,* ed. A.-M. Käppeli, 56–57. Geneva: Metropolis, 1993.

Karp, Carole. "George Sand and the Russians." In *George Sand Papers: Conference Proceedings, 1976,* ed. Natalie Datlof et al. New York: AMS Press, 1977.

Kennedy, Don H. *Little Sparrow: A Portrait of Sophia Kovalevsky.* Athens: Ohio Univ. Press, 1983.

Kero, Reino. "The United States during Its First Century of Independence as It Appeared in Finnish Print (1776–1880)." In *Old Friends—Strong Ties,* ed. Vilho Nütemaa et al., 35–63. Turku, Finland: Institute for Migration, 1976.

Kirkland, Caroline. *Holidays Abroad: Europe from the West.* 2 vols. New York, 1849.

Klancher, Jon. "Reading the Social Text: Power, Signs, and Audience in Early Nineteenth Century Prose." *Studies in Romanticism* 23, no. 2 (1984): 184.

Kleman, Ellen. *Fredrika Bremer and America.* Stockholm: Åhlén & Åkerlunds, 1938.

Knight, Anne. Annotations in *A Plea for Woman* by Mrs. Hugo Reid (1843), MS vol. s495, 146 Friends House Library, London.

Kolchin, Peter. *American Slavery, 1619–1877.* New York: Hill & Wang, 1993.

Kolmerten, Carol A. *Women in Utopia: The Ideology of Gender in the American Owenite Communities.* Bloomington: Indiana Univ. Press, 1990.

Konttinen, Riitta. "Finska konstnärinnors 1880–tal: Ljus, luft och färg: Elin Danielson, Amélie Lundahl, Helene Schjerfbeck, Helena Westermarck och

Maria Wiik." In *De drogo till Paris,* 221–53. Stockholm: Föreningen Norden, 1989.

———. *Suomalaisia naistaitelijoita 1880–luvulta.* Helsinki: Otava, 1988.

———. *Totuus enemmän kuin kauneus. Naistaiteilija, realismi ja naturalismi 1880–luvulla.* Helsinki: Otava, 1991.

Kramarae, Cheris, and Paula Treichler. *A Feminist Dictionary.* London: Pandora Press, 1985.

Krásnohorská, Elise. "Bohemia." In *The Woman Question in Europe,* ed. Theodore Stanton, 446–56. New York: Putnam, 1884.

Kuehl, Warren. "Concepts of Internationalism in History." *Peace and Change* 11 (1986): 26.

Landon, Margaret. *Anna and the King of Siam.* New York: John Day, 1943.

Lattek, Christine. "Women in Exile: German Women of the 'Generation of 1848' in London." Paper read at Southern Conference on Women's History, 1988, Converse College, Spartanburg, S.C.

Laumann, Edward O. "Network Analysis in Large Social Systems." In *Perspectives on Social Network Research,* ed. Paul W. Holland and Samuel Leinhardt. New York: Academic Press, 1979.

Leffler, Anne-Charlotte. *En Självbiografi (grumdad på dagböcker och brev).* Stockholm, 1922.

Leitenberger, Johanna. "Austria." In *The Woman Question in Europe,* ed. Theodore Stanton, 175–88. New York: Putnam, 1884.

Lengyel, Emil. *And All Her Paths Were Peace: The Life of Bertha von Suttner.* New York: Thomas Nelson, 1975.

Leonowens, Anna Harriette. *The English Governess at the Siamese Court.* Boston: Fields, Osgood, 1870.

———. *The Romance of the Harem.* Boston: James R. Osgood, 1872.

Lerner, Gerda. *The Feminist Thought of Sarah Grimké.* New York: Oxford Univ. Press, 1998.

———. *The Grimké Sisters from South Carolina: Pioneers for Woman's Rights and Abolition.* New York: Schocken, 1967.

Leslie, Rev. Canon J.B. "Biographical Index of the Clergy of the Church of Ireland," 1958. Typescript. Representative Church Body Library, Dublin.

Lesser, Margaret. *Clarkey: A Portrait in Letters of Mary Clarke Mohl (1793–1883).* New York: Oxford Univ. Press, 1984.

Levine, Philippa. Introduction to *Untrodden Peaks and Unfrequented Valleys: A Midsummer Ramble in the Dolomites* (1873), by Amelia B. Edwards. Boston: Beacon Press, 1987.

Liddington, Jill. *The Road to Greenham Common: Feminism and Anti-Militarism in Britain since 1820.* Syracuse, N.Y.: Syracuse Univ. Press, 1991.

Lott, Emmeline. *The English Governess in Egypt: Harem Life in Egypt and Constantinople.* 2 vols. London: Richard Bentley, 1866.

[Lowe, Emily.] *Unprotected Females in Norway; or, The Pleasantest Way of Travelling There, Passing through Denmark and Sweden.* London: G. Routledge, 1857.

————. *Unprotected Females in Sicily, Calabria, and on the Top of Mount Etna.* London: Routledge, Warnes, and Routledge, 1859.

Lugones, María. "Playfulness, 'World'-Traveling, and Loving Perception." In *Women, Knowledge, and Reality: Explorations in Feminist Philosophy,* ed. Ann Garry and Marilyn Pearsall, 282–98. Boston: Unwin Hyman, 1987. Reprinted from *Hypatia* 2 (Summer 1987): 3–19.

McFadden, Margaret. "Anna Doyle Wheeler (1785–1848): Philosopher, Socialist, Feminist." In *Hypatia's Daughters: Fifteen Hundred Years of Women Philosophers,* ed. Linda Lopez McAlister, 204–14. Bloomington: Indiana Univ. Press, 1996.

————. "Boston Teenagers Debate the Woman Question, 1837–38." *Signs* 15, no. 4 (1990): 832–47.

————. "Feminism." In *Women's Issues: Ready Reference,* 1:323–29. Pasadena, Calif.: Salem Press, 1997.

————. "The Ironies of Pentecost: Phoebe Palmer, World Evangelism, and Female Networks." *Methodist History* 31, no. 2 (1993): 63–75.

————. "Peace Movement and Women." In *Women's Issues: Ready Reference,* 2:656–57. Pasadena, Calif.: Salem Press, 1997.

————. "Rosina Wheeler Bulwer-Lytton." In *An Encyclopedia of British Women Writers,* 2d ed., ed. Paul Schleuter and Jane Schleuter. New York: Rutgers Univ. Press, 1998.

McFeely, William S. *Frederick Douglass.* New York: Norton, 1991.

McKenna, Kevin J. "George Sand's Reception in Russia: The Case of Elena Gan." In *The World of George Sand,* ed. Natalie Datlof et al., 227–33. New York: Greenwood Press, 1991.

Malmgreen, Gail. "Anne Knight and the Radical Subculture." *Quaker History* 71 (1982): 100–113.

Malmström, Synnöve. "Kvinnliga pionjärer inom finländsk bildkonst från 1840– till 1880–talet" [Female pioneers in Finnish art history, 1840–1880]. In *Nainen, Taide, Historia: Taidehistorian Esitutkimus, 1985–1986* [Women, art, history], ed. Riitta Nikula, 35–54. Helsinki: Society for Art History in Finland, 1987.

Mansfield, Blanche (McManus). *The American Woman Abroad.* New York: Dodd, Mead, 1911.

Markkola, Pirjo, and Alexandra Ramsay, eds. *Yksi kamari—kaksi sukupuolta: Suomen eduskunnan ensimmäiset naiset* [One chamber—two sexes: The first Finnish women parliamentarians]. Helsinki: BTJ—Kirjastopalvelu, 1997.

Martineau, Harriet. *Autobiography.* Vol. 1. 1877. London: Virago, 1983.

Marx, Karl. "Communist Manifesto." 1848. In *The Essential Works of Marxism*, ed. Arthur P. Mendel. New York: Bantam, 1961.

Mermin, Dorothy. *Godiva's Ride: Women of Letters in England, 1830–1880*. Bloomington: Indiana Univ. Press, 1993.

Meysenbug, Malwida von. *Rebel in Bombazine: Memoirs of Malwida von Meysenbug*. New York: Norton, 1936.

Mill, Harriet Taylor. "The Enfranchisement of Women." 1851. In *Essays on Sex Equality*, ed. Alice Rossi, 91–121. Chicago: Univ. of Chicago Press, 1997.

Mitchell, Juliet, and Ann Oakley, eds. *What Is Feminism?* New York: Pantheon, 1986.

Moers, Ellen. "George Sand: An Introduction." In *George Sand: In Her Own Words*, trans. and ed. Joseph Barry, ix–xxii. Garden City, N.Y.: Anchor Books, 1979.

Mohanty, Chandra, Ann Russo, and Lourdes Torres, eds. *Third World Women and the Politics of Feminism*. Bloomington: Indiana Univ. Press, 1991.

Montén, Karin Carsten. *Fredrika Bremer in Deutschland*. Neumünster, Germany: Karl Wachholtz Verlag, 1981.

Moon, S. Joan. "Feminism and Socialism: The Utopian Synthesis of Flora Tristan." In *Socialist Women: European Socialist Feminism in the Nineteenth Century*, ed. Marilyn J. Boxer and Jean H. Quataert, 19–50. New York: Elsevier, 1978.

Mooney, Catherine M. *Philippine Duchesne: A Woman with the Poor*. New York: Paulist Press, 1990.

Moses, Claire Goldberg. *French Feminism in the Nineteenth Century*. Albany: State Univ. of New York Press, 1984.

———. "Saint-Simonian Men/Saint-Simonian Women: The Transformation of Feminist Thought in 1830s France." *Journal of Modern History* 54 (1982): 240–67.

Mott, Lucretia. *Slavery and "The Woman Question": Lucretia Mott's Diary of Her Visit to Great Britain to Attend the World's Anti-Slavery Convention of 1840*. Ed. Frederick B. Tolles. Haverford, Pa.: Friends' Historical Association, 1952.

Murray, Amelia M. *Letters from the United States, Cuba, and Canada*. New York, 1856.

Murray, John. *Handbook for Travellers in Southern Italy*. London: John Murray, 1883.

Naginski, Isabelle Hoog. *George Sand: Writing for Her Life*. New Brunswick, N.J.: Rutgers Univ. Press, 1991.

"National Honor Sought for Madame Anneke," *Milwaukee Sentinel*, April 27, 1930.

Nevala, Maria-Liisa. "Women in the Finnish Literary Establishment." In *The Lady with the Bow: The Story of Finnish Women*, ed. Merja Manninen and Päivi Setälä. Helsinki: Otava, 1990.

Nikula, Riitta. "Women in the History of Finnish Art." In *The Lady with the Bow:*

The Story of Finnish Women, ed. Merja Manninen and Päivi Setälä. Helsinki: Otava, 1990.

Nuttall, Geoffrey. *Christian Pacifism in History.* New York: Seabury, 1971.

"Obituary: Salvation Army Leader in England." *Durham Morning Herald.* Oct. 4, 1987, 20.

O'Brien, Dennis. "George Sand and Feminism." In *George Sand Papers: Conference Proceedings, 1976,* ed. Natalie Datlof et al., 76–91. New York: AMS Press, 1977.

Offen, Karen. "Challenging Male Hegemony: Feminist Criticism and the Context for Women's Movements in the Age of European Revolutions and Counter-Revolutions, 1789–1860." Paper presented at the Stuttgart conference, "Nineteenth-Century European Feminisms," June 1995.

———. "Contextualizing the Theory and Practice of Feminism in Nineteenth-Century Europe (1789–1914)." In *Becoming Visible: Women in European History,* ed. Renate Bridenthal, Susan Mosher Stuard, Merry Wiesner, 3d ed., 327–55. New York: Houghton Mifflin, 1998.

———. "Defining Feminism: A Comparative Historical Approach." *Signs* 14, no. 1 (1988): 119–57.

———. "A Nineteenth-Century French Feminist Rediscovered: Jenny P. d'Héricourt, 1809–1875." *Signs* 13, no. 1 (1987): 144–58.

[Palmer, Phoebe]. *Four Years in the Old World; Comprising the Travels, Incidents, and Evangelistic Labors of Dr. and Mrs. Palmer, in England, Ireland, Scotland, and Wales.* New York: Foster & Palmer, 1866.

———. *Promise of the Father; or, A Neglected Speciality of the Last Days.* New York: W.C. Palmer, Jr., 1872.

Pankhurst, Richard K.P. "Anna Wheeler: A Pioneer Socialist and Feminist." *Political Quarterly* 25 (1954): 132–43.

Parker, Theodore. *The Collected Works of Theodore Parker.* Ed. Frances Power Cobbe. 14 vols. London: Trübner, 1866.

Patterson, Elizabeth Chambers. *Mary Somerville and the Cultivation of Science, 1815–1840.* Boston: Nijhoff, 1983.

Pemble, John. *The Mediterranean Passion: Victorians and Edwardians in the South.* New York: Oxford Univ. Press, 1988.

Polasky, Janet L. "Internationalism in the Age of Nationalism." *History of European Ideas* 15, nos. 1–3 (1992): 211–16.

———. "Utopia and Domesticity: Zoé Gatti de Gamond." *Proceedings of the Western Society for French History* 11 (1984): 273–81.

Porter, Dorothy B. "Sarah Parker Remond." In *Notable American Women, 1607–1950,* ed. Edward T. James, 3: 136–37. Cambridge, Mass., Harvard Univ. Press, 1971.

Price, A. Whigham. *The Ladies of Castlebrae: A Story of Nineteenth Century Travel and Research.* Gloucester, Eng.: Alan Sutton, 1985.

Pulszky, Francis, and Theresa Pulszky. *White, Red, Black: Sketches of American Society in the United States.* 2 vols. New York: Redfield, 1853.

Qvist, Gunnar. *Fredrika Bremer och kvinnans emancipation.* Göteborg, Sweden: Akademiforlaget, 1969.

Rahm, Berta. *Marie Goegg.* Schaffhausen, Switzerland: Ala Verlag, 1993.

Raser, Harold E. *Phoebe Palmer: Her Life and Thought.* Lewiston, N.Y.: Edwin Mellen Press, 1987.

Reed, Andrew, and James Matheson. *Narrative of the Visit to the American Churches, by the Deputation from the Congregational Union of England and Wales.* 2 vols. New York: Harper and Bro., 1835, 2:207.

Reid, Mrs. Hugo [Marion Kirkland]. *Woman, Her Education and Influence.* New York: Fowler and Wells, 1987.

Reinfeld, Barbara K. "Charlotte Garrigue Masaryk, 1850–1923." *Czechoslovak and Eastern European Journal* 8, nos. 1–2 (1989): 90–103.

Rendall, Jane. *The Origins of Modern Feminism: Women in Britain, France, and the United States, 1780–1860.* New York: Schocken, 1984.

Report of the International Council of Women. Washington, D.C.: Rufus H. Darby, 1888.

Richardson, Marilyn, ed. *Maria W. Stewart, America's First Black Woman Political Writer: Essays and Speeches.* Bloomington: Indiana Univ. Press, 1987.

Richter, Payton E. *Utopias: Social Ideals and Communal Experiments.* Boston: Holbrook Press, 1971.

Riot-Sarcey, Michèle. "La conscience feministe des femmes de 1848: Jeanne Deroin, Désirée Gay." In *Un Fabuleux Destin: Flora Tristan,* 157–65. Dijon: Editions Universitaires de Dijon, 1985.

———. *La democratie à l'epreuve des femmes: Trois figures critiques du pouvoir, 1830–1848.* Paris: A. Michel, 1994.

Ritchie, Gisela F. "Visions of a United Europe: European Emancipatory Women of the 19th and Early 20th Centuries." *History of European Ideas* 14, nos. 4–6 (1992): 543–47.

Robinson, Howard. *The British Post Office.* 1948. Ann Arbor: University Microfilms, 1969.

Rodgers, Richard, and Oscar Hammerstein II. *The King and I.* New York: Williamson Music, 1951.

Rogers, Everett M. "Network Analysis of the Diffusion of Innovations." In *Perspectives on Social Network Research,* ed. Paul W. Holland and Samuel Leinhardt. New York: Academic Press, 1979.

Rogers, Hester Ann Roe. *The Experience and Spiritual Letters of Mrs. Hester Ann Rogers with a Sermon, Preached on the Occasion of Her Death, by the Rev. Thomas Coke, Ll.D. Also an Appendix Written by Her Husband.* London, 1841.

Roos, Jane May. "Another Look at Henry James and the 'White, Marmorean Flock.'" *Woman's Art Journal,* Spring/Summer, 1983.

Roos, Rosalie. *Travels in America, 1851–1855.* Trans. and ed. Carl L. Anderson. Carbondale: Southern Illinois Univ. Press, 1982.

Rooth, Signe Alice. *Seeress of the Northland: Fredrika Bremer's American Journey, 1849–1851.* Philadelphia: American Swedish Historical Foundation, 1955.

Rossi, Alice, ed. *The Feminist Papers.* New York: Bantam Books, 1974.

———. "Social Roots of the Woman's Movement." In *The Feminist Papers,* ed. Alice Rossi, 241–281. New York: Bantam Books, 1974.

Ruether, Rosemary Radford, and Rosemary Skinner Keller, eds. *Women and Religion in America,* vol. 1, *The Nineteenth Century.* San Francisco: Harper & Row, 1981.

Rupp, Leila J. "Challenging Imperialism in International Women's Organizations, 1888–1945." *NWSA Journal* 8, no. 1 (1996): 9–27.

———. "Conflict in the International Women's Movement, 1888–1950." Paper presented to the Berkshire Conference on Women's History, New Brunswick, N.J., June 1990.

———. "Constructing Internationalism: The Case of Transnational Women's Organizations, 1888–1945." *American Historical Review* 99 (Dec. 1994): 1571–1600.

———. *Worlds of Women: The Making of an International Women's Movement.* Princeton, N.J.: Princeton Univ. Press, 1998.

Rupp, Leila J., and Verta Taylor. "Women's Culture and the Continuity of the Women's Movement." In *Moving On: New Perspectives on the Women's Movement,* ed. Tayo Andreasen et al., 68–89. Aarhus, Denmark: Aarhus Univ. Press, 1991.

Ryall, Anka. 1989. "Reisebeskrivelser—etnologisk kilde eller topografiske eventyr?" *Dugnad* 3, no. 15 (1989).

———. "Domesticating Geographical Exploration: Fredrika Bremer's American Travel Narrative." Paper presented to the Society for the Advancement of Scandinavian Study, Madison, Wis., 1990.

Rye, Maria S. *Emigration of Educated Women.* Paper read at the Social Science Congress, Dublin, 1861; reprinted from *English Woman's Journal.* London: Emily Faithful for the Victoria Press, [1861].

Sadleir, Michael. *Bulwer and His Wife: A Panorama 1803–1836.* London: Constable, 1931.

"Samuel Cunard." *Encyclopedia Britannica,* 1994 (15th ed.), 3:790.

Sand, George. *Histoire de ma vie.* 1854–55. In *Oeuvres autobiographiques,* ed. Georges Lubin, 2 vols. Paris: Pléiade, 1970–71.

———. "To Members of the Central Committee of the Left," Paris, April 1848. In *George Sand: In Her Own Words,* trans. and ed. Joseph Barry, 411. New York: Anchor Books, 1979.

Schappes, Morris U. "Ernestine L. Rose: Her Address on the Anniversary of West Indian Emancipation." *Journal of Negro History* 34, no. 3 (1949): 344–55.

Scott, Joan Wallach. *Only Paradoxes to Offer: French Feminists and the Rights of Man*. Cambridge, Mass.: Harvard Univ. Press, 1996.

Seacole, Mary. *Wonderful Adventures of Mrs. Seacole in Many Lands*. 1857. New York: Oxford Univ. Press, 1988.

Secci, Lia. "German Women Writers and the Revolution of 1848." In *German Women in the Nineteenth Century: A Social History*, ed. John C. Fout. New York: Holmes & Meier, 1984.

Shepperson, George. "The Comparative Study of Millenarian Movements." In *Millennial Dreams in Action: Essays in Comparative Study*, ed. Sylvia L. Thrupp, 44–52. The Hague: Mouton, 1962.

———. "Harriet Beecher Stowe and Scotland, 1852–3." *Scottish Historical Review* 32 (April 1953): 40–46.

Sherrick, Rebecca. 1982. "Toward Universal Sisterhood." *Women's Studies International Forum* 5, no. 6 (1982): 655–62.

Sklar, Kathryn Kish. "'Women Who Speak for an Entire Nation': American and British Women at the World Anti-Slavery Convention, London, 1840." In *The Abolitionist Sisterhood: Women's Political Culture in Antebellum America*, ed. Jean Fagan Yellin and John C. Van Horne, 301–33, 338–40. Ithaca, N.Y.: Cornell Univ. Press, 1994.

Slavin, Sarah. "Authenticity and Fiction in Law: Contemporary Case Studies Exploring Radical Legal Feminism." *Journal of Women's History* 3, no. 1 (1990): 124–5.

Smith, Agnes. *Eastern Pilgrims: The Travels of Three Ladies*. London: Hurst & Blackett, 1870.

Smith, Amanda. *An Autobiography: The Story of the Lord's Dealings with Mrs. Amanda Smith the Colored Evangelist*. 1893. Schomburg Library of Nineteenth-Century Black Women Writers. New York: Oxford Univ. Press, 1988.

Smith, Bonnie. *Changing Lives: Women in European History since 1700*. Lexington, Mass.: D.C. Heath, 1989.

Smith-Rosenberg, Carroll. "Beauty, the Beast, and the Militant Woman." *American Quarterly* 23 (1971): 562–84.

Snitow, Ann. "A Gender Diary." In *Feminism and History*, ed. Joan Wallach Scott, 505–44. New York: Oxford Univ. Press, 1996.

Somerville, Mary. *Personal Recollections, from Early Life to Old Age, of Mary Somerville, with Selections from Her Correspondence, by Her Daughter, Martha Somerville*. Boston: Roberts Brothers, 1874.

Sparrow, Walter. *Women Painters of the World, from the Time of Caterina Vigri, 1413-1463, to Rosa Bonheur and the Present Day*. London: Hodder & Stoughton, 1905.

Spencer, Donald S. *Louis Kossuth and Young America*. Columbia: Univ. of Missouri Press, 1977.

Spivack, Gayatri Chakravorty. *In Other Worlds: Essays in Cultural Politics*. New

York: Routledge, 1988.

Stansell, Christine. "Women, Children, and the Uses of the Streets: Class and Gender Conflict in New York City, 1850–1860." *Feminist Studies* 8 (1982): 309–35.

Stanton, Elizabeth Cady. *Eighty Years and More: Reminiscences, 1815–1897.* 1898. Boston: Northeastern Univ. Press, 1993.

Stanton, Elizabeth Cady, Susan B. Anthony, and Matilda Joslyn Gage. *History of Woman Suffrage.* 5 vols. 1881. New York: Arno Press, 1969.

Stanton, Theodore, ed. *The Woman Question in Europe.* New York: Putnam, 1884.

Stark, Freya. *The Freya Stark Story.* Condensation in one volume of *Traveller's Prelude, Beyond Euphrates,* and *The Coast of Incense.* New York: Coward-McCann, 1953.

Stendahl, Brita K. *The Education of a Self-Made Woman: Fredrika Bremer, 1801–1865.* Lewiston, Maine: Edwin Mellen Press, 1994.

Stenwall, Åsa. *Den frivilligt ödmjuka kvinnan: En bok om Fredrika Runebergs verklighet och diktning.* Bords, Sweden: Centraltryckeriet AB, 1979.

Stewart, Julia Gertrude. Letterbook. Dallas, Stewart, and Steel Families Papers, ML MSS 1219, items 4–8, Mitchell Library, State Library of New South Wales, Sydney, Australia.

Stites, Richard. *The Women's Liberation Movement in Russia: Nihilism, Feminism, and Bolshevism, 1860–1930.* Princeton, N.J.: Princeton Univ. Press, 1978.

Stowe, Charles Edward. *Life of Harriet Beecher Stowe, compiled from Her Letters and Journals.* Boston: Houghton Mifflin, 1889.

Stowe, Harriet Beecher. *Sunny Memories of Foreign Lands,* 2 vols. Boston: Phillips, Sampson, 1854.

Strachey, Barbara. *Remarkable Relations: The Story of the Pearsall Smith Women.* New York: Universe Books, 1982.

Strachey, Ray. *A Quaker Grandmother: Hannah Whitall Smith.* New York: Fleming H. Revell, 1914.

Sturge, Sophia. Letter to Aleksandra Gripenberg, July 30, [1890?]. Helsingin Yliopisto Kirjasto, Manuscript Collection, University of Helsinki Library.

"Sunny Memories: Harriet Beecher Stowe's 1853 Tour of Europe." Exhibit at the Stowe-Day Foundation, Hartford, Conn., June 1993–Dec. 1994.

Taylor, Barbara. *Eve and the New Jerusalem: Socialism and Feminism in the Nineteenth Century.* New York: Pantheon, 1983.

Taylor, Charles. *Hegel.* New York: Cambridge Univ. Press, 1975.

Taylor, Clare, ed. *British and American Abolitionists: An Episode in Transatlantic Understanding.* Edinburgh: Univ. of Edinburgh Press, 1974.

Thistlethwaite, Frank. *The Anglo-American Connection in the Early Nineteenth Century.* Philadelphia: Univ. of Pennsylvania Press, 1959.

Thomas, Evangeline, CSJ, ed. *Women Religious History Sources: A Guide to Repositories in the United States.* New York: R.R. Bowker, 1983.

Thomas, Hilah, and Rosemary Skinner Keller, eds. *Women in New Worlds: Historical Perspectives on the Wesleyan Tradition.* Nashville, Tenn.: Abingdon, 1981.

Thompson, Robert Luther. *Wiring a Continent: The History of the Telegraph Industry in the United States, 1832–1866.* 1947. New York: Arno Press, 1972.

Thompson, William. *Appeal of One Half the Human Race, Women, against the Pretensions of the Other Half, Men, to Restrain Them in Political and Thence in Civil and Domestic Slavery.* 1825. Intro. Richard Pankhurst. London: Virago, 1983.

Thomson, Patricia. "George Sand and English Reviewers: The First Twenty Years." *Modern Language Review* 67, no. 3 (1972): 501.

Tristan, Flora. *The London Journal of Flora Tristan, 1842.* Trans. and ed. Jean Hawkes. London: Virago, 1982.

———. *Nécessité de faire un bon accueil aux femmes étrangères.* Paris: Chez Delaunay, 1835.

———. *Peregrinations of a Pariah, 1833–1834.* Trans. and ed. Jean Hawkes. Boston: Beacon Press, 1986.

Trollope, Anthony. "An Unprotected Female at the Pyramids." In *Tales of All Countries.* London: Chapman and Hall, 1866.

———. "The Unprotected Female Tourist." In *Travelling Sketches.* London: Chapman and Hall, 1866.

"Trygg-Helenius, Alli." In *Kansallinen Elämäkerrasto* [Finnish National Biography]. Porvoo, Finland: Osa v. WSOY, 1934.

Tute, Warren. *Atlantic Conquest.* Boston: Little, Brown, 1962.

Tyrrell, Ian. *Woman's World, Woman's Empire: The Woman's Christian Temperance Union in International Perspective, 1880–1930.* Chapel Hill: Univ. of North Carolina Press, 1992.

Uglow, Jennifer. "Maria (Susan) Rye." In *The International Dictionary of Women's Biography,* 404. New York: Continuum, 1985.

"Uncle Tomitudes." *Putnam's* 1 (Jan. 1853): 97–99.

Usherwood, Stephen. "Travel Agents Extraordinary." *History Today* 22 (Sept. 1972): 650–51.

Veauvy, Christiane. *Parole oubliées: Les femmes et la construction de l'Etat en France et en Italie, 1789–1860.* Paris: A. Colin, 1997.

Vigée-Lebrun, Elizabeth. *Memoirs of Madame Vigée Lebrun.* 1903. Trans. Lionel Strachey, intro. John Russell. New York: George Braziller, 1989.

Voilquin, Suzanne. *Mémoires d'une Saint-Simonienne en Russie (1839–1846).* Ed. Maïté Albistur and Daniel Armogathe. Paris: Des Femmes, 1977.

———. *Souvenirs d'une fille du peuple, ou La Saint-simonienne en Egypte.* Ed. Lydia Elhadad. Paris: Maspero, 1978.

Volet-Jeanneret, Helena. "La Femme bourgeoise à Prague 1860–1895: De la philanthropie à l'émancipation." Thesis, University of Lausanne. 1988.

Von Alfthan, Märta. *Sju Årtionden med Unioni Naisasialiito Suomessa, Unionen Kvinnosaksförbund i Finland* [Seven decades with the Union of Finnish Feminists]. Helsinki: Söderström, 1965.

Von Asten-Kinkel, Adelheid. "Johanna Kinkel in England." *Deutsche Revue* 26 (Jan.–Mar. 1901): 71–76.

Waddington, Patrick. *Turgenev and George Sand: An Improbable Entente.* Totowa, N.J.: Barnes & Noble, 1981.

Wagner, Maria. "A German Writer and Feminist in 19th-Century America." In *Beyond the Eternal Feminine: Critical Essays on Women and German Literature,* ed. Susan L. Cocalis and Kay Goodman, 159–75. Stuttgart: Akademischer Verlag Hans-Dieter Heinz, 1982.

Walkowitz, Judith. *Prostitution and Victorian Society.* Cambridge: Cambridge Univ.Press, 1980.

Walz, Maggie. Letters. Aleksandra Gripenberg Collection, 318:27:1–5. Finnish Literature Society (SKS), Helsinki. Trans. Ann-Catrin Östman.

Webber, Everett. *Escape to Utopia: The Communal Movement in America.* New York: Hastings House, 1958.

Wein, Jo Ann. "The Parisian Training of American Women Artists." *Woman's Art Journal,* Spring/Summer, 1981.

Wellman, Barry. "Structural Analysis: From Method and Metaphor to Theory and Substance." In *Social Structures: A Network Approach,* ed. Barry Wellman and S.D. Berkowitz, 19–61. New York: Cambridge Univ. Press, 1988.

Wellman, Barry, and S.D. Berkowitz, eds. *Social Structures: A Network Approach.* New York: Cambridge Univ. Press, 1988.

Wells-Barnett, Ida B. *Crusade for Justice: The Autobiography of Ida B. Wells.* Ed. Alfreda M. Duster. Chicago: Univ. of Chicago Press, 1970.

————. *A Red Record: Tabulated Statistics and Alleged Causes of Lynchings in the United States, 1892–1893–1894.* Chicago: Donohue & Henneberry, 1895.

Werkmäster, Barbro. "Frigjord eller bunder? De kvinnliga konstnärnerna och 1880–talets emancipationssträvanden." In *De drogo till Paris,* 11–28. Stockholm: Föreningen Norden, 1889.

Wesley, Dorothy Porter. "Sarah Parker Remond." In *Black Women in America: An Historical Encyclopedia,* 2:972–74. New York: Carlson, 1993.

Wesley, John. Letter to Mary Bosanquet, 1771. In *The Letters of the Rev. John Wesley, A.M.,* ed. John Telford, 5:257. London: Epworth Press, 1931.

West, Robin. *Caring for Justice.* New York: New York Univ. Press, 1997.

Wharton, Edith. *The Buccaneers.* New York: Appleton-Century, 1938.

Wheeler, Anna Doyle. Letters to Charles Fourier, 30 July 1830 and 28 May 1833. Archives Nationales (Paris), Archives societaires, 10 AS 24 and 25, doss. 3.

————. "Rights of Women." *British Co-operator* 1, nos. 1–2 (1830): 12–15, 33–36.

————, trans. "Appel aux femmes," by Jeanne-Victoire [pseud.] *The Crisis,* June 15, 1833. In *Women, the Family, and Freedom,* ed. Susan Groag Bell and Karen Offen, 1:146–47. Stanford, Calif.: Stanford Univ. Press, 1983.

Wheelwright, Julie. *Amazons and Military Maids: Women Who Dressed as Men in the Pursuit of Life, Liberty, and Happiness.* London: Pandora Press, 1989.

Wikander, Ulla. "International Women's Congresses, 1878–1914: The Controversy over Equality and Special Labour Legislation." In *Rethinking Change: Current Swedish Feminist Research,* ed. Maud L. Eduards et al., 11–36. Uppsala: Humanistisk-samhällsvetenskapliga forskningsradet, 1992.

Willard, Emma. "Letter to DuPont de l'Eure on the Political Position of Women." *American Literary Magazine* 2, no. 4 (1848): 246–54.

Willard, Frances. *Woman and Temperance; or, The Work and Workers of the Woman's Christian Temperance Union.* Hartford, Conn.: Park, 1883.

Wilson, A.N. *Hilaire Belloc: A Biography.* New York: Atheneum, 1984.

Witt, Peter N., Charles F. Reed, and David B. Peakall. *A Spider's Web: Problems in Regulatory Biology.* New York: Springer-Verlag, 1968.

Wittke, Carl. "Mathilde Franziska Anneke." In *Notable American Women, 1607–1950,* ed. Edward T. James, 3:50–51. Cambridge, Mass.: Harvard Univ. Press, 1971.

Woodring, Carl. *Victorian Samplers: William and Mary Howitt.* Lawrence: Univ. of Kansas Press, 1952.

Woolf, Virginia. *Three Guineas.* 1938. New York: Harcourt, Brace, 1966.

Wright, Frances. "Of Free Inquiry." 1829. In *The Feminist Papers,* ed. Alice Rossi, 108–17. Boston: Northeastern Univ. Press, 1988.

————. "A Plan for the Gradual Abolition of Slavery in the United States, without Danger of Loss to the Citizens of the South." 1825. In *Women and Religion in America,* vol. 1, *The Nineteenth Century,* ed. Rosemary Radford Ruether and Rosemary Skinner Keller, 75–77. San Francisco: Harper & Row, 1981.

————. *Society and Manners in America.* London, 1821.

Wyman, Mark. *Round-Trip to America: The Immigrants Return to Europe, 1880–1930.* Ithaca, N.Y.: Cornell Univ. Press, 1993.

Yee, Shirley J. *Black Women Abolitionists: A Study in Activism, 1828–1860.* Knoxville: Univ. of Tennessee Press, 1992.

Yellin, Jean Fagan. *Women and Sisters: The Antislavery Feminists in American Culture.* New Haven, Conn.: Yale Univ. Press, 1989.

Zboray, Ronald J. *A Fictive People.* New York: Oxford Univ. Press, 1993.

Zimmerman, Judith E. "Natalie Herzen and the Early Intelligentsia." *Russian Review* 41 (July 1982): 249–72.

Zucker, Stanley. "German Women and the Revolution of 1848: Kathinka Zitz-Halein and the Humania Association." *Central European History* 13, no. 3 (1980): 237–54.

Index

Italicized numbers refer to illustrations.